The Origins of Grammar

The Origins of Grammar

Evidence from Early Language Comprehension

Kathy Hirsh-Pasek and
Roberta Michnick Golinkoff

The MIT Press
Cambridge, Massachusetts
London, England

Second printing, 1997

This book was set in Times Roman by Asco Trade Typesetting Ltd., Hong Kong Printed on recycled paper and bound in the United States of America.

Library of Congress Cataloging-in-Publication Data

Hirsh–Pasek, Kathy.
  The origins of grammar : evidence from early language
  comprehension / Kathy Hirsh–Pasek and Roberta Michnick Golinkoff.
     p. cm.
  Includes bibliographical references and index.
  ISBN 0-262-08242-X
  1. Language acquisition. 2. Grammar, Comparative and general—
Syntax. 3. Comprehension in children. I. Golinkoff, Roberta M.
II. Title.
P118.H57   1996
401'.93—dc20   95-44507
                                                       CIP

To
Jeffrey and Elliott
and to
Michael, Benj, Joshua, Allison,
and Jordan

Contents

Acknowledgments

The order of our names on this book is completely arbitrary. The book is the product of a long and successful collaboration and friendship. Indeed, in all of our joint work, we have reached that synergistic point where either one of us could finish (and even start) the other's sentences.

We dedicate this book to two men—Elliott Golinkoff and Jeff Pasek—whose constant support and love made it possible and to the five children—Michael Pasek, 5 years; Benj Pasek, 10 years; Josh Pasek, 12 years; Allison Golinkoff, 12 years; and Jordan Golinkoff, 16 years—who provided constant data (sometimes more than we wanted) for our immersion experience in language acquisition. We thank our husbands for encouraging our professional fervor and for overlooking phone bills for calls to each other that could have been the budget for a small nation. We thank our children for showing us that traditional assessment instruments far underestimate toddlers' knowledge of linguistic structure. We also thank them for the wonderful anecdotes they provide for our classes. (In fact, Michael recently announced that "*vampires* have very important roles to play in baseball games" and Allison admonished her brother not to be so "*controllive*"!)

Over the years, we have received help and support from so many individuals that it is impossible to thank them all. First and foremost, however, we have had the fortune of profiting from many conversations with Lois Bloom and Lila Gleitman. Both Lila and Lois spent many hours discussing theory with us and reading earlier versions of some of these chapters. We thank them, too, for serving as role models for the heights that women scientists can reach in the field of psychology.

Second, we have also collaborated with some first-rate graduate and undergraduate students. Kathy Cauley and Laura Gordon, former graduate students who were with us at the inception of the work, and former

undergraduates Anne Fletcher, Jessica Cone, Louise McNally, Kelly
Olguin, and Anthony Alioto contributed in a number of ways to the
success of the research reported in this book. Neill Wenger, Marcia
Mofson, and Diana Kaufman masterfully administered our labs just as
Judy Wiley, Carrie Maddox, Amy Rosenberg, and Melissa Schweisguth
do now. In addition, several of our colleagues have reviewed portions of
the manuscript and offered constructive feedback. We especially want to
thank Nora Newcombe and Gaby Hermon for their insightful comments.

The support from the University of Delaware's Department of Educational Studies and its Chair, James Raths, also deserves special mention,
as does assistance from his administrative assistant, Betty Perna.Vickie
Porch—a wonder woman who can turn labyrinthine handwritten inserts
into meaningful prose—provided us with outstanding secretarial assistance. It was sometimes hard for us to live up to her standards of excel-
lence for manuscript preparation. Further, the University's Instructional
Technology Center and its director, Fred Hofstetter, supplied us with
an electronics wizard in the person of George Harding, who reveled in
solving our technical problems and keeping us running. We were also
blessed with Bob Gorman, a statistician whose contribution to the project
far exceeded his paltry reward. Last but certainly not least, the University's Media Services Center, and its director Lonnie Hearn, has provided
us over the years with state-of-the-art video-editing facilities and highly
skilled technicians to help us select and maintain our equipment.

Finally, we were fortunate to have received funding for this project
from a number of sources, including a grant from the National Institute
of Child Health and Human Development (HD15964) awarded to both of
us, another grant from that agency awarded to us and to Paula Malone
and Charles Bean (HD19568), and three Pew Memorial Fund grants and
two Temple University Biomedical research grants awarded to Hirsh-
Pasek. Hirsh-Pasek's participation was partially supported by another
grant from the National Institute of Child Heath and Human Development (3U10HD25455-0552) awarded to Marcia Weinraub and Kathy
Hirsh-Pasek. Golinkoff was awarded a fellowship from the John Simon
Guggenheim Foundation, a James McKeen Cattell Sabbatical Award, a
University of Delaware Research Foundation grant, as well as Biomedical
funds from the University of Delaware. For 1993–1994, Golinkoff received a fellowship from the Center for Advanced Study at the University
of Delaware, which was essential for bringing this project to completion.

Chapter 1

Introduction

Language learning ought to be impossible. Consider what it must be like to be an infant learning a language: You are immersed in a world of transient events that are often accompanied by the melodic strings called language. Your task is threefold: (1) to discover the units of language represented within the melodic strings (e.g., sentences, phrases, and words); (2) to analyze the world's events in language-relevant ways (e.g., objects and actions); and (3) to uncover the link between the language units that you hear and your representation of the world around you (Gleitman and Wanner 1982). Any number of hypotheses could be entertained in each of these problem spaces. Why not assume, for example, that the label "book" means something entirely different when uttered in the vocal pitch used by a mother or a father? Why not assume that sentence boundaries occur at every fifth syllable? Fortunately, nature seems to equip language learners with strategies that help to guide them toward selecting the most reasonable hypotheses.

This book investigates these strategies and accompanying hypotheses in one area of language acquisition: syntax. Syntax is the sine qua non of language. It is the level of language that allows us to represent the world by mapping meanings onto forms. With a finite set of units and rules, an infinite number of sentences can be generated, symbolizing any number of events and relationships. This allows us to go beyond the "here and now" in communicating about the past, present, and future.

Although a good deal is known about the adult language system, investigators are still struggling to learn more about how children achieve adult grammatical competence. Children must induce the syntactic rules from the linguistic input that they hear as it covaries with the world that they see around them. Yet many form-to-meaning pairings are possible. How do children induce just the right set of rules and generalizations given that they apparently receive no relevant corrective feedback from the environment? This question is the crux of what Pinker (1989) calls "Baker's paradox" (Baker 1979). The problem is presented even more strikingly by Gold (1967), who, simulating language acquisition on a computer, argues that an unbiased learner who had to induce the rules of grammar from strings of input would require more than a human lifetime to accomplish the task. It is well known, however, that children acquire most of their grammar by the time they are three years old (Ingram 1989).

The reason that real children can achieve the "impossible" is that they differ from Gold's learner in two important ways. First, Gold's learner was an unbiased learner. It is now commonly accepted that young children (as opposed to hypothetical or machine learners) come to the task of grammatical learning with some sensitivity to the information available in the input. These sensitivities are realized in the strategies or "operating principles" (see Slobin 1973, 1985a) that young children impose as they analyze the input that they hear. Indeed, the major debates in language acquisition theory today concern not *whether* there are some sensitivities to syntactic information but *which* sensitivities children are endowed with and how they might be translated into the organizing principles that get syntactic learning off the ground.

Second, Gold's learner received syntactic information in isolation from other forms of input (e.g., input from the environmental context, prosody, or social interaction). That is, Gold's learner heard a series of sentence strings and had to induce the units and rules of language as if in a vacuum. Yet it is well known that linguistic units and relations can be highlighted by social interactions or prosody, for example. Hirsh-Pasek and Golinkoff (1993) have argued that the mechanism for discovering grammatical structure involves the child's capitalizing on a *coalition* of multiple and overlapping cues in the linguistic and nonlinguistic environment. Thus, to make the case for language learning, one has to abandon two of Gold's assumptions and look for alternative solutions to the language-learning problem. Each of these points, (1) that the learner is biased, and (2) that learners abstract the units and rules of language from a coalition of cues in the input, deserves further explication.

1.1 The Case for a Biased Learner

The suggestion that language learners might be sensitive to certain information in the input is not new. In 1973 and 1985, Slobin captured the language learner's biases in a set of operating principles that, "whatever their ultimate origin, are necessary prerequisites for the perception, analysis, and use of language in ways that will lead to mastery of any particular input language" (Slobin 1985a, 1159). By way of example, one of his 40 or so principles, called "OP (Position): Fixed Word Order," states that "[i]f you have determined that word order expresses basic semantic relations in your language, keep the order of morphemes in a clause constant" (Slobin 1985a, 1255). Such a principle equips the child with a procedural way of organizing the input. Unless there are salient morphological indications of semantic relations, children should adhere to strict word order. This and other operating principles, first suggested in 1973, formed the basis for a new, process-oriented approach to language acquisition. Given a set of principles, languages could be discovered from the input. This approach inspired researchers to look for evidence of operating principles in the development of languages around the globe (see Slobin 1985a,b, 1992).

There have been cogent criticisms of the specific set of operating principles that Slobin (1985a) proposed as well as of their conceptual framework (Bowerman 1985). However, the principle-based approach has been extremely useful to researchers in a number of areas of developmental psychology (Gelman and Gallistel 1979; Markman 1989; Keil 1981; Golinkoff, Mervis, and Hirsh-Pasek 1994). This is because principles give the child a starting point toward the acquisition of competence in a domain. As Gelman and Greeno (1989) write in discussing the growth of competence in a number of domains including language and mathematics:

The idea is that a skeletal set of principles is available to support the kind of selective attention and learning in the domain characterized by these principles. Initial representations serve as enabling devices. (p. 128) ... If we grant learners some domain-specific principles, we provide them with a way to define a range of relevant inputs, the ones that support learning about that domain. Because principles embody constraints on the kinds of input that can be processed as data that are relevant to that domain, they therefore can direct attention to those aspects of the environment that need to be selected and attended to. (p. 130)

A principle-based approach for the acquisition of grammar offers one way in which researchers can begin to account for how children discover the framework for their language. That is, children must be sensitive to and attend to things like order, constituent structure, and grammatical markers such as closed-class words (e.g., "for," "with") if they are ever to induce the way in which their particular language encodes meaning.

Slobin's operating principles were an explicit attempt to demonstrate how children can capitalize on these natural sensitivities to construct a grammatical skeleton for later language learning. Other theories of language acquisition have traditionally presupposed the existence of this grammatical skeleton, taking the output of these principles as prerequisites to the process of acquisition. For example, in a preface to their theory of acquisition Wexler and Culicover (1980) write that in order to make theoretical progress, the researcher must assume

that the learner imposes order on the raw information [in input] .... This assumption does not solve how (if at all) the preanalysis system is learned. Rather, this problem is ignored so that progress can be made in understanding a different level of learning. Ultimately, all such levels must be investigated if we are to have an adequate theory. (p. 61)

The quest for language researchers, then, is to determine what information in the language input infants and toddlers are sensitive to and how these sensitivities are reflected in the strategies that these children use to learn their native tongue. In other words, what are the minimal operating principles required to account for the universal and specific properties of language? Wexler and Culicover (1980) allude to what some of these might be. For example, any theory of language acquisition must document how children conduct a phonemic analysis of speech (Wexler and Culicover 1980; Landau and Gleitman 1985; Pinker 1984), how they are able to assign the words that result from this segmentation to the appropriate form classes (e.g., noun or verb), and how they are able to find constituents at the phrasal and clausal levels (Peters 1985; Berwick 1986; Gleitman and Wanner 1988; Pinker 1984; Wexler and Culicover 1980). In other words, most theories presuppose that infants are capable of segmenting the stream of speech into language-relevant units. Of course, speech segmentation is not enough. Children must also conduct a semantic analysis of the language units (Landau and Gleitman 1985; MacWhinney 1987; Pinker 1984; Slobin 1985a; Wexler and Culicover 1980), recognizing in the crudest analysis, for example, that certain words refer to objects and others to actions or object properties.

Equipped with some procedures for how to discover units in the linguistic stream, children must also come to detect the relationships between the units. Given that so many languages rely on order either in the affixation of morphological endings or in the order of lexical constituents, it would benefit children to notice the order of elements (be they morphemes or words) in the input (Slobin 1973, 1985a; Maratsos and Chalkley 1980).

A principle capturing this order generalization should prove central to learning and in fact is listed not only as one of Slobin's principles but also as a parameter in Chomsky's theory (1981).

In sum, even from this brief categorization of presumptions suggested by prior theories, a number of general principles emerge. Infants must be sensitive to some aspects of the input over others for language to be learnable. In chapters 4 through 6 we present data that bear on the question of infants' sensitivity to grammatical constructs.

1.2 The Case against Learning in Isolation

Albeit in the context of a computer simulation, Gold (1967) demonstrated that a learner who approached the task without any biases would take an eternity to learn language. Gold also highlighted the difficulty of learning language from strings of text without any accompanying context. Real children have the opportunity to discover linguistic representations from a number of covarying, and often complementary, sources of information—from the coalition of cues (Hirsh-Pasek and Golinkoff 1993). For example, children cannot learn about the structure of sentences if they have not discovered the nouns and verbs (among other form classes) that make up those sentences. How might they go about discovering what sentence units constitute the noun class? Several converging types of information are available. First, in general, nouns are among the more heavily stressed units in the sentence (Kelly 1992; Kelly and Martin 1994). Second, nouns in speech directed to children are more likely to occur in isolation or in final position in the sentence (Goldfield 1993; see also Aslin 1992). Third, many of the nouns directed to children tend to label concrete, bounded objects as opposed to concepts like "truth" and "beauty" (Gentner 1983, 1988; Maratsos 1988). Fourth, nouns are often signaled in the input with distinct morphology or markers such as the articles "the" and "a" in English (Maratsos 1988). Fifth, nouns are often introduced to young children as objects are being manipulated (either by them or by an adult), pointed to, or gazed at (Tomasello 1992; Schmidt 1991).

Again, the suggestion that children might cull information from a number of different sources is not new. Those belonging to the "interactionist" school of language learning, for example, were quick to challenge Chomsky's (1965) claims that syntactic input alone is enough to trigger grammatical competence (see Snow and Ferguson 1977, for a review). Social interactions, or the ways in which the linguistic message is delivered to the child through infant-directed speech and in the context of a shared environment, provide necessary and sufficient supports for language learning (Snow 1986; Nelson 1985; Bruner 1983a,b). Slobin's (1985a) work similarly emphasizes that language learning occurs through a coalition of sources:

The application of particular operating principles depends on a complex of existing linguistic and extralinguistic knowledge, processing constraints, the structure of social interaction, and the structure of the language being acquired. (p. 1245)

Bloom (1970) makes the same point when she describes the interaction of form (linguistic knowledge), content (cognitive knowledge), and use (social/functional knowledge) in developing language systems. Pinker (1987) also writes about a constraint satisfaction model for language acquisition in which a number of input systems operate through an interactive network to ensure that children learn the rule system for the adult language:

The *input* to the child consists of sentences heard in context. If we are charitable about the child's perceptual abilities, we can assume that he or she can extract a variety of types of information from that input: the set of words contained in the sentence; their order; prosodic properties, such as intonation, stress, and timing; the meanings of individual content words, insofar as they can be acquired before grammar learning begins; crude phonological properties of words, such as the number of syllables; the semantics of the utterance inferred from the nonlinguistic context, including its predicate-argument structure and relations of co-reference and predication; and finally, pragmatic information inferred from the discourse context, such as topic versus focus. (p. 399)

More recently Kelly and Martin (1994) argue that domain-specific problems like language acquisition can be solved by noting the probabilistic convergence of information from multiple sources (e.g., stress patterns and phoneme sequences). Finally, Hirsh-Pasek, Tucker, and Golinkoff (1995) and Tucker and Hirsh-Pasek (1994) demonstrate how dynamic systems theory can be used to explore the ways in which children use and weigh the coalition of language-relevant inputs throughout the course of language development. They posit that children constantly monitor varied input sources as they discover their native grammar. For example, prosodic cues may be the most salient aspect of the input at an early point in language acquisition, giving way to semantic cues as the analysis of linguistic units becomes more automatic. A little later, the 2-year-old child learns that emphases on syntactic form along with semantic analyses are crucial to the language structure.

This reliance on multiple sources of input whose degree of importance varies over time is a central tenet of a dynamic system. For example, Thelen and Smith (1994) argue that two characteristics of developing biological and psychological systems make a coalition view not only possible, but likely. First, all developing systems share the property that they call "reentry," or the ability to abstract related patterns from temporally simultaneous but varied inputs. Upon seeing an apple, for instance, the viewer also knows that it will be smooth, have substance, and have a certain taste because these experiences occurred in close temporal proximity when the apple was first encountered. In the case of language, reentry translates into the claim that, for example, the class called "nouns" is multiply determined (e.g., marked by the cooccurrence of a concrete object and a word uttered in sentence-final position). Second, systems have the characteristic of "degeneracy" such that there are many ways to reach or select the same endpoint. Even if a word does not exhibit all of the properties of a noun, the cooccurrence of a sufficient number of these properties will allow it to be identified as a noun. In short, concepts such as reentry and degeneracy that are used in the biological literature and that have been recently introduced to psychology through systems theory may provide a helpful way of thinking about how the child uses multiple sources of information in the service of acquiring grammar.

In sum, many investigators argue for some form of a coalition view of language acquisition. Indeed, the assertion that children cull from many different sources in developing the framework for their grammar should seem obvious. Yet throughout the history of psycholinguistic research investigators have nonetheless placed a premium on one type of input source over the others. Bloom and Lahey (1978) write:

Linguistic theory in the years before the '60s considered the form of the language as the only object of study and the goal of description could not include an account of meaning in messages. According to Bloomfield (1933), the realm of meaning embraces all possible events in the world and so was not a reasonable goal for linguistic inquiry. In contrast, Skinner's (1957) psychological explanation of verbal behavior centered on use and ignored form and content almost entirely. As a result, accounts of language before the 1970s described form most often and use less often, but did not consider their interaction with meaning or with one another in any systematic way. (p. 21)

The same statements concerning a singularity of focus can be made today. Although most current theories acknowledge the contribution of many sources of input for syntactic information, most choose one as the primary motivator for development. Landau and Gleitman (1985), for example, suggest that attention to syntactic markers will be the favored route for syntactic learning. Pinker (1987) argues that "... semantic information could continue to function in practice as the most important seeds that get the network started" (p. 439; see also 1984). Finally, for Bates and MacWhinney (1987), function-form mappings, or the linguistic realization of communicative goals, are the grist for the mill of grammatical learning. Thus, it is only through tying functions (such as topic and agent) to linguistic markings that the child acquires form (p. 177).

The task facing psycholinguists is to decide exactly which input sources are necessary for the acquisition of grammar and how each input in the coalition works *individually* and *interactively* throughout the course of linguistic development. In chapter 7 we develop this view more thoroughly, arguing that different input sources take precedence at different points in language development. To investigate how young children utilize multiple sources of information in the input, researchers must develop methods for testing language acquisition without fragmenting the natural coalition of cues that exist in the input. Traditional methods often look for evidence that one of these types of cues is used by stripping away the other cues that make up the natural coalition. For example, to test for the "pure" syntactic ability to interpret pronouns in sentences, some researchers have presented sentences such as "Grover thinks that Cookie Monster is touching him" without mentioning either of the characters in the prior discourse (McDaniel, Cairns, and Hsu 1990). Not surprisingly, children's performance improved when similar sentences did include previously mentioned discourse referents (Kaufman 1987). Other investigators test for linguistic competence by putting some of the covarying cues in competition with one another. If nascent learners rely on a coalition of cues to comprehend sentences that use word order to signal meaning, then experiments that look for the comprehension of semantically anomalous sentences like "The man bites the dog" will grossly underestimate the child's language faculty.

In sum, then, conceptualizing the problem of language learning as one that depends upon culling information from a number of inputs puts a new burden on experimenters. Language researchers must recognize that early sensitivities to aspects of the syntax may only be unearthed in testing environments that allow children to use all of the resources at their disposal. They may need to develop new methods for examining early language processes that enable children to use prosody, social cues, environmental information, and syntax in interpreting grammatical materials.

1.3   Goals and a Look Ahead

In this book we conceptualize the language acquisition process as the product of a biased learner who reaps information from a coalition of input sources. In most of the book we focus on the grammatical sensitivities that this biased learner brings to the task of language acquisition and on introducing and validating a new method of exploring the sensitivities through language comprehension. In the rest of the book we present our preliminary view of how infants use these sensitivities in a coalition framework for language learning. Language comprehension provides the medium for this exploration. It is in comprehension that the biases the learner brings to the task and the coalition of input cues meet for the first time.

Our goals in writing this book are fourfold. First, we empirically demonstrate early sensitivities to properties of very general language structure (i.e., constituent structure, word order, and verb subcategorization cues). Second, we offer a new method for exploring children's language sensitivities through comprehension. The method, which is a type of intermodal preferential looking paradigm, can be used with children as young as 13 months of age to investigate their nascent knowledge of language structure. Third, we offer a new way of thinking about the process of language comprehension itself through a coalition analysis. Our analysis borrows insights from theories about the development of mental models and systems theory. It begins to explain how the various language cues might work together to enable language comprehension. It provides some speculation about what processes might be involved in comprehension, why comprehension might precede the production of language, and why the intermodal preferential looking paradigm is so effective in uncovering early language comprehension. Fourth, a secondary (but, we believe, no less important) goal is to make the domain of language acquisition accessible to psychologists through clear and relatively jargon-free exposition.

In keeping with these goals, in chapter 2 we review current language acquisition theories in an attempt to abstract a common set of presumptions about language learning. These common theoretical presumptions provide the fodder for the strategies that learners might use when analyzing syntax in the input that they hear. In chapter 3 we briefly review problems and progress in the study of language comprehension, and we introduce a new procedure that alleviates many of the problems discussed. It promises even greater progress in the empirical investigation of the principles that children employ as they map form onto meaning. In chapters 4, 5, and 6 we present a series of experiments designed to uncover the working strategies that guide infants' and toddlers' interpretation of language input, focusing on children's attention to constituent structure (chapter 4), their sensitivity to word order, (chapter 5), and their burgeoning knowledge of verb subcategorization frames or the language that surrounds the verb (chapter 6). Finally, in chapter 7 we focus directly on the process of language comprehension. We develop a speculative model of comprehension and examine the role that learner biases and the availability of coalitions of cues might play within this theory of comprehension.

Chapter 2

Theories of Language Acquisition

In chapter 1 we argued that Gold's (1967) machine language learner was handicapped because it possessed no biased learning mechanisms and it learned language in isolation without the benefits of contextual cues. Although the learner needs both of these factors, different theories of acquisition have been developed that rely heavily either on the internal biases of the learner (Chomsky 1965; Wexler and Culicover 1980; Lightfoot 1989; Bickerton 1984) or on how the learner might acquire grammar through attention to contextual cues in the input language (Snow 1986; Bates and MacWhinney 1987). Although these theories are perceived as quite distinct in the literature, there are common threads that link them together. Upon analysis, these common assumptions provide clues to the kinds of sensitivities that learners might share when they approach the language-learning task. In this way, theory can be used to guide the understanding of process.

This chapter is divided into four sections. In an attempt to make language acquisition theory accessible to individuals who work in other areas, we devote section 2.1 to introducing the uniqueness of language and the phenomenon that current theories of acquisition must explain, and we pose three questions that motivate this review. Section 2.2 is further divided into two parts, corresponding to two hypothetical families of theories of language acquisition. Explication of each type of theory is followed by an evaluation. In section 2.3 we collapse the dichotomies that appear to divide the two families of theories, and in section 2.4 we revisit the three questions. Our aim is to reach a compromise between what have traditionally been called the nativistic and interactionist theories of language acquisition. Although we lean slightly toward the nativistic side of the debate (for reasons to be outlined here and in the rest of the book), we believe that language acquisition is best described through the dynamic interplay of a number of forces (the coalition model; see chapter 7). Thus, in this chapter we seek to outline the assumptions that theories of language acquisition share and the way in which the studies to be presented in this book begin to address these assumptions.

2.1 Language Acquisition and Theory in Linguistics

Some researchers have urged their colleagues to "hang loose!" (Miller 1981) with respect to commitments to any particular theory of grammar. Yet the first step in developing a theory of language acquisition must be to specify what it is that the child must acquire. Without a vision of the adult state, the questions that researchers ask might lack precision and relevance. Thus, the researcher who wishes to conduct a theory-based research program must be guided by descriptions of the adult state, and such descriptions are theory laden. The safest course, as Pinker (1984) has cogently argued, is to study aspects of language that all theories of grammar—regardless of what else they do—seem to agree on. For example, most theories seem to have the "same small set of grammatical categories and relations, phrase structure rules, inflectional paradigms, lexical entries, lexical rules, [and] grammatical features" (p. 25). Studying topics such as these fairly ensures that the researcher will avoid "parochialism" or "impending obsolescence" (p. 25) since, whatever theory is currently in vogue, they are topics it will have to ideal with.

In this book we have followed Pinker's (1984) advice with respect to commitments to theories of language. Indeed, we have carried his advice a step further and have also not committed ourselves to any particular theory of language acquisition. Instead of making such a commitment, we focus on questions that all theories must address. Thus, this review is organized around three questions:

1. What is present when grammatical learning begins?
2. What mechanisms are used in the course of acquisition?
3. What types of input drive the language-learning system forward?

The first question is concerned with what the child brings to the task of language learning. This includes cognitive, social, and linguistic knowledge that may either be innate or originate in prior learning. On the surface, theories identified as "nativistic" seem to presuppose far more at the start than theories that emphasize how the child makes use of the linguistic and nonlinguistic environment.

The second question focuses on the actual processes that children use to acquire language. For example, do children use domain-general learning procedures that are common to, say, perception and problem solving, or do they use domain-specific learning procedures that are peculiar to language processing?

The third question asks what types of inputs drive the language-learning system forward. Do children rely primarily on increasing knowledge of social conventions as in the pragmatic account, or do they perform increasingly sophisticated structural analyses of the linguistic stream? Does the environment play a relatively large or a relatively small role in assisting children to uncover the rules of their native tongue?

Whether explicitly or implicitly, all theories of language acquisition presuppose their own answers to these questions. Before we look at the various answers, however, the problem of language acquisition, or what must be learned in the first place, needs to be described in more detail. In what follows we outline a general view of the nature of language and what is necessary to acquire a language. In so doing, we provide readers whose own research may be outside the area of language acquisition with a brief introduction to these issues (for a fuller treatment see Fletcher and Macwhinney 1995 and Ingram 1989, for example).

Among the insights about language that are widely accepted by both linguists and acquisition theorists are that all languages comprise (1) units at a number of levels that encode meaning (e.g., words, phrases, and clauses) and (2) relations or ways of arranging those units to express events and relationships. Languages are also hierarchically organized. Units at one level (e.g., phrases) are embedded in units at a higher level (e.g., clauses). Thus, any theory of acquisition must account for how children become sensitive to the types of units that exist and to the relations or arrangements of these units in their native language. Only with these sensitivities could children work toward achieving adult competency.

All theories of grammar and of acquisition presuppose that words are the basic building blocks of language, despite the fact that words are composed differently in different languages. For example, in languages like Chinese and English, words carry relatively few grammatical markers and may consist of a single morpheme. In a sentence such as "You saw me," each word serves a separate grammatical function. To say the same thing in a language such as Imbabura Quechua, a speaker uses a single word containing much grammatical information:

riku- wa-   rka- nki
see   first person object past second person subject

Thus, a single word in Imbabura Quechua can be composed of a rich combination of affixes and stems that carry much of the linguistic burden that is expressed by separate words in languages like English. From a psychological perspective, one might speculate that languages that contain mostly separate wordlike units are easier for children to acquire than the so-called agglutinative languages that "paste" together different grammatical elements into a single word. The actual data on children acquiring these languages, however, suggest otherwise. Regardless of the properties of the language, the milestones of acquisition seem to occur at about the same ages around the world (Lenneberg 1967; Slobin 1985a,b).

Despite differences in the way languages use words to transmit grammatical content, the words in all languages fall on a continuum that ranges from what are referred to as "open-class" words to what are referred to as "closed-class" words. Prototypically, open-class words bear content (e.g., "chair," "psychology," "think") and closed-class or "function" words (e.g., pronouns, articles, and prepositions) contain no content, in the traditional sense, but rather serve as operators to signal different meaning relations and grammatical units. Closed-class items are essential for specifying the architecture of the phrases within sentences. In general, across languages, children acquire open-class words, which label the objects and actions in their environment, before they acquire the closed-class words, which carry more abstract meanings (Brown 1973; but see Nelson 1973 for some strategic differences in children's early vocabulary).

Across all languages, the open-class words may be further subdivided into a finite set of "form classes" such as "nouns," "verbs," "adjectives," and "adverbs." Not all languages contain all these categories, but all choose from this limited set (see Greenberg 1963; Comrie 1981). In all languages where acquisition has been studied, the preponderance of children's first words appear to come from the class of nouns (Gentner 1983; but see Bloom, Tinker, and Margulis, in press; Nelson, Hampson, and Shaw 1993), although one need not claim that children are aware of these adult designations for grammatical categories. Indeed, nouns even appear first in languages such as Korean that are characterized by much noun ellipsis and that have verbs in sentence-final position (Au, Dapretto, and Song 1994). These form class units in turn provide the core for larger constituents such as noun phrases (e.g., "the big red book") and verb phrases (e.g., "jumped happily"). All grammatical theories attempt to account for the composition of phrases and clauses.

In sum, to learn a language, a child must first find the units that compose that language. Although languages seem to draw universally from the same finite set of units, the child faces a somewhat different task in uncovering what these units are depending on the language to be learned. Nonetheless, all children in the second year of life show evidence of having found the units used for grammar building by the way in which they begin with the smallest unit (words) and gradually create phrase- and then clause-sized units.

With regard to the relations between words, languages also share a number of common features. Of these, the most important is that languages are "structure dependent" (Chomsky 1972) rather than "serial-order dependent." This means that "... knowledge of language depends on the structural relationships in the sentence rather than on the sequence of items" (Cook 1989, 2). This fact has a number of implications for language acquisition. For example, even though the subject and the verb may be separated by a variable number of words, children must be able to find these elements in order to create agreement between them (e.g., "*John*, the boy next door, works for ... "). Thus, children must be able to find the units in their particular language and detect which units are structurally dependent on what other units in that language. This in turn involves recognizing the hierarchical structure of the language and learning what grammatical devices (e.g., word order, inflectional markings, or tones) the language uses to create various types of syntactic units.

Structure dependency is best illustrated by the simple example of questions in English. For instance, the structure of "Will John come?" implies that questions are formed by inverting the second word in the parallel declarative sentence, in this case "John will come." However, such a rule quickly runs into trouble since it would generate ungrammatical questions like "Sister John's will come?" This simple example demonstrates that inverting the word in any particular *position* in a sentence could never work; what counts is the *type* of word involved.

Syntactically speaking, "will" is an auxiliary. Perhaps the rule of question formation involves movement of the auxiliary. But this generalization is not specific enough. Consider a sentence with a relative clause, such as "The man who will come is John." "Will" and "is" are both auxiliaries. Which one should be moved? Moving the first auxiliary, "will," yields the ungrammatical question "Will the man who come is John?" Moving the second auxiliary, "is," yields the acceptable question "Is the man who will come John?" Jumping to the conclusion that moving the second auxiliary is the correct rule also runs up against any number of counterexamples. The answer is that in English, the auxiliary from the main clause—and not from the relative clause—is the one that is moved. Thus, any movement in a sentence must take syntactic categories (such as main and relative clause, subject of the sentence, object of the sentence) into account and not the order of the words. Rules of question formation in English (or any other language) must be described with respect to the grammatical structure of the sentence, not the serial order of the words.

How children become aware of the syntactic categories over which the rules are written in language is a continuing topic of debate in theories of language learning (see Pinker 1984). Although children generally don't learn how to identify these categories consciously until perhaps a 7th-grade grammar class, their linguistic behavior (such as question formation, subject-verb agreement, and numerous other phenomena) illustrates that syntactic categories must be unconsciously present at least by the time they are using four- and five-word sentences. The question for acquisition researchers is when and how such grammatical concepts enter the child's linguistic armamentarium. At least by age 3, children do not appear to violate rules for structure dependency (Crain and Nakayama 1987).

In sum, the question of how learners acquire the units and relations of their native language *is* the question of how they learn language. Acquisition involves becoming sensitive to linguistic structures, not just to the serial order of the words. Theories of acquisition must therefore account for how learners acquire linguistic units and linguistic rules.

2.2 Two Varieties of Language Acquisition Theories: Sketches of a Field

Despite the fact that theories of language acquisition are relatively immature, the current theories provide a starting point from which to consider how language learning gets off the ground. For the purposes of this discussion, theories of language acquisition will be classified into two families defined broadly by their commitment to what the child brings to the task, the processes used to acquire language, and the input considered central for acquisition. As in any exercise of this sort, "shoehorning" a theory into a family may do some violence to the details of that theory.

Table 2.1
Distinction among the major theories

	THEORY TYPE	
	Inside-out	Outside-in
Initial structure	Linguistic	Cognitive or social
Mechanism	Domain-specific	Domain-general
Source of structure	Innate	Learning procedures

What will be gained in exchange for some imprecision, however, will be an efficient way to present some of the major theoretical cuts in the field. By way of preview, the distinctions between these families of theories are presented schematically in table 2.1.

Outside-in theories. One family of theories, which we characterize as the "Outside-in" group, contends that language structure exists outside the child, in the environment. Children attend to the salient objects, events, and actions around them and *construct* language from rather meager linguistic beginnings. Indeed, early grammar is sometimes posited to be a transparent mapping of salient perceptual events onto linguistic form. The hypotheses the child entertains about what might constitute language-relevant data are derived and constrained either by the social environment or by the child's inherent cognitive capabilities, not by any specific linguistic knowledge. In this scenario, therefore, the language-learning problem is not privileged, but rather is one that is solved by domain-general learning procedures—by the same procedures that allow the child to analyze the environment into ongoing events composed of actions and objects. Thus, as table 2.1 indicates, all Outside-in theories must of necessity focus on the processes by which language is acquired since they do not grant that the child has been endowed with any language structure a priori. These processes must, in turn, be very powerful given that the Outside-in theories do not constrain them or the grammar ultimately acquired in any way. Thus, in general, Outside-in theories identify language learning as a totally bottom-up process, no different from learning that takes place in other domains. There are two identifiable subtypes of Outside-in theories —social-interactional and cognitive—differing mainly on which type of input is presumed to contribute most to language learning.

The *social-interactional theories* hold that the social interactions in which the child participates provide the route into language acquisition by highlighting just those aspects of events that will be translated into linguistic forms. The *cognitive theories*, emphasize the role played by the child's prior understanding of events and relations in the nonlinguistic world as well as the child's cognitive processing capabilities. Children use language to label the cognitive categories (e.g., agent, action) they have constructed. They then use distributional evidence or pattern detection of a general sort to cross-classify cognitive categories into linguistic ones like "noun phrase" and "subject of the sentence."

Inside-out theories. The second family of theories, which we characterize as the "Inside-out" theories, contends that language acquisition occupies its own separate niche or module in the brain and has its own unique mechanisms (Fodor 1975; Chomsky 1981). Language acquisition is the process of finding in the linguistic environment instantiations of the considerable innate linguistic knowledge the child already has. In the sense that the child works to find counterparts for a priori categories, the process of language acquisition is Inside-out in character. It is a process of discovery instead of construction.

There are also two subtypes of Inside-out theories. One subtype, the *structure-oriented* theories, places primary emphasis on the content of the grammar to be acquired. For example, such theories are concerned with how children select between grammatical options to "set" the "parameters" that correspond to their native language (Hyams 1986; Lightfoot 1989) and how they give evidence of the operation of universal linguistic principles such as the "binding" principles that apply to the interpretation of nouns, pronouns, and anaphors (e.g., Wexler and Chien 1985). In general, these theories presuppose rich linguistic structure that primes the child's entry into the linguistic system.

The second subtype of Inside-out theories, the *process-oriented* theories, also grants that the child must be innately endowed with domain-specific linguistic knowledge, such as a version of Chomsky's (1981) Principles-and-Parameters Theory or Bresnan's (1978) Lexical-Functional Grammar. The difference between these theories and the structure-oriented ones lies in their emphasis on uncovering the mechanisms the child uses to acquire language (Landau and Gleitman 1985; Gleitman 1990; Pinker 1984, 1989). Given the emphasis on mechanisms, some of these theories concern themselves with the acquisition sequence from its earliest point.

As is evident even from this cursory review, the Outside-in and Inside-out theories appear to offer very different assumptions about what the child brings to the task, what mechanisms guide acquisition, and what inputs the child uses. However, we will show that under the two theories learners actually approach the task with more in common than a superficial analysis suggests. Indeed, the two theories and their subtypes all seem to posit a learner who comes to the task with fairly sophisticated linguistic knowledge. In section 2.4 what are often considered dichotomies between the theories will be shown to be hyperbolic statements that actually obscure the theories' commonalities of position on the three questions listed above. Theories of language acquisition, we will argue, differ more in degree than in kind.

Outside-in Theories
Most of the Outside-in theories, be they social or cognitive in character, were developed as a direct response to Chomsky's (1965) nativistic and domain-specific view of language acquisition. Outside-in theories have been attractive to researchers for three reasons. First, they emphasize development, change, and culture more than the older nativistic theories. Second, because the social or cognitive categories that form the substrate for acquisition appear prior to language itself, researchers can investigate emerging language-relevant phenomena prior to the time when children begin to use multiword speech. Third, the Outside-in view (it is claimed) allows language learning to be accounted for by the same sorts of domain-general mechanisms that account for other types of learning. That is, according to outside-in theories, a child works to learn language structure; it does not come for free.

Social-Interactional Theories   The intellectual roots of researchers in the social-interactional group trace back to the speech-act theorists (Austin 1962; Searle 1969), who emphasize the functional uses of language. The social-interactionists believe (to varying degrees) that children construct their native language through social commerce. Nelson (1985) puts this position succinctly:

Language learning takes place within the framework of social interaction, and the nature of the particular kinds of interaction experienced determines not only the function and content of the language to be acquired but which segments will be learned first and how these segments will subsequently be put together or broken down for reassembly. (p. 109)

The sense of this quotation, embedded in a discussion of individual differences in language development, is that depending on the kind of cultural, social, and linguistic environments children are exposed to, they will learn not only different "function and content" but different-sized linguistic units and different grammatical rules for their recombination. For example, depending on the kinds of speech children hear directed to them, they may first learn unanalyzed "gestalts" (e.g., social expressions like "What's that?" uttered as a single unit) instead of learning single words that are then freely recombined (see also Peters 1985). The source of linguistic knowledge here is Outside-in: there is little discussion of what linguistic knowledge the child brings to the task other than the ability to participate in and profit from these social encounters.

An early proponent of a strong version of the social-interactional position was Bruner (1975), who argued that the structure of social interaction could be mapped transparently onto linguistic structure. On this view, when infants engage in give-and-take games with their caregivers in which they alternately play the role of "agent of action" and "recipient of action," they are essentially learning language. As Bruner later wrote in representing that position, "... something intrinsic in the nature and organization of concepts ... predisposes language to be the way it is—including the grammar" (1983a, 27). Bruner (1983a) subsequently recanted this position and concluded that "... systems of language ... are autonomous problem spaces, that however much their conquest may be aided by non-linguistic knowledge or external support from others, they must be mastered on their own" (p. 28). Despite his later retraction, a portion of the study of language acquisition was redirected by Bruner (among others) to the study of the ways in which the social environment supports—and in stronger versions, accounts for—such acquisition.

Under these formulations, repeated interactions with the environment provide the material for the child's construction of increasingly detailed scripts that serve as the substrate for initial language learning (Nelson 1985). Children can memorize sentences and phrases embedded in "formats" (Bruner 1983a,b) or "routines" (Snow 1986; Nelson 1985) and can later attend to the relationships between the stored sentences, deriving from them a set of sentence "rules." As children advance, the social environment might provide recasts and corrections of their grammatically incorrect utterances, facilitating and refining their early productions (Hirsh-Pasek, Treiman, and Schneiderman 1984; Hirsh-Pasek et al. 1986; Nelson 1977; Sokolov and Snow 1994; Moerk 1983; Bohannon and Stanowitz 1988; Furrow, Nelson, and Benedict 1979). Under this view, social interactions provide a cultural classroom for language learning. Children are presumed to bring little specifically linguistic knowledge to the task of language learning. Rather, they must have some way of interpreting the social interactions around them, of setting up and interpreting joint attentional episodes, of understanding some global relations between the input sentences and represented meaning, and of detecting the corrections that caregivers provide in what are often subtle and inconsistent responses to their sentences (see Bohannon and Stanowitz 1988, for a discussion of how this might work). Thus, the child begins language learning as a social partner. Social processes like joint attention, script construction, "fine-tuning" of caregivers' utterances to the level of the child's, and correction from the environment form the foundation for the abstraction of linguistic units and the continuing revision of linguistic rules. The motivation that drives the system forward is often an instrumental one: the child is eager to fulfill various social functions, many of which are best carried out through linguistic means. It is the child's interpretation of the social environment that propels the language-learning system onward.

The work of some social-interactional theorists does not appear to answer the question posed here, namely, how children break into the grammar of their native language. Rather, it seems to center more on issues surrounding the uses to which language is put. As Bruner (1983b) writes:

Whatever else language is, it is a systematic way of communicating to others, of affecting their and our own behavior, of sharing attention .... Let us not be dazzled by the grammarian's questions. Pragmatic ones are just as dazzling and mysterious. How indeed do we ever learn to get things done with words? (p. 120)

On the other hand, some social-interactional theorists' work is motivated by a desire to understand how social interaction supports language acquisition per se. As Snow (1989) writes:

No one denies that social interaction is a prerequisite to normal development, in language as in other domains. The question arises about *special features* of social interaction—whether there are aspects of the ways in which adults or older children interact with infants and young children that are crucial or helpful to language development, and if so, what those features are and how they help. (p. 2)

In short, some social-interactional theorists, like Snow, continue to focus on what it is about social interaction that might facilitate the learning of grammar. Others appear to be concerned with the pragmatic aspects of language and not the syntactic (e.g., Berko Gleason 1993).

Cognitive Theories   Because children appear to interpret their environment in terms of cognitive categories made up of agents, patients, actions, locations, and so on, cognitive theorists such as Schlesinger (1971, 1988) and Braine (1976) argue that these cognitive categories can provide a solid foundation for language learning. Unlike those who have argued from a more social perspective, these theorists (who do not negate the role of social input) have also developed models of language learning.

For example, in describing his semantic assimilation model for language acquisition, Schlesinger (1988) argues that children begin the task of language learning with early relational categories that are

semantic case-like categories (such as agent, patient, location) rather than syntactic ones. [These semantic categories] ... reflect the way the child interprets the world around him.... The child interprets the environment in terms of semantic relations and learns how these are expressed in his native language by means of word order, inflection and function words. (p. 122)

Evidence from studies of early event perception and memory adds credence to Schlesinger's claims. Children may indeed come to the language-learning task equipped with language-relevant categories like agency (Golinkoff 1981), animacy (Golinkoff et al. 1984), causality (Cohen and Oakes 1993), and possibly path or location (Mandler 1988, 1992).

The developers of the most detailed of these models, Bates and Mac-Whinney (1987, 1989), endorse a domain-general view of language learning in which minimal language structure is given from the start. Building on Maratsos and Chalkley's (1980) analysis of how children discover form classes through unconstrained distributional analysis, MacWhinney and Bates (1989) write:

[T]he universal properties of grammar are only indirectly innate, being based on interactions among innate categories and processes that are not specific to language. In other words, we believe in the innateness of language, but we are skeptical about the degree of domain-specificity that is required to account for the structure and acquisition of natural languages. (p. 10)

According to Bates and MacWhinney's "Competition Model," based on connectionist-type learning mechanisms, the child looks for form-function mappings through the use of such constructs as "cue validity" and "cue strength." "Cue validity" describes the extent to which a particular cue for how a language works is available (i.e., present in the surface structure) and reliable (i.e., leads to the same outcome when it is available). Cue validity can therefore be assessed by looking at what grammatical devices a language uses to mark certain meanings. "Cue strength" is how much weight the learner gives to units of linguistic information. A particular cue will be weighted more heavily if it has high cue validity. Thus, for English, preverbal position tends to be a highly reliable and often available cue for agency. It will correspondingly be assigned greater cue strength than it would in a language like Italian, where word order is less rigidly constrained and semantic roles are marked in other ways.

The Competition Model has undergone extensive additions and revisions, although the assumptions underlying it have not changed:

> [L]anguage acquisition becomes a problem of pattern detection that may or may not require the application of innate linguistic knowledge. We suspect that more general principles of pattern detection and distributional learning are sufficient for the task ... (Bates and MacWhinney 1989, 26)

Thus, children note distributional evidence in the input and piece together the grammar of their language. The claim is that far less linguistic knowledge needs to be in place at the start of the language-learning process than would be supposed by the nativistic or Inside-out theories to be discussed below. General-purpose cognitive mechanisms such as induction and hypothesis testing can be employed in the service of language acquisition, and these processes are sufficient to guarantee successful grammatical learning. Theories like Bates and MacWhinney's are being extended in connectionist treatments in which computer simulations are used to model a distributional theory of language acquisition (Plunkett 1995).

Summary of the Outside-in Position   To the three questions posed above, then, Outside-in theorists would offer the following answers:

1. What is present when grammatical learning begins? The child brings to the language-learning task a rich social and/or cognitive system that includes cognitive categories such as agent and recipient. The child also brings the ability to attend to and organize linguistic data, although this ability does not emanate from any language-specific module apart from general cognition.

2. What mechanisms are used in the course of acquisition? Although some theories do not explicitly mention mechanisms, the thrust of the Outside-in theories is that children are equipped with domain-general learning procedures, not particularly constrained in any way, which enable them to analyze events into cognitive categories and to detect the covarying language forms. For grammatical learning the chief mechanism

appears to be distributional analysis, since children form ever wider, more abstract concepts that ultimately overlap with adult linguistic concepts.

3. What types of input drive the language-learning system forward? In the Outside-in theories, burgeoning social knowledge and/or cognitive skills provide the impetus for continued language learning. At the earliest stages, language is simply a transparent overlay onto social or cognitive categories.

Critique of the Outside-in Position   Four criticisms have been leveled at the Outside-in approaches to language acquisition (see Golinkoff and Gordon 1983; Snow and Gilbreath 1983; Pinker 1984); some of these have been prefigured in the above review. The account offered by these theories appears to have the advantage of parsimony in that domain-general abilities—presumably the same abilities that service, say, perception or number knowledge—are seen as supporting language acquisition (Piatelli-Palmarini 1980). Yet these general accounts, even in their more advanced instantiations, fall far short of explaining some of the basic facts of language acquisition.

The first problem is that although the Outside-in theories profess to make minimal nativistic assumptions about what the child brings to the language-learning task, they presuppose much in the way of nonlinguistic and linguistic knowledge at the start of language acquisition without often explicating the source or process by which that knowledge was gained. For example, Bates and MacWhinneys' Competition Model requires the "early availability" of the following concepts (from MacWhinney 1987, 259):

Major item type: nominal, verbal, operator
Nominal status: common, proper, pronoun, and dummy
Number: singular, plural, and dual
Individuation: mass, count, and collection
Tense: present, past, and future

This list represents only part of the linguistic material that the model explicitly presumes to be present at the start of language learning. Likewise, Schlesinger (1988) proposes that

the child indeed does have access to relational categories underlying sentences, since these are at first not abstract, formally defined categories ... but categories that reflect the relationship in situations referred to by the sentence he hears: the agent of an action, the location of an entity, and so on. If anything, it is these cognitively based categories that must be assumed to be innate. (p. 123)

Thus, the Outside-in approach presumes a host of possibly innate and abstract givens that include ways of (1) interpreting the environment in terms of categories like agents and actions; (2) segmenting the speech stream into linguistically relevant units; (3) attending to the order and frequency of these units; (4) memorizing the units for purposes of comparing and computing their frequency in order to resolve competition (Bates and MacWhinney 1987); and (5) creating categories of ever-expanding power such that they approximate grammatical categories like "subject of the sentence" (Bates and MacWhinney 1987; Braine 1976; Bowerman 1973; Schlesinger 1988).

To sum up, the first problem faced by Outside-in theories is that they contain many hidden assumptions about the linguistic knowledge that the child brings to the task. Indeed, these linguistic assumptions are necessary for their arguments to go through. As Kelly and Martin (1994) state with respect to theories that rely on distributional analyses:

[R]eference to the statistical structure of the environment will not be sufficient to characterize learning since the nature of the environment is partly defined by how the learner categorizes items within it. Furthermore, these categories may in fact be intrinsically linguistic in nature. Hence we are back to a basic problem in language learning: What notions about the nature of language do children bring to the task at hand? Reference to statistical regularities has not eliminated this problem at all. (pp. 115–116).

The second problem faced by some Outside-in theories is that they treat linguistic knowledge as though it is reducible to knowledge in other domains. That is, Outside-in theorists have tended to treat language as though it is a transparent mapping between cognitive or social categories and linguistic forms. But this view faces several obstacles and questions. If there is any such transparency, children quickly go beyond it when they master the complexity of their language. Furthermore, if the transparency assumption were true, why wouldn't all languages be the same? Why wouldn't all languages rely on the same order of elements if it was more "natural" to use the sequence *doer − action − result*? Humans presumably construct these categories as a result of universal cognitive processes.

The fatal flaw in this assumption is that cognitive and social categories do not map transparently onto linguistic forms; nor is linguistic knowledge the same as social or cognitive knowledge. One argument to this effect is made by Roeper (1987), who points out that the cognitive category of "agent" is not the same as the linguistic category of "agent." For example, one can say "the robber of the bank," but not "the thief of the bank." Robbers and thieves are both agents, but the words "robber" and "thief" cannot fill the same grammatical slots in the phrases given. Thus, knowing the cognitive agent would not be sufficient for expressing this idea linguistically.

The third problem faced by Outside-in theories is the need to explain how the child starts with one kind of linguistic system based on cognitive and social categories and transforms it into the adult linguistic system based on abstract syntactic categories. As Bloom, Miller, and Hood (1975) first pointed out:

> Braine's (1974) formulation, and pragmatic explanations in general, establish a serious discontinuity with later development. Such claims fail to contribute to either a) how the child eventually learns grammatical structure, or b) the systematic (semantic-syntactic) regularities that are manifest among the earliest multiword utterances. (p. 33)

Gleitman (1981) humorously refers to this problem of discontinuity as the tadpole-to-frog problem. What we have called Outside-in theories begin with cognitive categories—the tadpole—and must transform them into more abstract linguistic categories—the frog. For example, if children begin with the category of agent and not the category of sentence subject, they must somehow transform the former into the latter. Since sentence subjects can be agents, patients of action, locations, and so on, there is no one-to-one mapping between cognitive and linguistic categories. Yet the Outside-in theories cannot adequately explain how this transformation occurs. They are unable to offer workable solutions to this problem of discontinuity for two related reasons: some of the Outside-in theories conflate language and communication and therefore do not see it as a problem; others seem to rely on unarticulated assumptions about the grammar that the child must ultimately acquire (Golinkoff and Gordon 1983).

One response to this problem of discontinuity is to note that there may be no discontinuity problem at all. Perhaps syntax (and not just semantic categories) is there from the beginning. There is reason to believe that children can use syntactic information; that they can even use abstract syntactic categories from a very early age; and that if there is some shift from a semantically or communicatively based system to a syntactic one, it occurs quite early in the language acquisition process. Evidence from children as young as 17 and 18 months of age, for example, suggests that children are keenly aware of syntactic structure and that syntax is not reducible to semantics (see Levy 1988; Pinker 1984; Bloom 1990; Choi and

Bowerman 1991). Further, in an exquisite demonstration of the impact of syntax, Choi and Bowerman (1991) show that young children (17 months of age) use syntax in interaction with semantic information to carve up the domain of spatial relations. In English, for example, the notion PATH (*into* or *out of*) is marked in the same way whether it results from a spontaneous or a caused motion (e.g., "John rolled the ball OUT OF the box" vs. "The ball rolled OUT OF the box"). In Korean different words are used to represent PATH depending on whether the movement is caused or spontaneous. Thus, the same semantic space is carved up differently by different languages, a fact that seems to be internalized by children who are but a year-and-a-half old. Syntax here is influencing semantic organization; form is influencing function. (This result is perhaps most striking given that Bowerman (1973) was one of the early proponents of an Outside-in, semantically based approach to language acquisition.) In short, there may not be a tadpole-to-frog shift on this view.

The fourth problem is perhaps the most toublesome for the Outside-in theories. It falls under what has been referred to as the "poverty-of-the-stimulus" argument. In Chomsky's (1988) words, "As in the case of language, the environment is far too impoverished and indeterminate to provide this system to the child, in its full richness and applicability" (p. 153). Three examples will illustrate what the environment fails to contain. The first example of how the linguistic stimulus (sentences that the child hears, in isolation from their context) cannot provide sufficient data for distributional analysis is what are often called "empty categories" (Chomsky 1981). These are categories that are presumed to exist at some abstract, underlying level but that are not realized in the surface structure of the sentence. Psycholinguistic research with adults (e.g., Bever and McElree 1988; see Fodor 1989, for a review) has demonstrated that on-line sentence processing reflects the existence of these categories. In imperative sentences (e.g., "Get dressed!"), "you" is implied but is not present in the surface form. Children (who hear many imperative sentences) do not produce sentences like "Get dressed himself!" although they do produce sentences like "Get dressed yourself!" Since they cannot be performing a distributional analysis on a "you" that is not present in the speech they hear, children must, in some way, be aware of its existence at a deeper level. No amount of pattern detection will supply learners with the clairvoyance needed to retrieve the nonexistent "you"; some other mechanism must account for their sensitivity to this category.

Structure dependency provides a second example of how the stimulus presents insufficient data for pattern analysis. The sentence cited earlier, "The man who will come is John," makes this point in that its surface form gives little indication of how it is hierarchically organized (but see Lederer and Kelly 1991). Yet this sentence is composed of a main clause ("The man is John") and a subordinate noun phrase ("who will come"), and only the "is" from the main clause may be fronted to form a question. Thus, only the question "Is the man who will come John?" is grammatical; the question "Will the man who come is John?" is not. No amount of "ground up" surface structure analysis will allow learners to stumble on the fact that not all noun phrases are treated equally; the grammatical role the noun phrase plays in the sentence determines what alterations it may undergo. Without this structural knowledge, however, children will make many incorrect generalizations about the grammar of their language.

A third piece of evidence in favor of the poverty-of-the-stimulus argument is that reliance on the surface cues provided in the input often leads to the wrong generalizations. Consider the following examples provided by Gibson (1992) in his critique of Bates and MacWhinney's Competition Model:

The chicken cooked the dinner. (chicken = agent)
The chicken was cooked. (chicken = theme)
The chicken cooked. (chicken = theme)

Under the Competition Model, cue validity and cue strength predict that preverbal position here should be identified with agency. It is not. Children do not seem to make the overgeneralization errors that would be expected if they were analyzing the input in ways suggested by the Outside-in theories. In fact, there are no surface cues in the impoverished input that can assist the child in these cases.

In sum, the following four limitations make the Outside-in theories less than plausible accounts of how children learn language: (1) the problem of hidden assumptions embedded within the theories; (2) the conflation of language and communication that leads theorists toward reductionist accounts of language (e.g., linguistic knowledge as reducible to cognitive or social knowledge); (3) the problem of discontinuity in grammatical development; and (4) the poverty-of-the-stimulus argument. Although almost all Outside-in theories suffer from one or more of these limitations, one is more or less free from all of them.

Bloom's Version of a Cognitive, Outside-in Theory Bloom (1970, 1973, 1991a, 1993) is an Outside-in theorist who has consistently appreciated that linguistic knowledge is not reducible to other kinds of knowledge: "... linguistic development is neither isomorphic with nor a necessary result of cognitive development" (Bloom, Lightbown, and Hood 1975, 30); "... how they [children] have learned to think about the objects, events, and relations in their experience is something apart from how they have learned to represent such information in linguistic messages" (p. 29). Thus, Bloom saw language as a "separate problem space" early on and does not view language acquisition as a simple one-to-one mapping between cognitive knowledge and linguistic forms.

Yet Bloom is an Outside-in theorist because to the question of what the child brings to language acquisition, her answer is completely "bottom-up." That is, she does not believe that the child begins with any a priori linguistic categories (Bloom, Lightbown, and Hood 1975; Bloom 1991a, personal communication); instead, she believes that the child applies domain-general cognitive principles (as opposed to principles specific to language) to the task of language learning. She writes:

The processes involved in this learning [grammatical learning] are the same as for learning anything else (physical knowledge, biology, etc.) and consist of 1) detection of novelty, identity, and equivalence ... and 2) abstraction, coordination, and integration, for connections between categories. These processes themselves no doubt have a biological basis (categorization, for instance) but depend upon such garden variety context factors as salience, frequency, and the like. (personal communication)

Further, although Bloom believes that children express notions like "agent" and "location" in their earliest multiword utterances, she avoids the problem of discontinuity by claiming that the child is able to make use of syntactic categories from the first multiword utterance (although not before; see Bloom 1973). Counter to Outside-in theorists who argue for the separate acquisition of semantics and syntax (see Schlesinger 1988; Braine 1976; Bowerman 1973; Bates and MacWhinney 1987; Brown 1973), Bloom maintains that children learn semantics and syntax together, as opposed to deferring syntactic learning to some unspecified future time (Bloom 1970; Bloom, Lightbown, and Hood 1975; Bloom, Miller, and Hood 1975). The basis for this claim is that Bloom found sentences such as "Lamb go here" and "Put lamb here" among children's earliest utterances. In "Lamb go here," "lamb" serves as sentence subject and as patient (or object affected); in "Put lamb here," the unstated "you" is the sentence subject and "lamb" is the grammatical direct object and patient. Such sentences, produced by the same child, revealed too much linguistic sophistication to be reducible exclusively to semantic relations. If the child had access only to semantic relations, the same noun playing the same semantic role should not vary in its syntactic function. On the other hand, if children are sensitive to syntactic requirements—in this case, the argument structure required by particular verbs—"lamb" may play the same semantic role but have two different syntactic functions depending on the verb. Bloom's data revealed that children consistently made complex mappings between meaning and form, respecting the syntactic subcategorization requirements of verbs that were highly similar in meaning.

Given increasing evidence that children do indeed treat language as a formal object—as opposed to a system isomorphic with cognitive or social knowledge—many researchers have returned to Bloom's position, crediting young children with knowledge of both form classes (e.g., noun, verb) and syntactic categories (e.g., subject of the sentence) (Pinker 1984; Bowerman 1988; Ihns and Leonard 1988; Valian 1986; Levy 1988). Some researchers, such as Pinker (1984), indeed go further than Bloom does. According to Bloom's view, although children are engaged early on in formal linguistic analysis, their original categories are not identical to adult categories but smaller in scope. Nonetheless, Bloom's emphasis on the child's ability to engage in formal linguistic analyses provides a bridge between the Outside-in and Inside-out theories. A foundational assumption for Inside-out theories is that young children conduct linguistic analyses and use syntactic as opposed to only semantic categories. Inside-out theories differ from Bloom's Outside-in account, however, on the source of the child's ability to perform linguistic analyses and on the nature of the learning mechanisms.

Inside-out Theories

A key difference between the Inside-out and Outside-in theories is that the Inside-out theories begin with the premise that the complexities of language, as well as its species-specificity, could not be accounted for without innate constraints on the "language faculty." As Karmiloff-Smith (1989) writes:

I fail to see how it could be biologically tenable that nature would have endowed every species except the human with a considerable amount of biologically specified knowledge. (p. 273)

Inside-out theories grant the child domain-specific linguistic knowledge (hence the term "language faculty") and emphasize grammar *discovery* rather than grammar construction.

Compared with the Outside-in theories, the inside-out theories deemphasize the role that the environment plays in language acquisition. This is a direct result of the stance these theories take on what constitutes language. Since on the Chomskyan (1975, 1981) view, there are linguistic phenomena such as empty categories that are not "visible" (or "audible") in the linguistic input, linguistic knowledge cannot in principle be wholly discovered through inspection of the available input. Hence, the Inside-out theorists often allude to the notion "poverty of the stimulus."

The existence of grammatical elements like empty categories is central to the Inside-out arguments. On this view, the child could never *learn* about something that is absent from the surface structure of the sentence and present only at an abstract level. If one grants these linguistic facts, no corpus of utterances, however vast, could ever advance the child's grammatical learning. The child must be genetically "prepared" to encounter these empty categories. Indeed, there is mounting evidence that both child and adult processors are sensitive to some types of empty categories (such as traces left behind by various movement processes) (see Goodluck 1991).

The Chomskyan Basis of Inside-out Theories   Current Inside-out theories represent an advance over previous formulations based on Chomsky 1965. In the older versions, the child's mind was likened to a black box whose contents defied inspection. Into this box, commonly known as the "Language Acquisition Device," were dumped all the linguistic generalizations that could not arguably be derived from linguistic experience (Chomsky 1972). When the number of linguistic rules and transformations became unwieldy—both in the grammar and by extension in the child's Language Acquisition Device—Chomsky (1981) developed the "Principles-and-Parameters Theory" of what he (1988) refers to as the "language faculty," which consists of

a set of invariant principles and a set of parameters that are set by some linguistic environment, just as certain receptors are 'set' on exposure to a horizontal line. (Lightfoot 1991, 647).

Thus, this theory replaced a grammar in which rules and transformations had proliferated with an elegant, more streamlined grammar. Multiple and contradictory rules were replaced by a finite set of principles and parameters; multiple transformations by a single transformation ("Move α"). By "principles," Chomsky means something very different than Slobin (1985a,b), namely, universal statements about how language works. One such principle, the Projection Principle (Chomsky 1981), states that "[t]he properties of lexical entries project onto the syntax of the sentence" (Cook 1989, 11). For example, nouns "project" into noun phrases; verbs into verb phrases. Thus, once learners know the form class of a lexical item (e.g., "chair" is a noun), they will also know how it may behave syntactically. Knowledge of the Projection Principle allows children to recognize that individual lexical items are part of larger constituents that compose sentences.

With the construct of "parameters," Chomsky captures the ways different languages handle various grammatical phenomena. One suggested parameter called "pro-drop" captures whether or not a language allows sentences without subjects. For example, English does not permit subjectless sentences and even requires the use of expletives or dummy elements to avoid this (e.g., "*It*'s raining"). However, Italian does allow subjectless sentences (e.g., "It's raining" is expressed simply by the verb "Piove"). To say that children begin the language-learning process in possession of such a parameter implies that they need to hear (in theory) no more than a few key sentences to set the switch of this parameter to match their target language: either "subjectless sentences *are* allowed" (Italian) or "subjectless sentences *are not* allowed" (English).

Thus, the development of Principles-and-Parameters Theory represented a clear advance for Inside-out theories of language acquisition. First, it acknowledged the many important ways in which languages differ while at the same time making the Inside-out acquisition account seem more universal. Second, by positing a "menu" for the setting of parameter switches, it introduced a powerful metaphor. According to Chomsky (1988), "... universal grammar is an account of the initial state of the language faculty before any experience" (p. 61). All children need to do in language acquisition is set a few switches, corresponding to the language they are immersed in—an act whose repercussions will extend throughout the grammatical system—and acquire the vocabulary items particular to that language (Cook, 1989). Third, since there was no agreement on what these parameters were, a whole new program of linguistic research was initiated. Once again, acquisition research was central to this enterprise. If the proposed parameters were the correct ones, they should be able to account for acquisition.

Types of Inside-out Theories: Structure- Versus Process-Oriented Theories
The basis for separating the Inside-out theorists into two groups rests on presuppositions about how the process of language acquisition gets underway. The structure-oriented theorists begin their story *after* the initial stages of language learning, presupposing answers to our first question, "What does the child bring to the language-learning task?" Also, until recently (Lightfoot 1989), theorists in this camp have been relatively less concerned with finding answers to our second question, "What mechanisms does the child use to acquire language?" The process-oriented theorists, on the other hand, are dedicated to understanding the origins of grammatical acquisition and the mechanisms that make it possible. Thus, although both subgroups presuppose that nature prepares the child for the task of learning language, the process-oriented group provides more complete answers to the questions that motivate this review.

Structure-Oriented Theories   The prototypical structure-oriented theorist is Chomsky himself (1988), who has articulated the strongest version of this position. Along with other structure-oriented theorists (e.g., Wexler 1982; Hyams 1986, Lightfoot 1989), he assumes that whatever the exact array of principles and parameters turns out to be, nature has given these to the child. Thus, to the question of what the child brings to the task of language acquisition, structure-oriented theorists answer that the child has been endowed with considerable, explicit, domain-specific, linguistic knowledge. The social or cognitive framework for language acquisition so important to the Outside-in theories is reduced to a given by Chomsky (1988), who writes that the child

approaches language with an intuitive understanding of such concepts as physical object, human intention, volition, causation, goal, and so on. These constitute a framework for thought and language and are common to the languages of the world ... (p. 32)

For structure-oriented theorists the interesting questions have to do with children's manifestation of the principles and parameters of universal grammar; entry into the domain-specific system is a given. These theorists presuppose that the child comes to the language-learning task with the ability to segment the linguistic stream, find word classes and grammatical categories, conduct phrase structure analyses, and set parameters. What interests these theorists is (1) exactly what principles and parameters children begin with and (2) what constitutes the "primary linguistic data" (Chomsky 1988) for setting the switches of the parameters.

According to Chomsky (1988), parameters can be set, and the basis for principles revealed, by exposure to only a few sentences of the language to be learned. This position is sometimes referred to as the "instantaneous" view of language acquisition. When the actual data produced by children contradicted this extreme position (see e.g., Wexler and Chien 1985, on the late appearance of Principle B of the binding theory), the explanation endorsed by some structure-oriented theorists was biological maturation. Thus, with regard to the question of the mechanisms responsible for language acquisition, some Inside-out theorists assume that biological maturation, parallel to the maturation of bodily organs, is primarily responsible. Further, structure-oriented theorists eschew traditional notions of learning as explanations for language growth. Chomsky (1988) has written that learning a language is not really something that the child does. Rather, it is something that "happens" to the child in an appropriate environment. The analogy that Chomsky (e.g., 1988) consistently uses is visual perception. Just as one would never argue that an organism had "learned" to develop sense receptors on the retina for the perception of horizontal and vertical lines, so one should not argue that language is "learned."

Finally, for the structure-oriented group, the input that drives the system or "triggers" parameter setting is certainly linguistic input. Since not all sentences are usable by the child, the language faculty selects relevant data from the linguistic input (see Lightfoot 1989 for discussion of what constitutes the "primary linguistic data"). In addition to having a critical role in the setting of the parameters, the environment is treated as playing a role analogous to the one that nutrition plays in the onset of puberty: an impoverished environment may restrict or suppress language growth in the same way that poor nutrition may delay the onset of puberty (Chomsky 1988).

Process-Oriented Theories   The differences between process-oriented and structure-oriented theories are slight. Structure-oriented theorists tend to focus on the emergence of particular linguistic structures as a way to validate aspects of grammatical theory. Process-oriented theorists, however, emphasize the means through which children discover their grammar by focusing on the mapping between function and form. Not surprisingly, structure-oriented theorists are often linguists and process-oriented theorists tend to be psychologists. Like the structure-oriented theorists, the process-oriented group grants that nature has endowed the child with domain-specific linguistic knowledge that makes language learning possible. These Inside-out theorists, however, focus on how the child breaks into language. Thus, the fact that the child is seen as being *prepared* to learn certain linguistic facts does not remove the mystery of *how* the child actually accomplishes this feat. As the name we have given them reveals, process-oriented theorists, such as Gleitman and her colleagues (1990; Gleitman and Wanner 1988; Gleitman and Gillette 1995) and Pinker (1984, 1989) and his colleagues, are concerned with *how* initial linguistic representations are formed and *how* acquisition continues once children have produced their first words.

Pinker (1984) offers the most explicit overall theory of language acquisition to date. To the question of what the child brings to the task of language acquisition, Pinker answers that "... the child is assumed to know, prior to acquiring a language, the overall structure of the grammar, the formal nature of the different sorts of rules it contains, and the primitives from which those rules may be composed" (p. 31). That is, Pinker believes the child is equipped with word classes like noun and verb, syntactic categories like subject and object, and other grammatical knowledge.

Gleitman (1990; Gleitman and Wanner 1988), too, begins from the premise that a child operating without any constraints on how to interpret the linguistic input (or the nonlinguistic world, for that matter) would wallow forever in a hypothesis space too large to chance upon the correct interpretation of a word, let alone a sentence. For this reason the child needs considerable language-specific knowledge to even begin the task of language learning—knowledge about how to parse sentences, knowledge of potential sentence structures, and so on. The task that children face is somehow to derive instantiations of this knowledge from their particular language. One glimpse into the learning problem from this perspective is provided by word learning. Without constraints on the myriad hypotheses a child might generate, the word "cat," uttered in some nonlinguistic and linguistic context (e.g., the caregiver points to a cat lying on a pillow and says, "See the *cat*?"), could be interpreted in any number of ways. It could refer to the cat's tail, which happens to be swishing, the union of the cat and the pillow it is lying on, or perhaps some property of the cat like its fur. Clearly, the child must be predisposed to interpret words in specific ways, compatible with the way already accomplished speakers seem to use them. Markman (1989) and Golinkoff, Mervis, and Hirsh-Pasek (1994) discuss a set of principles for lexical acquisition that would do this work.

The acquisition of lexical items is only the beginning of the story, however: the child must cross-classify these words into word classes. Inside-out theories grant the child the universal set of word classes. However, as Pinker (1984) points out, it is not enough to say that children are born with word classes such as "noun" and "verb"; they also need to be able to find instantiations of these classes in the input. To solve this problem, Pinker (1984) posits a mechanism that he calls "semantic bootstrapping," based on related proposals by Grimshaw (1981) and Macnamara (1972). On this proposal, children who encounter labels for persons, places, or things are prepared to link these back to their linguistic counterpart, namely, the word class "noun." The semantic bootstrapping proposal goes well beyond this example. In Pinker's (1987) words:

> [T]he claim of the Semantic Bootstrapping Hypothesis is that the child uses the presence of semantic entities such as "thing," "causal agent," "true in past," and "predicate-argument relation" to infer that the input contains tokens of the corresponding syntactic substantive universals such as "noun," "subject," "auxiliary," "dominates," and so on. In the theory outlined in Pinker (1984) this knowledge is used by several sets of procedures to build rules for the target language. (p. 407)

Note that Pinker's account presupposes that (1) children can parse incoming sentences; (2) they can figure out which word in the string corresponds to the object label; and (3) they (innately) possess "linking rules" for joining the word for the referent to the class "noun" and further to "sentence subject."

Gleitman (1990) points out that each of these issues constitutes a significant research problem in its own right. For example, upon seeing a rabbit jump and hearing "See the rabbit jump!", how is the child to know that the phonological segment "rabbit" (assuming it has been discriminated from the stream of words around it) maps to the object in motion? In this regard, Pinker may be overestimating the transparency of the mapping between language and environmental events (Gleitman 1990). Despite their disagreements, however, Pinker and Gleitman would answer the first question in somewhat similar ways. Children come to the language-learning task with a linguistic endowment that predisposes them to make certain hypotheses rather than others about words and about grammar.

With regard to our second question on the nature of the mechanisms for language learning, both Pinker and Gleitman believe that children use domain-specific *and* domain-general processes to analyze the linguistic input. From a domain-general perspective, both theorists would agree that children must apply general learning devices (e.g., pattern detection) to uncover the details of the way their language works. On the domain-specific side, children are predisposed (because of their innate grammatical endowment) to come up with certain hypotheses rather than others as they analyze the linguistic stream. Indeed, theorizing far more explicitly than previous researchers, Pinker (1984) posits a set of six procedures to describe how the child conducts syntactic analyses. According to the "structure-dependent distributional learning" principle, for example, children use what they already know about grammar to assist them in learning about words whose semantic and syntactic features are not immediately transparent. So, a child who hears the sentence "John told the truth" can tell from the fact that the article "the" precedes the word "truth" that it is probably a noun. This allows the child to continue to parse the sentence without having to stop.

Once children have worked out something of the grammar, it would be very useful for them to exploit the frames in which words appear to figure out the nuances of their meanings. The clearest case is that of blind children, who although they cannot observe environmental contexts of use, nonetheless seem perfectly able to distinguish between such verbs as "look" and "see." To account for this phenomenon, Landau and Gleitman (1985) propose the mechanism called "syntactic bootstrapping." For example, if a noun occurs immediately before and after a verb (as with "push"), the verb may be causative. If a noun occurs only immediately before (as with "run"), the verb is likely to be noncausative. Obviously, in order for syntactic bootstrapping to be possible, there must be correlations between syntax and meaning that the child must be able to exploit at a relatively early age. A number of current research projects suggest that these correlations do exist and that adults and children exploit them (see Fisher, Gleitman, and Gleitman 1991; Naigles 1990; Fisher 1994; Gleitman and Gillette 1995).

Regarding the third question (What inputs drive the language-learning system forward?), there is again considerable agreement between Gleitman and Pinker. The input that propels language learning is linguistic in nature, although the role of the extralinguistic environment is far from minimal. Unlike the structure-oriented theorists, Pinker and Gleitman do not talk of the environment as a "trigger" but instead focus on the nature of the information available in the language input, as well as in the child's observation and interpretation of events. On both accounts the semantic system can be used to help learners bootstrap their way into the syntactic system at the same time that the syntactic system helps learners narrow down particular facets of the semantic interpretation. In this sense, both Pinker's and Gleitman's positions allow for a dialectic process. Nevertheless, although both authors acknowledge strong contributions from semantics and syntax (Pinker 1990; Gleitman 1990), Pinker puts relatively more weight on the semantic input in the dialectic whereas Gleitman puts relatively more weight on the syntactic input.

In sum, the process-oriented Inside-out theorists, although granting that nature has prepared the child for language learning, are distinguished from the structure-oriented Inside-out theorists by their emphasis on the question "how"; that is, they ask, "How do children actually operate on the linguistic stream to uncover the categories nature has prepared them to search for?" In their attention to mechanism, the process-oriented theorists seem to resemble Bloom (1991a), an Outside-in theorist who grants that children actively construct grammar. Where Pinker and Gleitman differ from Bloom is on their insistence that children do not begin the task with exclusively domain-general learning procedures or structures; both Pinker and Gleitman permit nature to narrow the child's hypothesis space considerably and to endow the child with domain-specific processes that facilitate grammar acquisition.

Critique of the Inside-out Position   Several criticisms can be leveled at the Inside-out theories, especially at the structure-oriented branch. First, the relegation of linguistic insights to innate constraints built into the grammar itself is open to question. Specifically, Inside-out theories are vulnerable to the criticism that claims of innateness make a theory unfalsifiable because, as Fodor and Crain (1987) argue, "A theory which admits substantive innate principles can all too easily add another one to the list, in response to a new observation about natural languages" (p. 46).

The next three criticisms stem from the first. Given that much linguistic knowledge is innate, Inside-out theories (particularly the structure-oriented branch) often appear (1) to be nondevelopmental; (2) to reduce the role of the environment to serving as a trigger; and (3) to rely on the nonmechanism of maturation when structures do not appear instantaneously.

With respect to whether acquisition has a developmental curve, it is only in recent years (in response to data showing that children do not get it all right from the start) that structure-oriented Inside-out theorists have begun to grapple with the actual course of acquisition. Bates and MacWhinney (1987) point out that this literature is still characterized by too much of an emphasis on language structures emerging cleanly in a single trial, never to be used incorrectly again. Yet the course of acquisition is not a smooth, ascending curve. Children have been known to use correct structures alongside incorrect structures for years (see Kuczaj 1977). Infant perception may be a good analogue for how development occurs in other domain-specific, encapsulated areas where children start out with innate knowledge. As Spelke (1990; Spelke et al. 1992) argues, infants appear to begin the process of perception with the expectation that objects have solidity, take up space, and so on. However, infants do not operate according to the Gestalt principles that older children and adults operate with in perception; for example, they do not employ "completion"—the notion that objects that are partially occluded continue behind their occluder. Thus, innate knowledge provides the starting point, or the skeleton around which later learning is organized.

In emphasizing that input sentences "trigger" linguistic progress, the metaphor of the child as a passive reactor—ironically, as in the mechanistic model—has been reasserted. Inside-out theorists of the structure-oriented type minimize psychological mechanisms such as imitation, comparison, storage, and concept formation that the child undoubtedly uses to acquire language. As Bloom (1991a) writes:

A developmental perspective assumes that children play an active part in acquiring language. They are in effect, "the agents of their own development" .... Most learnability-theoretic research has an essentially *mechanistic* world view, in which language depends on inborn, specifically linguistic constraints triggered by relevant instances in the input. Developmental research and theory has an *organismic* world view, with an emphasis on change, integration, and process. (pp. 13–14).

The lack of a developmental approach seriously impedes the structure-oriented Inside-out theories from being able to explain *when* particular structures are triggered by the input available from the environment. Since for the Inside-out theories the environment can be presumed to be a constant, it must be something within the organism that allows the triggering to take place at time 2 when it did not occur at time 1.

This point brings us to the next criticism. For the structure-oriented Inside-out theorist the role of the environment in language learning is likened to the role that nutrition plays in human growth: it is necessary—and no more. Other than containing the linguistic input, and the extra-linguistic situations that covary with the input, the environment serves a minimal function in the process of language acquisition. Inside-out theorists (e.g., Lightfoot 1989) are just beginning to grapple with what it means to say that the environment serves as a "trigger" for the acquisition of linguistic structures, even though research on how children use the environment to service acquisition has been going on for years (Snow and Tomasello 1989). Linguistic and extralinguistic features of the environment appear to be coincidentally arranged in a coalition that assists the child in learning language.

The last criticism is that some of the Inside-out theorists either posit no mechanisms for learning language or else rely on maturation when the principle or structure of interest does not appear in a timely fashion. Chomsky, again anchoring one end of the continuum, repeatedly likens the process of acquisition to what takes place in the development of the retina. Other than having visual experiences, the organism has no control over the increase in the density of the receptors on the retina. For Chomsky, language is analogous. Referring to it as the product of "learning" is a misnomer; instead, like vision, it is something that just happens to the child. When it doesn't happen fast enough, biological maturation is sometimes invoked as an explanation (Borer and Wexler 1987). And yet as Weinberg (1987) writes:

By assuming maturation [as an account for the sequenced appearance of various grammatical structures] we are led to a theory that merely catalogues points in time when different principles come into play without searching for any understanding of why particular principles come in any given order. (p. 25)

Summary
Even a cursory review of the literature like this one highlights basic differences among the leading theories of language acquisition (recall table 2.1). Among the most obvious is that Outside-in theories are likely to be domain general, with an emphasis on the learning process, whereas Inside-out theories are likely to be domain specific, with an emphasis on both internal structure and processes. In Outside-in theories, the learning processes evolve from general cognitive or social bases and are sensitive to external input that allows children to construct grammar from rather meager beginnings. Notice, however, that these processes must somehow be sensitive to language-relevant information in the environment; otherwise, children could randomly abstract units and relations that would lead them to generate incorrect grammatical hypotheses. By contrast, Inside-out theories assume the child to be endowed with a strong internally consistent structural foundation (a universal grammar) that drives the

learning process. Processes are thus "informed" of what kinds of things to look for, and learning can be thought of as a process of discovery rather than one of construction.

Given these basic distinctions, other attested differences follow. First, in Inside-out theories, language learning rests on the child's possession of linguistic structure; in Outside-in theories, it rests on cognitive and social structures. Second, Inside-out theories use domain-specific processes to construct language; Outside-in theories use domain-general processes. Third, because of the Inside-out theories' strong reliance on an a priori internal grammar, language learning is thought to rely more on innate knowledge in these theories than in Outside-in theories. Fourth, compared to Outside-in theories, language learning is considered to be relatively instantaneous in Inside-out theories because as some argue, much less needs to be learned and what must be learned need only be triggered by the appropriate environmental stimuli (at least for those who hold that the source of linguistic structure is innate).

These distinctions provide a sketch of the major families of language acquisition theories. But are these theories really as polarized as the literature suggests? Are the sketches offered in this chapter accurate portrayals of how each group of theorists believes that language is learned? We think not. Closer inspection of the theories reveals that many of the proposed dichotomies are "hyperboles." That is, these dichotomies are a product of exaggerated statements that differ more in degree than in kind. If it is true that theories of language acquisition have more in common than has generally been assumed, then it logically follows that points of consensus may emerge with regard to the three questions around which this chapter is organized.

2.3   Collapsing Dichotomies: How Theories of Language Acquisition Rely on Hyperbole

In this section we refine our look at the theories by discussing why characterizations of differences among them may be more hyperbolic than real. We argue that the dichotomies that have historically characterized theories of language acquisition are better cast in terms of continua than in terms of polar extremes. By collapsing theories onto continua, we do not intend to downplay the significance of prior work in language acquisition. Rather, adopting this treatment allows us to show the perhaps unanticipated commonalities among the theories that guide our research. Indeed, in section 2.4, we discuss what might be common answers to the three questions guiding this chapter. The research reported in this book empirically investigates this common ground—namely, in our view, the basic sensitivities that form the foundation for language acquisition.

The first of the three hyperboles that characterize theories of language acquisition is this:

Hyperbole 1
Outside-in theories account for grammatical development in terms of cognitive and social categories. Inside-out theories account for grammatical development in terms of the discovery of facts about an a priori grammatical structure.

Like all hyperboles, this one contains some truth and much exaggeration. Panel (a) of figure 2.1 exposes the hyperbole by characterizing the major families of theories with respect to the kinds of categories that children are thought to bring to the language-learning task. That is, Outside-in theories do postulate that children start with cognitive and social categories like agents and actions that somehow turn into linguistic categories like nouns and verbs. In stark contrast, Inside-out theories provide the child with a rich linguistic structure at the outset, although the nature of this endowment depends on the particular theory.

What makes this dichotomy collapse is that neither group of theorists relies exclusively on the categories shown on its side of the opposition. That is, even Chomsky (1988), the most extreme of the Inside-out theorists, acknowledges the role played by social understandings and cognitive processes in the acquisition of language. For example, Chomsky assumes that the child has a knowledge of "theta roles," which are the action role categories (e.g., agent, recipient) of the Outside-in theorists. On the other hand, the Outside-in theorists use linguistic scaffolding to get their models off the ground. For example, Schlesinger's (1971, 1988) model presupposes a child who is sensitive to inflectional markings in the input. Thus, both families of theories grant that the child has at least some linguistic sensitivities at the start (if not a full grammar) and is capable of conceptualizing the environment in terms of language-relevant cognitive and social categories.

Given that each of these families of theories requires linguistic, cognitive, and social categories, the dichotomy between theories that rely on linguistic structures and those that rely on cognitive or social structures collapses into a continuum (see figure 2.1, panel (a)). Anchoring the

A.   TYPE OF INITIAL LANGUAGE STRUCTURE

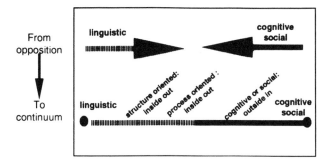

B.   MECHANISM USED FOR LANGUAGE LEARNING

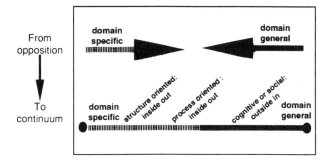

C.   SOURCE OF INITIAL STRUCTURE

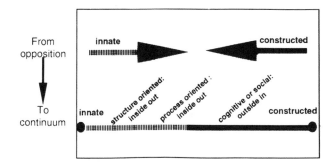

Figure 2.1
Collapsing the hyperbolic dichotomies that characterize theories of language acquisition results in three continua

continuum at one end would be a theory that relied totally on linguistic categories, apart from any categories constructed through environmental interaction. Notice that there is no theory that falls at that end, except perhaps for the incorrectly stereotyped view of Chomsky's theory. Anchoring the other end of the continuum would be a theory that allowed for no linguistic structure at all at the outset of language learning. No modern-day theory is to be found here either, given the Outside-in theorists' claims about what is presumed to be present as children start learning language (MacWhinney 1987; Schlesinger 1971, 1988). The two families of theories, although still not totally overlapping in their distribution, are now seen to have much more in common than previously thought. Indeed, they differ more in degree than in kind.

The same picture emerges when we examine the learning mechanisms implicated in language learning.

Hyperbole 2
Outside-in theories rely on domain-general learning processes; Inside-out theories rely on domain-specific learning processes.

This hyperbole implies that Outside-in theories allow the child to construct language via the same domain-general learning procedures first used to construct cognitive and social knowledge. Thus, as language-learning mechanisms these theories tend to rely on general learning procedures, identical to those used to acquire knowledge in other domains. On the other hand, Inside-out theories are said to rely exclusively on processes tailored to detect and form linguistic generalizations. Panel (b) of figure 2.1 illustrates the kinds of mechanisms each family of theories claims that children use to build language.

For a number of reasons, however, turning attention to processes does not sharpen the line between the theories. First, as Sternberg (1988) writes:

Processes need a knowledge base on which to operate, and the extent of the knowledge base in large part determines what processes can operate under which circumstances, as well as how effectively they can operate. (p. 277)

The Outside-in theorists' domain-general learning procedures operate on (minimally) a knowledge base that includes the identification of linguistic elements; otherwise, the child could not form linguistic generalizations. Second, the Outside-in theories include procedures or mechanisms that are themselves domain specific. For example, in the accounts of Schlesinger (1979) and MacWhinney and Bates (1987), children "look for" patterns of word order, inflections, or tense markers. More recent instantiations of the Competition Model posit a learner who can identify a word as having occurred immediately before (or after) a verb. To accomplish this task, a learner must have some way of identifying a verb (as opposed to words from other classes) in the input stream (see Gibson 1992). In order for acquisition to proceed under these theories, then, children must, a priori, be able to identify linguistic units. Note the effect that this has on the hyperbolic dichotomy we have drawn between the theories (panel (b) of figure 2.1, and table 2.1). Domain-general learning in the Outside-in theories has become open to the linguistic categories present in the Inside-out, domain-specific theories. Once we incorporate linguistic unit identification into the mechanisms for language learning, these mechanisms begin to look increasingly domain specific. Building linguistic sensitivities into the process rather than into the knowledge base—as the Outside-in theorists have done—is but a backdoor way to acknowledge that the child must use some domain-specific knowledge to acquire language. The result is to blur the line that separates the families of theories with regard to the source of linguistic structure and process. It becomes impossible to distinguish whether some implicit knowledge of language guides the operation of the processes or whether the activation of language-relevant processes guides the construction of linguistic structure. Thus, on this analysis, the two families of theories begin to resemble one another. Both contain some reference to domain-specific learning procedures—whether couched in terms of the knowledge base (as in the Inside-out theories) or in terms of the processes employed (as in the Outside-in theories). Also, both contain references to domain-general learning processes, as when children extract a particular morphological pattern by noting its frequency in the input. It is therefore false to conclude that Outside-in theories rely exclusively or even primarily on domain-general mechanisms. Rather, both families of theories fall on a continuum with regard to domain-specific claims (see figure 2.1, panel (b)). In the following passage Gelman and Greeno (1989) capture the sense of why both families of theories include domain-specific knowledge of language, whether they place that knowledge in structure or in process:

If we grant learners some domain-specific principles, we provide them with a way to define a range of relevant inputs, the ones that support learning about that domain. Because principles embody constraints on the kinds of inputs that can be processed as data that are relevant to that domain, they therefore can direct attention to those aspects of the environment that need to be selected and attended to. (p. 130)

In other words, without some structural knowledge of what the processes are to operate on, the organism's hypothesis space would be far too wide to form the correct linguistic generalizations.

In sum, all theories of language acquisition require a learner who has access to both domain-specific and domain-general learning procedures. Domain-specific procedures are necessary if the child is to become sensitive to peculiarly linguistic information such as "hidden" elements or empty categories (see Fodor 1989). Domain-general procedures such as categorization, abstraction, and weighting of cues can also play an important role in acquiring linguistic knowledge (MacWhinney 1987).

This hyperbole exposed, a third follows:

Hyperbole 3
Outside-in theories avoid claims for innateness whereas Inside-out theories are replete with such claims.

This hyperbole is represented in panel (c) of figure 2.1. It is clear that Inside-out theories assume that children enter the language-learning task in possession of a veritable armamentarium of linguistic principles, parameters, and categories, depending on the theory. The collapsing of the hyperbolic dichotomy here hinges on whether the Outside-in theorists truly avoid such presuppositions. If we grant, as in the above discussion, that even Outside-in theorists build in some domain-specific linguistic constraints so that the processes responsible for language acquisition will (1) "look for" appropriate input in the environment and (2) derive a limited class of linguistic generalizations, the innateness dichotomy also collapses into a continuum (again, see panel (c) of figure 2.1). The thorny nature of the innateness issue for many developmental questions (see Aslin 1981), along with the fact that it is difficult to evaluate these claims empirically, leads us to avoid that quagmire. Instead, we think this argument is best cast in terms of the *availability* of information by the time that language acquisition begins.

As pointed out earlier, although they claim to be minimalists, all Outside-in theorists (save L. Bloom (1991a)) posit that certain language-relevant information must be available by the time language learning begins. It is often the case that the origins of this knowledge are glossed over and its existence simply stated as a given. It may be that these theorists believe this knowledge is a product of the domain-general processes that (they would argue) construct linguistic structure. However, as we pointed out in discussing hyperbole 2, the fact that this information is written into the procedures for learning rather than into the structure makes the information no less available at the start of language acquisition.

The question that should be asked is, "How much language-specific knowledge and what kinds of domain-specific processes are needed at the outset of language learning to ensure that grammatical learning takes place?" Otherwise put, how much does the child need to know to be able to learn about syntax? Indeed, this question is at the heart of the current attempts to define the conditions for language learnability. Once the innateness argument is cast in these less dogmatic terms and redefined as availability, it is clear that this dichotomy, too, collapses into a continuum. Again, no theory occupies the extremes. Even those from the structure-oriented Inside-out camp assume that *some* learning takes place in the form of parameter setting; and even the staunchest Outside-in theorist posits that some linguistic information is available to learners as they begin their journey toward linguistic competence. Panel (c) of figure 2.1 illustrates the new continuum.

By way of analogy, no good archaeologist would jump to a conclusion after uncovering one piece of pottery. Rather, equipped with procedures designed to unearth the relevant data, the archaeologist, like the child, would look for confirming evidence and for patterns in the uncovered shards. To continue the analogy, the archaeologist knows to "look for" certain types of clues like particular markings or carvings on earthenware, just as the child knows to "look for" evidence like word order and inflections in the linguistic input. Both the archaeologist and the child are guided by a constrained set of hypotheses. This does not, however, negate the need for learning, nor does it argue that learning should be instantaneous.

In sum, we have reexamined the earlier analysis of the two families of theories. We derived three hyperboles often used to characterize these theories in the literature. In all cases, these hyperbolic differences have exposed the artificial dichotomies on which these theories have traditionally been distinguished, and have revealed that the theories are much better described in terms of continua.

2.4 Language Acquisition Theories: Common Ground

Given that there is more agreement between these families of theories than would be assumed from a surface analysis, in this section we consider whether some consensus can be reached on the answers to the three questions raised earlier. In doing so, we also present our own view of the language acquisition process.

Question 1: What is present when language learning begins? Whether the theory is Outside-in or Inside-out, the child is viewed as being sensitive to and able to detect a number of linguistic units and potential arrangements of those units. The Inside-out theories capture this knowledge in structure and the Outside-in theories in the processes the child brings to bear on linguistic input. The result, however, is the same: children must have access to linguistic units (nouns, verbs, phrases, and clauses) and must be sensitive to the possible relations between those units if they are to proceed in the learning of grammar.

Question 2: What are the mechanisms used in the course of language acquisition? Minimally, all theorists seem to agree that children must be sensitive, a priori, to language-relevant data. Children come equipped with strategies that enable them to "look for" language units like clauses, phrases, and words. Unless these units are detected, the abstraction of grammatical patterns is impossible. Even those arguing in favor of initial categories composed of agents and actions must at some point account for how these agents and actions become the epiphenomenal linguistic categories that are functionally equivalent to nouns and verbs. For the purposes of a consensus view, then, one need only argue that there must be some processes capable of detecting sentencelike units, phrasal units, word units, and form classes (e.g., nounlike units and verblike units), and some processes that can come to distinguish open-class words from the smaller set of closed-class words (e.g., inflectional markings).

These processes must also "look for" organizational patterns in the data to detect linguistic relations. All theories of acquisition require that children attend to the order of units, be it the order of words, of inflectional markers relative to words (Levy 1988), or of phrases relative to the larger constituents in which they are housed. The theories also need to account for the child's knowledge that all nouns (agents and themes) or clauses are not alike—for the knowledge that language is hierarchical and that there can be embedded clauses and main clauses.

In answer to the second question, then, our opinion is aligned with a kind of process-oriented, Inside-out view (see figure 2.1) in which children come to the learning task with some sensitivities to properties in the input that are informed by internal grammatical knowledge. It is essential not only that children learn about the units and patterns in the input but also that they be able to recover the hidden grammatical elements and to recognize dependencies within the input that they hear. We believe that there are multiple and overlapping cues for grammatical structure in the input; infants must be primed to detect these inputs and extract these correlations. In chapter 7 we develop this idea further as a mechanism we call "guided distributional learning." Indeed, there is ample evidence from the literature on animal learning that animals come prepared to form certain kinds of associations or to pick up certain kinds of information from the world around them. For example, Gallistel et al. (1991) describe how migratory songbirds, as nestlings, use specialized computational mechanisms to store an image of the stellar constellations, which they use later to guide their migration. In the following passage, the word "infant" could easily be substituted for "bird", and the context understood to be about language learning rather than the learning of stellar configurations:

[W]e have a domain-specific learning mechanism that determines what in the bird's environment will be attended to at a certain stage in its development, how that input will be processed, and the structure of the knowledge that is to be derived from that input. (p. 18)

As the wall between process and structure crumbles, so too does the distinction between the first two questions. The mechanisms used in the course of development will be those processes used to abstract language-relevant data from the input—those processes that lie at the intersection of the various theories. Sometimes these processes will be guided by structural constraints and operate in a language-specific way: for example, "Look for inflectional markings." At other times they will be guided by more domain-general learning procedures: for example, "Attend to ordering relationships." Thus, children perform guided distributional learning—finding regularities in the input that they have been primed to notice. Guided distributional learning, therefore, entails an intertwining of the domain-specific and domain-general processes.

Question 3: What types of input drive the system forward? With regard to this question, we propose that consensus among the various theories be identified not by examining the intersection of the possible input sources they presume, but by examining the *union* of these sources. This coalition of input sources was introduced in chapter 1 and will be developed further in chapter 7. As the theories were reviewed above, it became evident that many theorists concentrate on one type of input as more central than others for ensuring grammatical development. The very fact that input sources as diverse as environmental events, social interaction, prosody, and syntactic patterns are all viewed as criterial for different theories of grammatical learning should give one pause. Perhaps a more eclectic stance will better explain how children come to abstract or to discover the units and relations embedded within the grammar. Indeed, the recent proliferation of bootstrapping theories leads one to suspect that children live in a benevolent world in which these input sources covary reliably with one another (Shatz 1978; Landau and Gleitman 1985; Gleitman 1990; Pinker 1984, 1987; Grimshaw 1981). In English, for example, the highly stressed noun is usually found in last position in the utterance (Goldfield 1993), is commonly found preceded by an article ("the" or "a"), and is often the focus of joint attention in a social context (Messer 1983). It is this coalition view that represents the eclectic position that we adopt as our answer to the question of what types of input drive the system forward.

2.5 Summary: Early Sensitivities to Language Input

In sum, then, this review of current acquisition theories provides a sense of the foundation that children have for later language learning. By the time that language (grammatical) learning begins, children are sensitive to certain language-relevant information in the input. Using previously undiscovered consensus among the theories as a guide, we propose that very early on, children are sensitive to information in the input that will allow them to "look for" such basic units of language structure as words, phrases, and clauses (chapter 4). Children are also sensitive to basic relations such as agency and location, to order (e.g., of words (chapter 5) and inflections), and at some point to the syntactic configurations in which words appear (chapter 6).

With early attention to these basic units and relations, children can begin the journey to full linguistic competence by noting the distribution of units and markers within the language input that they hear. The process by which this occurs is the guided distributional learning mentioned above and discussed further in chapter 7. In fact, it is only when these foundations are in place that children will be sufficiently developed to learn language in ways suggested by some of the theories.

Given the linguistic presumptions noted above, we must ask, "How do children come to discover these basic units and relations in the input?"

Here we suggest that the processes that children bring to the task are sensitive to language-relevant information from a number of sources concurrently. Units of language emerge amid a kind of multimedia display in which the notes of prosody, context, syntactic position, and so on, form a chord or coalition that children can reliably identify as a nounlike or verblike unit. These smaller units then act consistently within sentence patterns that also covary with certain types of environmental events and prosodic/intonational patterns. In short, children try to use all the pieces of information at their disposal, although not necessarily at the same time, in abstracting the units and relations of grammar. This multimedia display will be explored in greater detail in chapter 7 when we outline a framework of language comprehension.

Infant and toddler sensitivity to many pieces of the multimedia program has already been discovered. For example, during the last decade researchers have made significant progress in uncovering some of the ways in which children segment the speech stream (see Hirsh-Pasek and Golinkoff 1993, for a review). A number of studies have also investigated infant sensitivity to semantic information in the input (e.g., Bowerman 1988; Bates, Bretherton, and Snyder 1988; Mandler 1992). Less research, however, is available that focuses on the infant's sensitivity to linguistic or syntactic organization. This is largely because such information has been very difficult to obtain from preverbal infants. In the research that follows, we address this gap and report the development of a new method for studying early language comprehension. This method provides a way of looking at language processing in very young children (beginning at 13 months) and a way of permitting children to use the coalition of sources at their disposal. After describing the method in some detail, we demonstrate how it has been used to unveil some of the early processes that children bring to the language-learning task.

In sum, if the account we have developed about the origins of grammar is plausible, then unlike Gold's learner, the real learner is a biased one who lives in a real social world. To learn more about the kinds of language processes that young children bring to the task of grammatical learning, we must begin to develop methods of investigating early language sensitivities, that can be used with very young children who are just beginning to learn language, and that allow children to capitalize on their sensitivities to the coalition of language-relevant inputs. In what follows, we present a method of language comprehension that meets these criteria.

Chapter 3

The Intermodal Preferential
Looking Paradigm

... it seems to me that, if anything far-reaching and real is to be discovered about the actual grammar of the child, then rather devious kinds of observations of his performance, his abilities, and his comprehension will have to be obtained, so that a variety of evidence may be brought to bear on the attempt to determine what is in fact his underlying linguistic competence at each stage of development.

Chomsky, "Formal Discussion"

During the past two decades researchers have devised a number of clever and devious ways to peer in on the strategies that infants and young children use as they embark on their language-learning journey. Many have observed early language *production* for clues to how children solve the language-learning problem. Others have developed ingenious ways of eliciting utterances from young children by enriching the linguistic contexts that stimulate the production of particular language structures (see Crain and Thornton 1991). If children can be "tricked" into generating certain rarely produced structures, their otherwise hidden competencies can be revealed. Many have also studied emergent language through tests of language *comprehension*. This work rests on the assumption that children may be capable of understanding structures that they cannot or do not yet produce.

In this chapter we review some of the methods used to investigate early language knowledge. In doing so, we have three goals. First, we make the case for studying language comprehension as opposed to just studying production. Second, we briefly evaluate existing methods for studying language comprehension and highlight some of the limits inherent in these methods. Third, and most prominently, we present a new method for studying language comprehension, one based on the intermodal preferential looking paradigm developed by Spelke (1979). In chapters 4, 5, and 6 we then demonstrate how this method can be profitably used to investigate infants' and toddlers' grammatical sensitivities.

3.1 Reasons for Studying Language Comprehension?

There can be little doubt that studies on young children's language production in the past 25 years have provided a rich source for language acquisition theories. Language production, the observable half of the child's language performance, however is only part of the story. Just as astronomers were not satisfied to study only the light side of the moon, so researchers in language acquisition have long recognized that access to data from the "dark" side of their topic—namely, language comprehension—illuminates the language acquisition process far more than the study of production alone. In particular, language comprehension data serve three useful purposes. First, by looking at comprehension researchers can obtain a more accurate picture of the content of the child's emerging language system. It has sometimes been assumed, for example, that the syntactic variability found in a set of transcripts accurately reflects the breadth of the child's grammatical knowledge. However, since children talk in environments that are rich in contextual and social supports, it is likely that their productions underrepresent their grammatical knowledge. That is, children typically select speech topics from the "here-and-now." Because of this, and because of willing adults who interpret for them, children can often get away with saying less, and saying it in a less sophisticated manner, to achieve their goals. Without comprehension assessments, the researcher is forced to wait for the child to spontaneously produce the structure of interest. In comprehension experiments, one can test for a wide range of syntactic sensitivities, whether they have been produced or not. These syntactic sensitivities become the bases for more accurate theories of language acquisition.

A case in point illustrating how comprehension data may be indispensable in falsifying theoretical assertions about the young child's linguistic competence, comes from work by Radford (1990). Radford states that young children's language productions provide no evidence of a determiner system or an inflectional system. One possibility is that Radford is correct: the absence of these linguistic elements from children's speech is what gives early speech its telegraphic character. On the other hand, Radford may be wrong. Although these elements do not appear in *speech*

—because of currently unspecified limitations on production—perhaps the child is sensitive to and aware of these systems in comprehension. Gerken and her colleagues (e.g., Gerken, Landau, and Remez 1990; Gerken and McIntosh 1993; and see Shipley, Smith, and Gleitman 1969) have shown that children who do not use function words in their own speech do seem to expect them. When these words are missing or altered, children's sentence comprehension suffers. In other words, if children's sentence comprehension is adversely affected by the absence or mutilation of some linguistic feature, then children may operate with such a system— even if the system is not apparent in production.

A second reason for focusing on comprehension studies is that they may provide an alternative window onto the *process* of language acquisition. Arguably, by the time children are producing a particular structure, they have already acquired it. Yet the steps leading up to the analysis and mastery of that structure would be less visible without studies of sentence comprehension. For example, by studying language comprehension, one can ask what kinds of organization children impose on a word string or what strategy children are using to interpret a new word. One can present novel or nonword stimuli (see experiment 6, chapter 6), too, to "trick" children into revealing their apparent processing strategy. Although language production also yields insights into process by virtue of the errors and omissions children make, we can sometimes verify hypotheses generated from production by designing tests of language comprehension. More questions about the relationship between comprehension and production processes will be addressed in chapter 7.

The third reason why comprehension data are useful has to do with *methodological control*. In the real world there may be circumstances in which children appear to comprehend certain structures when in fact they do not. With comprehension experiments, researchers interested in a certain structure and the circumstances under which it is used can create situations of a type that control for extraneous variables. For example, Shatz (1978) argued that children are biased to respond to sentences with action, whether or not an action is being called for. To test this hypothesis, Shatz created conditions in which it was clear to *adults* that action was *not* being called for to see whether children could resist the temptation to act. By controlling the experimental situation in this way, Shatz increased the likelihood that she could unambiguously interpret children's action responses. (In fact, children interpreted many such sentences as requests for action.)

In sum, studies of language comprehension have three advantages over studies utilizing spontaneous production: they permit researchers to probe for structures that are not yet produced; they offer a new window onto the process by which the child acquires a particular structure before that structure emerges full-blown; and they permit a degree of methodological control not available from observing production.

3.2   Evaluating Methods for Studying Language Comprehension

Several procedures have dominated language comprehension assessment in both the lexical and grammatical domains. First, researchers have used "enactment tasks" such as providing children with dolls or miniature objects and asking them to (for example) "Make the boy kiss the girl!" Second, they have used a related technique called "acting out tasks" in which children are asked to carry out actions themselves: for example, "Kick the ball!" These enactment and acting out tasks are easy to administer and are fun for children. Yet comprehension tasks that require children to either act out events or follow commands may underestimate children's linguistic knowledge because of their competing action biases. It is well known, for example, that children have a tendency to act, and to act in particular ways, when surrounded by objects. Their predisposition to "act like x" may override the instruction to "act like y," even if the information in the sentence has been understood. This problem has been explicitly acknowledged in a number of studies (see, e.g., Shipley, Smith, and Gleitman 1969; de Villiers and de Villiers 1973) and documented by Shatz (1978). Alternatively, young children may simply refuse to act on command. Therefore, a biased response or a failure to respond cannot be taken as evidence of noncomprehension, but only as evidence of noncompliance.

Other studies have used a third method for generating comprehension data: picture-pointing tasks. Children are presented with a choice of pictures and are asked to point to the picture that a sentence describes. For example, Fraser, Bellugi, and Brown (1963) asked children to "Point to the picture that shows 'The deer are jumping.'" The pictures showed one or more deer jumping, so that the child's discrimination hinged on the number specified by the auxiliary verb ("is" vs. "are"). Other examples come from Lovell and Dixon (1967), who tested the comprehension of a number of language structures in children from $2\frac{1}{2}$ through 7 years of age.

Pictorial tasks have been very popular in psycholinguistic research. Like enactment tasks, they are easy to administer. Like enactment tasks, however, they also pose some problems. In addition to requiring the action of pointing, pictorial displays may fail to provide young children with sufficient motivational incentive and may fail to make sought-after distinctions salient and unambiguous. Studies by Friedman and Stevenson (1975) and Cocking and McHale (1981), for example, show that young children do not understand the function of conventions such as curved lines around joints to indicate that movement is taking place. Thus, the depiction of dynamic relationships involving action is problematic.

A fourth method is to infer children's comprehension by observing their comprehension in situ and recording the observations in diaries (Nelson 1973). These studies may overestimate the young child's grammatical knowledge. For example, a mother may state that her child understands the sentence "Go get a diaper." Yet when she typically utters this sentence, she performs a unique action (e.g., peering into the child's diaper), which signals that a diaper change is about to occur. The child may understand no more about the sentence frame than does a dog who sees his master pick up a leash while uttering the sentence "Do you want to go for your walk?" Credit for comprehension can come only from tests in controlled settings.

Given these methodological problems, Golinkoff et al. (1987) argue that most studies of sentence comprehension that use enactment or picture-pointing techniques have been biased *toward* nouns, *against* an understanding of action terms, and *against* an understanding of the relationships embedded in grammatical constructions. That is, the current methods used to study comprehension are not optimal for studying the strategies that children may rely upon in the learning of grammatical relationships. Note that to make this claim does *not* dismiss the significant gains that have been reaped from research on language comprehension. It does, however, make clear that methods are needed that (1) do not require children to perform actions and (2) represent dynamic events in a more natural way.

In recent years a few new methods have been introduced that appear to answer this need. One of these methods depends on the child's differential visual fixation responses; it thus has the advantages of being based on a response already in the child's repertoire and of requiring no explicit action on the child's part. Thomas et al. (1981) developed a signal detection procedure to test for lexical comprehension. A child is shown an object at one of four corners of a rectangular apparatus as the object is named aloud. Using a signal detection analysis, the question is whether a naive observer will judge that the child then looks more to the corner containing the named object than to the other corners. Although promising, this method has had only limited use, and only with static (as opposed to dynamic) stimuli.

Another method with great promise is just beginning to be used to study children's sentence processing: the assessment of cortical event-related potentials (ERPs). When electrodes are placed on a subject's scalp, it is possible to record the ongoing electrical activity of the brain (Molfese 1983). ERPs establish strict temporal relationships between the onset of a discrete stimulus event and changes in the resulting ERP pattern in different regions of the brain. ERPs have been used to study the infant's grasp of word meanings (e.g., Molfese, Morse, and Peters 1990; Molfese et al., in press), as well as children's sentence processing (e.g., Holcomb, Cofey, and Neville 1992). For example, Mills, Cofey, and Neville (in press) demonstrated that infants between 13 and 20 months show a distinct ERP response when they listen to a word their parent reports they comprehend but not when they listen to a word their parent reports they do not comprehend. As with the visual fixation method, the main virtue of the ERP paradigm is that it does not require that the child speak or act. All the child has to do is listen to a linguistic stimulus, which may or may not be accompanied by a visual stimulus. Thus, this method can also be used with infants.

Finally, a group of researchers has refined and validated a parent report measure of children's language comprehension, the MacArthur Communicative Development Inventory (Fenson et al. 1994). The first part of the inventory ("Words and Gestures") can be administered to parents of infants between the ages of 8 and 16 months. It requires nothing from the child and can be used to ask parents about the child's understanding of verbs, nouns, and closed-class items such as prepositions. Parental responses have been shown to correlate positively and significantly with the child's subsequent language ability (Dale et al. 1989; Fenson et al. 1994). This instrument, validated in a number of ways on hundreds of children (Fenson et al. 1994), provides useful data on what lexical items parents think their infants understand at various ages. It is therefore also useful as a clinical screening device. However, other than the questions on closed-class items, the first part of the instrument was not designed to explore early syntactic sensitivities.

In sum, numerous studies have been conducted using an array of methods, some of which may be better suited than others to infants' and young children's natural response repertoires. The most recent paradigms have been designed to alleviate some of the assessment problems inherent in the enactment and picture-pointing methods. However, none of the new methods has been sufficiently refined to enable researchers to look at grammatical development in ways that require no overt action on the part of the child and that can portray grammatical relationships through dynamic stimuli. The intermodal preferential looking paradigm incorporates both of these advantages.

3.3   The Intermodal Preferential Looking Paradigm

Introduction and Rationale
The intermodal preferential looking paradigm is depicted in figure 3.1. An infant is seated on a blindfolded parent's lap 2' 2" back from the center of and exactly between two television monitors, which are 30 inches apart. A concealed audio speaker midway between the two monitors plays a linguistic stimulus that is consonant with or "matches" only one of the displays shown on the screens. Mounted atop the speaker is a light that comes on during each intertrial interval to ensure that the infant makes a new choice about which screen to look at on each trial. The infant's task is to look at one of the two video screens. In all such studies the logic is the same: infants will choose to allocate more attention to the video event that matches what they are hearing (in this case, a linguistic message) than to the video event that does not match.

To see how the paradigm works, consider a pair of stimuli in what is arguably the simplest case: noun comprehension (Golinkoff et al. 1987). In one trial a shoe appeared on one screen and a boat on the other. The linguistic message (produced in child-directed speech) was "Where's the shoe? Find the shoe!" The hypothesis, which was confirmed, was that infants would look more quickly and longer toward the screen displaying the shoe than toward the screen displaying the boat.

This paradigm has been successfully used to investigate early language comprehension in a number of previous studies. For example, in the first set of studies (Golinkoff et al. 1987), whose goal was to see whether the paradigm would work for both syntactic and lexical assessments, we purposely selected 28-month-olds who were using two- and three-word utterances in their own speech; these children showed word order

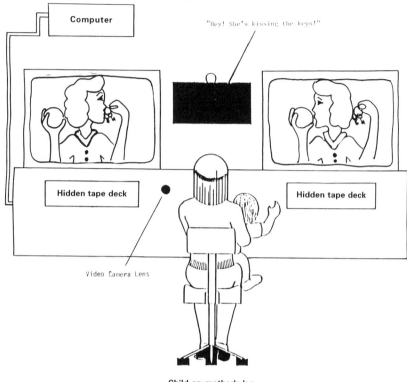

Figure 3.1
A depiction of the intermodal preferential looking paradigm showing a sample
stimulus set from experiment 1. On the left screen a woman is kissing keys while
holding a ball in the foreground. On the right screen a different woman is kissing
a ball while holding keys in the foreground.

comprehension in the paradigm. In the same set of studies we also showed,
using a random sample of 17-month-olds, that the paradigm worked for
noun and verb comprehension. Naigles (1990) has used the paradigm to
demonstrated that 2-year-olds are sensitive to the meaning implications
of transitive and intransitive sentence frames; and Fernald, McRoberts,
and Herrera (in press) have used it to examine the effects of prosodic
manipulations on the comprehension of familiar words.

The intermodal preferential looking paradigm seems capable of revealing linguistic knowledge in young children for two reasons, both of
which will be treated further elsewhere in this book. First, unlike many

other assessments of language comprehension, this paradigm does not require children to point, answer questions, or act out commands. Children need merely employ a response already in their repertoire—visual fixation—in order to fulfill the task requirements. Second, the paradigm usually does not set natural cues for comprehension in conflict with each other, nor does it omit the contribution of these sources. That is, in this paradigm children have access to syntactic, semantic, prosodic, and contextual information. When these are all provided, children may take advantage of the coalition of cues normally used in language comprehension, those discussed in chapters 1, 2, and 7, to demonstrate the upper limits of their knowledge.

The intermodal preferential looking paradigm was adapted from the work of Spelke (1979), who developed it to study intermodal perception. For example, 4-month-old infants saw two events (e.g., a person clapping hands and a donkey falling onto a table) and heard a nonlinguistic auditory stimulus that matched only one of the events (say, the sound of hands clapping). Infants watched the screen that matched the auditory stimulus significantly more than the screen that did not match. When linguistic stimuli are used—as in the present studies—children can show relatively more visual attention to the match only if they *understand* the language used. For this reason our adaptation of the preferential looking method is fundamentally different from its use in studying intermodal perception.

Indeed, it could be argued that the rationale behind the paradigm— namely, that infants will prefer to watch the screen that matches the linguistic stimulus more than the screen that does not—apparently contradicts much of the research indicating that infants prefer to watch novel or discrepant stimuli (see Cohen, DeLoache, and Strauss 1979). However, techniques that have found a preference for novelty differ from the one presented here in two fundamental ways.

First, novelty preference appears to be the rule for *intra*modal experiments in which two visual events are paired and presented with no accompanying auditory stimulus. In addition, intramodal experiments specifically manipulate novelty by presenting the same stimuli repeatedly and then varying the next stimulus in some systematic way to see if the child can discriminate the new from the old. *Inter*modal experiments do not manipulate novelty but ask a different question: Can children find the invariance or link between stimuli presented in two different modalities (e.g., visual and auditory)? Throughout the literature on intermodal perception, studies show that infants prefer to find the matching rather than the nonmatching stimulus. For example, Starkey, Spelke, and Gelman (1983) showed that 10-month-olds, presented with two screens, would watch the one that displayed the same number of objects (randomly arranged) as the number of taps they heard. Similarly, Meltzoff and Borton (1979) found that 29-day-old infants would look longer at a shape they had explored by touch than at one they had not explored. Finally, Kuhl and Meltzoff (1982) found that 4-month-old infants preferred to look at a face whose mouth was moving in concert with a speech sound they heard rather than at a face whose mouth was articulating another sound.

Second, unlike intramodal experiments, intermodal experiments are not designed as discrimination tasks in which a concept or category is built up and then altered systematically. Rather, in intermodal experiments (like ours) that yoke symbolic stimuli with referents, researchers ask about infants' ability to use a symbolic stimulus to find a referent. That is, these studies do not address the issue of novelty and discrimination—indeed, they present two equally novel stimuli. The question is whether children can use their understanding of the language to find the corresponding stimulus in the other modality.

In a sense, the intermodal preferential looking paradigm duplicates the language-learning situation. When a parent says, "See the dog!", for example, the child's task is to *match up* the linguistic stimuli he is hearing (the word "dog") with something in the environment (a dog). Thus, this paradigm may work because its requirements mimic those found in language learning: infants might prefer the matching screen over the non-matching screen because there is some ecological validity in looking for a "match" in the environment when they are presented with symbolic stimuli like words. For this reason and the reasons stated above, in no studies performed in our laboratories have children ever shown a significant (or even approaching significant) preference for the nonmatch.

Description
Given that the intermodal preferential looking paradigm was used in all the experiments to be reported, a detailed description of it will be helpful.

Construction of the Video Events   Two videotapes are developed for each study. These tapes are constructed so that they work in synchrony, trial for trial, down to the same number of frames. This level of precision is essential given that the paradigm relies on preferential visual fixation, which can be biased by a number of incidental factors—not the least of which is one tape in a pair coming on before the other. Trials on a pair of tapes start and end at the same time, and the tapes stay in synchrony as they are played. In addition, although achieving perfect control is impossible, every effort is made to balance the amount of action and color on the two screens so as to reduce any potential salience problems. For example, the characters used in each tape in a pair are of equivalent size, and if a repetitive action is being performed on one screen, it is balanced against another repetitive action—taking place the same number of times —on the other screen.

Videotapes for the studies are filmed with a color camera against a white background. The best exemplars of each type of desired event are then selected and duplicated exactly for the number of trials needed for a particular study. Editing is done at the University of Delaware's Media Services Center. The videotapes used for the original footage and editing are $\frac{3}{4}''$ performance-quality tapes, although the $\frac{1}{2}''$ medium works as well. Copies of the original edited masters to be used for testing are then made on both $\frac{1}{2}''$ tape (for the Temple University laboratory) and $\frac{3}{4}''$ tape (for the University of Delaware laboratory).

Trials and Intertrial Intervals By way of illustration, table 3.1 shows a typical layout of a pair of tapes using a set of stimuli to be described further in chapter 4. There are three kinds of trials, all 6 seconds in length, called "sequential trials," "simultaneous trials," and "test trials," and one type of intertrial interval.

Intertrial Intervals Each trial is preceded and followed by a 3-second intertrial interval. During this period both screens are blank, and a low-wattage light bulb (mounted atop the hidden speaker centered between the two screens) is illuminated. The intertrial interval serves an important function: it draws the child's attention back to the center area between the two screens, allowing the child to make a "clean," independent choice for each trial. If children do not attend to the central fixation light for longer than .30 seconds during the intertrial interval before the test trial, their data for that trial are discarded. (Well over 97% of all trials are retained using this criterion.)

Sequential Trials As table 3.1 shows, in the sequential trials the child first sees an event on only the left screen while the right screen remains blank. This is followed by a 3-second intertrial interval. Then the child

Table 3.1
Experiment 1: The video events and linguistic stimuli for one block of trials

Tape 1	Linguistic stimuli	Tape 2
	Sequential trials	
Woman kissing ball while dangling keys in foreground	"Oh, what's going on?"	Blank screen
Blank screen	{Center light} "Hey, what's going on?"	Blank screen
Blank screen	"Look! What is she doing?"	Woman kissing keys while holding ball in foreground
	Simultaneous trial	
Blank screen	{Center light} "Wow, what's happening!"	Blank screen
Woman kissing ball …	"What are they doing?"	Woman kissing keys …
	Test trials	
Blank screen	{Center light} "Hey, she's kissing the keys!"	Blank screen
Woman kissing ball …	"Wow, she's kissing the keys!"	Woman kissing keys …
Blank screen	{Center light} "Where is she kissing the keys?"	Blank screen
Woman kissing ball …	"Oh! She's kissing the keys!"	Woman kissing keys …

sees an event on the right screen while the left screen remains blank. These trials serve to (1) introduce the video events before the child has to find the match for the linguistic stimulus, and (2) create the expectation that something will appear on each screen. The audio presented during sequential trials, as well as the audio presented during the intertrial interval that precedes each sequential trial, is "neutral" in the sense that it "matches" or is equally consistent with both events. For example, it might be something like "What's going on?"

Simultaneous Trials A simultaneous trial, during which the video scenes are presented synchronously on both screens, follows the sequential trials.

Simultaneous trials show the child that events will appear concurrently on both screens. They also provide a check on stimulus salience. That is, if the visual stimuli have been well balanced for perceptual factors, and while the linguistic stimulus is still neutral (see above), it is predicted that attention should be distributed equally to each member of the simultaneous pair across children.

Test Trials Two pairs of test trials always follow the simultaneous trial. The test trials differ from the simultaneous trial in a single way: the linguistic stimulus that accompanies these trials now exhorts the child to look at the screen that matches the linguistic stimulus. The linguistic stimulus, which describes one of the video events, is first heard during the 3-second intertrial interval that precedes the test trials and again during the test trials themselves so that the language, not merely the video, drives the looking response. For three of the four studies described here, the procedure of introducing the video events with sequential trials, next showing a simultaneous trial, and finally showing two test trials is repeated four times to test four different exemplars of the structure in question. (In one study—see chapter 4—six blocks of trials were presented.)

Linguistic Stimuli The linguistic stimuli for the test trials are given first during the intertrial interval that precedes the test trials and then during the test trials themselves. The rationale for presenting the linguistic stimulus during the intertrial interval is that by the time the intertrial interval that precedes the first test trial comes on the screen, the child has already had ample opportunity to observe the scenes on both screens.

Depending on the particular study, the linguistic stimulus is presented either once or twice during each test trial. From pilot work it became clear that the linguistic stimulus should be present for the duration of the event to maximize the amount of time the infant looks toward the matching screen.

All studies use "motherese" or child-directed speech produced by female voices. Although the use of child-directed speech has not been systematically manipulated as a variable, several research findings indicate that infants prefer to listen to child-directed rather than adult-directed speech (Fernald 1985; Kemler Nelson et al. 1989; Cooper and Aslin 1990) —even in nonnative languages (Werker, Pegg, and McLeod 1994). Further, despite the added linguistic complexity, all the linguistic stimuli are full sentences. The rationale for the use of full sentences again comes from the literature on child-directed speech: young children are more likely to be addressed in sentences that are grammatically complete than sentences that are incomplete and grammatically incorrect (Shipley, Smith, and Gleitman 1969).

Independent, Dependent, and Counterbalanced Variables   The independent, dependent, and counterbalanced variables are more often than not the same across experiments.

Independent Variables   Typical between-subjects independent variables in these studies are age and sex. Sometimes children of the same age are also divided on the variable of linguistic level. The within-subjects variables are match versus nonmatch and stimulus. "Stimulus" refers to a pair of test events. Most of the studies have used four pairs of events to test the structure in question. Each pair is seen twice and the data are always averaged across these two trials to increase the reliability of children's responses.

The Dependent Variable   Visual fixation time or the total amount of time in seconds (measured to the tenth of a second) the child spends watching the matching versus the nonmatching screen is the dependent variable.[1] It is cumulated from the time that the child looks at the light between the screens for more than .30 seconds during the intertrial interval. Recall that the linguistic stimulus for a test trial is first heard during the intertrial interval that precedes it. By that time children have seen (in most of our studies) two sequential trials and one simultaneous trial, so they presumably know what events to expect on each screen. Thus, we have found that children look to the matching screen even *before* the test trials come on. Furthermore, analyses that began measuring the dependent variable during the intertrial interval or that measured only during the test trials had the same results. In order for a look at either screen to feed into the cumulation of visual fixation time, it must exceed .30 seconds, considered the lower limit on the observer's reliable judgment of visual fixation.[2]

The hypothesis in each study is that significantly more visual fixation time will be allocated to the matching than to the nonmatching event. Note that it is never hypothesized that the child will look *exclusively* at the matching screen. In fact, looking times are expected to be distributed between the two video events since, for control purposes, visual displays in a pair are designed, as much as possible, to contain equivalent activity, bright colors, and complexity.

Coding of the Dependent Variable Infants' visual fixation responses are recorded either off-line (and coded after the child's visit) or on-line by a hidden observer. Figure 3.1 depicts the off-line situation; figure 5.1 the on-line situation. When visual fixation is coded *off-line*, the child's viewing of the tape is recorded on another videotape by an observer manipulating a video camera whose lens protrudes slightly from between and below the two monitors. The observer, hidden from the child's view, keeps the camera focused on the child's face. After the child's visit, a coder sets up the computer to receive the data and then plays the child's record back without sound. The coder, blind to the sequence of matches the child has seen, depresses hand-held buttons that correspond to the left and right screens to record the child's visual fixation on the tapes. The coder holds down the appropriate button for the duration of the child's gaze at a screen; both buttons simultaneously if the child looks to the center; and neither button if the child looks at neither screen. A computer program, especially designed for the purpose of calculating the data and depicting them trial by trial, receives the output of the coder's button presses.

When visual fixation is coded *on-line*, the observer is behind the apparatus holding the visual fixation coding buttons. The observer can hear the audio but is blind to the sequence of matches the child is seeing. In both the on- and off-line cases, observers report that they cannot keep track of the sequence of the matches; capturing the direction and duration of the child's gaze is all-consuming. Further, since sequential and simultaneous trials intervene between test trials, there is no easy pattern of matches to be memorized.

Interrater reliability was calculated in two ways because coders should agree on both the *direction* (left, right, center, or away—to neither screen) of a child's gaze and the *duration* of each look. Reliability was computed on data from the Delaware laboratory, which were coded off-line from videotapes. First, Cohen's Kappa (1960) was computed to compare coders' agreement for the direction of a child's gaze. That is, two coders each coded the performance of 10 randomly selected children independently. A different set of random numbers was generated for each child's data printout to allow us to sample 10 interspersed data points. The direction in which each coder thought the child was looking was recorded for each of these points. This was a very stringent way to measure reliability of coding gaze direction because it selected a single instant rather than measuring reliability during a whole event. Thus, although coders might have shown excellent agreement across any 6-second event (and they usually did), they might fail to agree on the single instant chosen. Cohen's Kappa was calculated on these data. Its value was .771 with a standard error of .052 ($p < .001$). This indicates an extremely high level of agreement between coders on the direction of a child's gaze.

Second, to compare coders' agreement on the duration of each gaze (when they agreed on its direction), the intraclass correlation coefficient (ICC) (Shrout and Fleiss 1979) was used. Since coders agreed on 85 out of 100 gazes selected (see above), data from 85 different gazes were entered into this analysis. ICC Model 2 was used so that we could generalize our results to a larger population of raters. The ICC was calculated to be .88. Generally, an ICC above .75 is considered adequate; an ICC of .90 is considered excellent. Since the 95% confidence interval for the ICC extends from .81 to .92, the ICC of .88 obtained here indicates that observers show a high degree of agreement in their coding of visual fixation time.

The same two analyses were conducted on the data resulting from 6 randomly selected children who were tested in the Temple laboratory, where visual fixation is coded on-line. Cohen's Kappa was .676, with a standard error of .077 ($p < .001$). The ICC was calculated to be .91, with a confidence interval between .84 and .95. This represents a high degree of agreement between coders. Since the confidence intervals from the two laboratories overlap, the ICCs do not differ statistically from each other. This means that on- and off-line coding yield the same high degree of reliability.

Missing Trials   Averaging across studies, approximately 3% of children's trials are not included in the data analysis. Trials can be missed for two reasons. First, if a child fails to watch the center light for at least .30 seconds during the intertrial interval that precedes each test trial, that trial is not counted. Second, if a child looks at neither screen for the duration of a trial, that trial is not counted. When a missing trial occurs, the child's mean visual fixation time to the matching and nonmatching screens across all the other test events is entered into the empty data cell.

Counterbalanced Variables   Five factors were counterbalanced in all experiments within a pair of videotapes. First, the first sequential trial (see table 3.1) appeared half the time on the left screen and half the time on the right screen within the four (or six) blocks of trials. Second, the match occurred the same number of times on the left screen as on the right screen. Third, for half of the subjects tape 1 was shown in the left deck;

for the other half of the subjects, it was shown in the right deck. This had the effect of producing two orders of the matching events that were mirror images of each other. Fourth, the linguistic message matched one stimulus of a test pair for half of the subjects and the other stimulus of a test pair for the other half. This was achieved by rerecording the audio message. Thus, if positive results emerge in a study, this critical counterbalance allows us to conclude that they are not a function of some peculiar synergism between the linguistic stimulus and the video event. Fifth, when a study required two actors on a screen, the left-right position of the actors was counterbalanced so that location on the screen could not serve as an artifactual cue to the matching screen.

Matches always occurred in the order left-right-right-left (or its mirror image) to ensure that subjects were basing their performance on finding the match for the linguistic stimulus and not on ordering strategies. Orders avoided were a strict alternating pattern (e.g., left-right-left-right) and starting out with two "winners" on the same side (e.g., left-left-right-right).

Additional Experimental Controls   Two additional controls were built into the studies. First, the parent (usually the child's mother) wears a visor so as not to be able to see the stimuli and unwittingly influence the looking patterns of the infant. The observers who code infants' eye fixations (either on- or off-line) discard the data from any child whose parent directs more than a passing glance toward the videotapes. Second, the parent sits facing forward with uncrossed legs, having been instructed not to speak to the child so as not to unduly bias the infant's looking preference.

Apparatus and Lighting   All equipment—except for the two 20-inch color monitors—is shielded from the child's view. The videotapes (filmed with a Newvicon 3150 color video camera) are shown on either $\frac{1}{2}''$ or $\frac{3}{4}''$ video decks, at the Temple and Delaware laboratories, respectively. The linguistic stimulus, dubbed onto the first channel of the videotape, is shunted to an audio speaker between the two monitors (see figure 3.1). Thus, infants cannot find the match by looking at the monitor that plays the linguistic message.

Videotapes have two auditory channels. The first channel contains the linguistic message the child hears. The second, inaudible channel contains a 1-kHz tone recorded for the duration of each trial. Thus, when any of the three types of trials is playing, the tone is on; when there is an intertrial interval (blank screen), the tone is off. These tones are "read" by a specially designed tone decoder that has two functions: (1) it turns the light on during the intertrial intervals and off during the trials; and (2) it signals the beginning and end of each trial to the computer (an Apple 2e), which has been programmed to compile a record of each child's looking responses throughout all trials and the intertrial intervals. The output from the observers' button presses enters the computer through the game port control panels.

Ambient lighting in the testing room is kept dim to heighten the salience of the monitors, minimize other distractions, and maximize attention to the screens. Although overall attention to the videotapes can be affected by the ambient lighting (as a serendipitous difference in lighting between the Temple and Delaware laboratories revealed; see chapter 5), these overall differences in visual fixation do not affect looking preferences to the matching screen.

Subject Solicitation   Subject families for all experiments were found through birth announcements in local newspapers. They were contacted first through a letter explaining the project and then by phone to set up an appointment. All appropriate human subjects procedures were employed. Parents were fully informed about the purpose of the study and signed a release form at the laboratory before testing began. After their visit parents received a letter thanking them for their participation. Later they received another letter summarizing the results of the study.

Procedure   The children came to our university laboratories, where they first played with an experimenter using a small set of toys. For some of the studies (as will be detailed below), items relevant to the tapes they were about to see were among the toys used. While the child played, the parent heard an explanation of the research. The parent signed a human subjects release form and then filled out the Rescorla Language Inventory (1991). The latter requires checking off the words that the child understands or produces (depending on the child's age) from a large set of words commonly produced by 3-year-olds. (Depending on the child's age, parents were differentially reassured that their children were not expected to know more than a subset of the words.) The parent was also asked to report examples of the longer word combinations that the child used. Children's utterances during the laboratory visit were recorded by an experimenter so that they could be crudely classified as one-, two-, or three-word speakers.

The parent was then asked to put on a tennis visor that was to be pulled down to block vision during the actual testing. Putting the visor on in the playroom removed some of the novelty of the "hat" so that it did not distract the child's attention during testing. The vast majority of parents complied readily with the request to keep the visor over their eyes during testing.

Parents sat facing forward with uncrossed legs and were asked to keep their children centered on their lap and not to speak to them during the video presentation. If the child seemed to want to get off the parent's lap, the parent was told to say something neutral to the child, like "Just another minute." The experimenter darkened the laboratory, started the two videotapes, and left the room. Testing was discontinued at any point if the child became fussy or upset. Finally, the parent and child were invited to see the experimental tapes immediately after each test was completed.

Subject Loss   Our subject losses in this procedure parallel those found in other studies of infant development and, in particular, in other studies that use visual fixation as a dependent variable (e.g., Cohen and Oakes 1993). Although this procedure has an advantage in that it often utilizes movement in its visual displays, infants are notoriously difficult subjects.

Although subject loss information will be given for each experiment, we describe here the criteria used for discarding data. The most obvious reason to discard a child's data was fussiness. Clearly, this decision required a judgment call. In our view, the goal was for the child and parent to have a positive experience. If the child persevered in leaving the parent's lap or began to squirm and/or cry, testing was stopped. Another reason to discard data was equipment failure or experimenter error. For example, an experimenter who observed the testing from behind the parent and child discarded the child's data if the tapes were not well synchronized (i.e., one tape in a pair came on before the other). Data were also discarded from any child who showed a preference for one screen that exceeded 75% of the total looking time or who watched the tapes less than 35% of the time (these criteria were calculated by the software); from any child whose parent watched the tapes; and from any child who failed to return to the central fixation point on more than 33% of the trials in a given experiment. Failure to return to the central fixation point might imply that the child was watching the same screen (perhaps in a daze?) across several trials.

Of course, the possibility always exists that when children's data are discarded for their failure to engage in the task, it is because they do not understand the linguistic stimuli. On the other hand, the children who complete our studies are not a homogeneous group. Their productive and receptive language varies widely, as do their visual fixation patterns.

The experience level of the laboratory can also affect subject losses. For example, we lost more subjects in earlier studies because of experimenter error and equipment failure than in later studies. (See, for instance, the differences in subject loss in experiments 1 and 2 in chapter 4.)

3.4 Summary and a Look Ahead

In this chapter we suggested that studies of language comprehension may offer researchers a unique view of the emergent language system and of the strategies that children use to discover their native language. In fact, comprehension procedures have a number of advantages over those that rely on production, not the least of which is that they allow the researcher to probe for particular language structures that are not yet produced. Despite these advantages, many comprehension studies have been plagued by having to rely on children's compliance with requests for action. They have also been hampered by the inability to represent dynamic relations.

The intermodal preferential looking paradigm, described in this chapter in detail, avoids some of these pitfalls. It is a procedure that requires minimal action (a looking response) and that can portray dynamic relationships in a video format, thereby making available new ways to study the mapping between language and events. Across a number of experiments, in addition to those reported here (e.g., Naigles 1990; Fernald, McRoberts, and Herrera, in press), this paradigm has proven effective in unveiling young children's hidden linguistic competencies. Yet the paradigm has its drawbacks, too. For one thing, only four to six pairs of stimuli can be examined in any study, given current designs and subject fatigue. Further, all stimuli are presented in a forced-choice procedure so that very few alternatives can be examined at a single time. Finally, the use of the paradigm requires a relatively complacent child. Nevertheless, as we will shown in the next three chapters, the paradigm can effectively make headway in revealing very young children's sensitivities to structures in the language that they hear—in particular, to constituent structure, word order, and subcategorization frames.

Chapter 4

Infants' Perception of Constituent Structure

We have suggested that language learning is possible because children are biased to interpret input in particular ways. In chapter 2 we asked what presumptions current theories of language share with respect to the information required to get language learning off the ground. One presumption held by all theories is that, at the outset of language learning, children must be sensitive to constituent structure at a number of levels and to the fact that words combine into larger units over which the grammar operates. In this chapter we investigate infants' sensitivity to constituent structure using the intermodal preferential looking paradigm presented in chapter 3. As we will show, one-word speakers, as young as 14 months of age, seem to know that words presented in strings are not isolated units, but are part of larger constituents.

As noted in chapter 2, sentences are composed of subunits called phrases, like noun phrases and verb phrases; these phrases are themselves composed of constituents called words. Thus, to learn a language, children must be sensitive to the fact that the input is packaged into units like phrases, which determine meaning. Several examples illustrate the impact of constituent structure on language comprehension. First, consider the sentence "The big bus pushed the small car." To interpret this sentence, a child must realize that the words combine in restricted ways to represent events—in other words, that sentence meaning is not constructed from a random combination of these words. "Big cars" and "small buses" are not being referenced. Rather, constituent structure demands that the child focus on the "big bus" and the "small car." Another example comes from ambiguous sentences. Here the same string of words (e.g., "She slipped on a sweater") can have two meanings, but the organizational packaging of a particular utterance, as in (1a) or (1b), signaled by the prosody of the utterance, determines the particular meaning that should be imposed.

(1) a. {(She)(slipped)(on a sweater.)}
    b. {(She)(slipped on)(a sweater.)}

(1a) conjures up the sense of tripping over the sweater, whereas (1b) refers
to getting dressed. A final example is provided by the ways in which
constituents operate in the grammar. For instance, "the young boy with
the black hair" is a single noun phrase and can therefore be moved as a
unit (2a–b) or replaced by a single (2c).

(2) a. The young boy with the black hair kissed the girl.
    b. The girl was kissed by the young boy with the black hair.
    c. He kissed the girl.

Language is not organized serially—as strings of isolated words—but in
terms of structural units. Speakers of English, for example, know "he" in
(2c) stands for the entire phrase "the young boy with the black hair" in
(2a). Thus, if children are to learn the grammar of their language, they
must become aware of constituent structure, for only with that knowledge
will they be able to derive meaning from form.

   Little is known about the child's appreciation of constituent structure.
On the production side, accounts of early utterances do at least provide a
glimpse into the syntactic structure used by young talkers. Bloom (1990),
for example, found that children from 18 to 34 months of age respect
constituent structure in their first spontaneous utterances. Even the
youngest children in the study seemed aware that adjectives like "big" can
precede common nouns like "dog" but not proper nouns like "Fred."
Thus, children do not utter possible but ungrammatical noun phrase
constituents like "big Fred," but from the start they do produce grammatical noun phrases like "big dog." Valian (1986) also argues that young
children (mean age = 2 years) appreciate constituent structure since the
children in her study used forms like "one" and "it" to represent fuller
noun phrases that were unrealized in the sentence. That is, these children
were aware that the "it" and "one" forms were coreferential with full
noun phrases.

   On the comprehension side, however, little is known about the assumptions that preverbal infants or one-word speakers make about constituent
structure as they listen to language input. In this chapter we specifically
address this gap and examine whether children's comprehension is guided
by knowledge of constituent structure or whether leaner interpretations of
their apparent comprehension of simple sentences are in order. Three

questions frame the discussion. First, do prelinguistic children know that words "go together" or form units? Second, do children know which words in the sentence form units? And finally, if the answer to the first two questions is yes, we can ask the third: do children understand that words that form units map to specific events in the world? Regardless of how any particular language carries out the mapping between language and the world (e.g., Japanese puts the action—the verb—at the end of the sentence and English puts it in the middle), the expectation that such mapping occurs must, at some implicit level, be present for grammatical learning to proceed.

The first question, whether preverbal infants know that words in a sentence somehow form units, is the focus of much current research (Fernald 1991; Hirsh-Pasek, Tucker, and Golinkoff, 1995). Indeed, recent evidence suggests that by $7\frac{1}{2}$ months infants can locate words in the speech stream (Jusczyk and Aslin, in press). Evidence is also mounting that during the first year of life children seem to be sensitive to the acoustic cues that indicate the major constituent boundaries of clause and phrase (Jusczyk et al. 1992). In these experiments 9-month-old infants demonstrated their preference for intact prosodic envelopes of both noun and verb phrases. They attended longer to stimuli in which 1-second pauses were inserted at the natural noun and verb phrase boundaries than to stimuli in which 1-second pauses were placed within noun or verb phrases, where they do not ordinarily occur in child-directed speech (Bernstein Ratner 1995; Fernald 1991). The fact that these results continued to emerge when the experimenters used filtered speech that removed the linguistic segments suggests that infants were probably relying solely on acoustic cues to the phrasal units. Just what this acoustic finding means with respect to what infants know about linguistic constituent structure is unclear. At minimum, these results suggest that infants in the first year of life are able to detect at least the breaks between constituents and possibly even the organizational packaging in the input. They say nothing about whether infants know (1) which words go together to form units or (2) that linguistic units map to events in the world. The importance of the findings by Jusczyk et al. (1992) is clear, however, in that they indicate that infants can find constituents in the linguistic stream even if these constituents initially "hang together" exclusively on shared prosodic features. Later the infant may become capable of looking within these acoustic units to discern the distributional dependencies they contain and how these acoustically defined units map to events in the world. This possible movement from finding the constituents to looking within them will be a feature of the coalition framework developed in chapter 7.

The evidence regarding the second question, whether infants know which words in sentences form units, is scant but suggestive. Earlier we described the work of Bloom (1990) and Valian (1986), both of whom found that toddlers have knowledge of constituent structure by the latter half of the second year of life. Additional support for these claims comes from the work of Gerken and her colleagues (Gerken, Landau, and Remez 1990). Although infants often omit closed-class items in their own speech, Gerken, Landau, and Remez (1990) and Gerken and McIntosh (1993) report that by 2 years of age infants nonetheless expect to find these units in the speech they hear and are surprised when they are missing or altered. Using an elicited imitation task, Gerken found performance was disrupted when functors like "the" and "was," which indicate noun phrases and verb phrases, respectively, were omitted from the sample sentences, replaced by nonsense words, or placed in the wrong type of phrase. Thus, it appears that by 2 years of age—if not sooner (see Bloom 1990)—infants know what kinds of words typically form units in the speech they hear. If 2-year-olds show evidence of having performed distributional analyses "within" previously identified acoustic constituents, perhaps even younger children recognize when words in an acoustic constituent go together to make up a joint meaning. The experiment described in this chapter examines infants' ability to find meaning in the verb phrase in sentences.

The third question presumed by any study of constituent structure is the mapping question: when do children first realize that language "refers"—or that constituents of language should map onto some meanings? Golinkoff, Mervis, and Hirsh-Pasek (1994) claim that by the end of the first year of life infants are already guided by what they call the "Principle of Reference": namely, words can be mapped onto children's representations of objects, actions, or attributes in the environment. Obviously, this definition hinges crucially on the meaning of "word" and "map," concepts that have proven notoriously difficult for philosophers, linguists, and psychologists alike. Equally mysterious is the nature of the mapping relation between words and referents in the environment. As Gauker (1990) points out, a word does not refer just because presentation of a specific object or event elicits its production. For example, one can say "Yikes!" each time one sees a particular cat, but that is not necessarily the same thing as referring to the cat. "Yikes" could merely be an emotional reaction; it could also be a trained associate (as in paired-associate learning).

Suffice it to say that a word (or group of words) that is used to make reference is a phonological shape that has an arbitrary relationship to the concept it represents (Lyons 1977). "Mapping" refers to the symbolic relationship between the word (be it spoken or signed) and the event or object it represents. The problem is figuring out how the form "gets hooked up with" the meaning. Put another way, how does the form come to symbolize, or stand for, the referent and not just "go with" it, as in a paired-associate relationship? It is very difficult, indeed virtually impossible, to diagnose a clear-cut case of linguistic reference in young children, although much research on early lexical development shows that infants appear to comprehend and produce some words as early as 12 months of age (Benedict 1979; Nelson 1973; Clark 1994; Huttenlocher 1974; Barrett 1995).

If infants operate with the Principle of Reference, it should be possible to show that words affect their attention, perception, categorization, and memory for events differently than do other acoustic stimuli. This is because if words bear a "stands for" rather than a "goes with" relationship to referents, they should make referents more distinct and promote categorical thinking. In general, the research supporting the Principle of Reference is sparse and somewhat contradictory (see Golinkoff, Mervis, and Hirsh-Pasek 1994). Waxman and Balaban (1992), for example, pitted words against sine wave tones of the same duration and amplitude in a categorization task with infants aged 9 months. Only when a word, and not a tone, accompanied slides of animals did infants appear to form a category by watching an out-of-category object longer at test. Even if future research shows unequivocally that words are interpreted as symbols by infants, it is logically possible to know that a single word can label an object or event but not to integrate the meaning of a string of words in a sentence. For example, an infant could know the meanings of the words "dog," "boy," and "kiss" in a sentence such as "The dog kisses the boy" but not recognize that the separate word meanings taken together describe a unique event. And yet all theories of language acquisition build upon the child's ability to find a mapping between words and the world. Unfortunately, little is known about when young children make the assumption that groups of words work together to represent particular meanings. For example, it is perfectly possible to imagine that young children around the end of the first year of life, in the single-word period, would, as one of Slobin's (1973, 1985a,b) principles predicts, process only the first word or the last word heard. On this account the child might only notice the word "dog," with no understanding of the fact that the following word, "kisses," had anything to do with the dog. Indeed, as Sachs and Truswell (1978) point out, many researchers have argued that

> in most everyday situations, young children do not need to integrate various words from an utterance in order to interact appropriately in a conversational situation. Many investigators (e.g., Bloom, 1973, 1974; Clark, Hutcheson, and Van Buren, 1974) have suggested that children in the one-word stage who appear to understand more than they can say may typically be responding on the basis of a key word or cues from the situational context. (p. 17)

Bloom (1973), for example, argues that children cannot integrate words in sentences to form units until they themselves are producing multiword speech (see also Atkinson 1985). Bloom writes:

> [B]efore the use of syntax in their speech, children have little if any knowledge of linguistic structure (p. 20) [and] ... when a sentence is redundant with respect to the context in which it occurs, then the amount of information which the child needs to get from the linguistic message is probably minimal. (p. 59)

Alternatively, if some of the lexical items in a sentence are known, and if sentences are seen as specifying particular relationships in the world, children might be able to do more than just notice a key word and rely on context. The extreme version of this position would be that of McNeill, (1970), who claims that new grammatical relations are constantly emerging, even during the one-word stage.

Without crediting the child with syntactic or grammatical relations (e.g., subject of the sentence), however, it is possible to assume an intermediate stance: even before children produce ordered speech themselves, they may expect the items in a sentence that they hear to map in some particular way to the world. Thus, upon hearing the sentence "The dog is kissing the boy," children might expect to observe an event in which the boy is being kissed as opposed to just being present in the scene. If children are integrating words in the sentence to derive a semantic representation, then they should not consider a scene in which something other than the boy is being kissed to be an accurate portrayal of the sentence.

In sum, then, we have asked three questions pertinent to the experiment to be described in this chapter, and we can answer them as follows. First, it appears that infants in their first year of life can isolate the units of language in ways that would make attention to constituent structure possible. Second, at least by the middle of the second year, toddlers have some appreciation of which words within these constituents ordinarily form units (e.g., "the" precedes nouns in noun phrases). Third, there is also some evidence in the literature to suggest that by the end of the first year of life, infants have achieved the insight of reference, or the principle that single words map to objects, actions, and attributes. What is still unclear, however, is whether infants interpret sentences as if *groups* of words function together as units of meaning, to specify particular relationships in the world. Moreover, very little is known about infants' sensitivity with respect to *which* words go together to form a constituent. For example, upon hearing an admittedly odd sentence like "She's kissing the keys," do infants know that the words predicate a particular nonlinguistic relationship? That is, do they know that a scene that depicts some keys on a table, and a woman kissing something that is not keys, would *not* represent the gist of the sentence? The experiment to be described here was designed to investigate this fundamental property of constituent structure.

4.1 Experiment 1: Can Infants Perceive Constituent Structure?

The purpose of the experiment, then, was to explore whether children producing only a few single-word utterances appreciate the fact that language maps to particular ongoing events. To have this knowledge implies that children have isolated linguistic constituents (not just the acoustic counterparts of such constituents), appreciate that word groups map to unique events, and can identify which groups of words (in the present case, the verb phrase) form a semantic unit. To comprehend language and to build a grammar, the child must have such knowledge, being capable of more than just noting key words and relying on nonlinguistic context.

Thus, the null hypothesis is that infants—especially at the beginning of single-word speech—are unable to integrate word meanings within the sentence. Consistent with Bloom's (1973) argument, the ability to map sentences to events may come only when children have achieved some degree of productive language. In stark contrast, our hypothesis was that young children are capable of finding constituents larger than the single word in the sentence and can make a reasonable guess about which words go together to denote meaning.

To evaluate whether infants hearing a sentence attend to single words or to larger units—that is, whether infants are sensitive to constituent structure, and in particular to the composition of the verb phrase—we designed experiment 1. This experiment was fashioned after one by Sachs and Truswell (1978) that investigated whether young children can follow two-word commands like "Tickle book" and "Kiss keys." The reasoning behind Sachs and Truswell's experiment was as follows: if young speakers can correctly carry out two-word commands—especially bizarre ones like "Kiss keys"—then they must realize that words in a string form units to specify particular relationships. If, on the other hand, children are focusing on individual words in the input and are using familiarity or semantic probability to carry out these commands, then they should fail to correctly carry out bizarre commands.

In Sachs and Truswell's study, the children ranged in age from 16 to 24 months, with a mean of 19.6 months. Many of these children were arguably on the verge of two-word speech. Sachs and Truswell reported that all of the children were able to carry out some of the unusual commands they gave and that this ability increased with age. The children who participated in the study described here were considerably younger (13–15 months) and produced very little single-word speech, let alone multiword combinations. Despite their young age, they were predicted to show sentential integration because of the minimal demands of the intermodal preferential looking paradigm.

The logic of experiment 1 is identical to that of Sachs and Truswell's study. Table 3.1 illustrates one of the six stimulus sets employed, and figure 3.1 shows a sample stimulus. Each of the two videotapes in a given stimulus set depicted a different woman carrying out the same action (e.g., kissing) at the same time. As table 3.1 illustrates, in this particular pair of tapes both women kissed something while moving an object in the foreground. On one screen, the woman kissed a set of keys while moving a ball in the foreground. On the other screen, a different woman kissed the ball while moving the keys in the foreground. If children organize their input into packages of words that map onto relationships in the environment, then the linguistic stimulus "She's kissing the keys" should direct attention toward the interactive scene in which the woman is, in fact, kissing the keys and not the ball.

Children could not select the match over the nonmatch by paying attention only to segments of the full linguistic stimulus. Since each screen displayed a woman, the pronoun "she" could not be used to find the match; and since each screen displayed the act of kissing, the verb alone could not be used either. Each screen also displayed a set of keys, and on the nonmatching tape the keys were made prominent by moving them in the foreground. If children paid attention only to the word "keys," they might have distributed their looking equally between the events since keys were present on both screens. Alternatively, they might even have preferred the nonmatch since the keys were moving prominently in the foreground in that case. Thus, in order to find the match, children could rely only on the fact that the keys were the recipient of the action of kissing. Children would have to detect the verb phrase "kissing the keys" and treat it as a unit that specified a particular event. That is, they would have to know that words operate within packages or constituents, and they would have to know which words in the stimulus went together. Of course, whether the child considered this phrase to be the "verb" phrase, or merely a group of words that expressed the action and object of the action, is beyond the scope of this study.

Method

Stimuli
Table 3.1 and figure 3.1 present one of the six pairs of video events used in experiment 1, with its accompanying linguistic stimuli. The audio might change from trial to trial, yet video events throughout a block of trials testing one of the stimulus sets did not change. Each of the sets of test stimuli was constructed in the same way as the sample, except for counterbalancing the side of the first appearance of a sequential event. The total length of the tapes was 4.5 minutes.

This study conformed to the pattern of introducing the video events with sequential and simultaneous trials and then presenting the test trials (see chapter 3 for more detail). Table 4.1 presents all six stimuli and the accompanying test sentences. Half of the subjects (those tested in the Delaware laboratory) heard a linguistic stimulus that matched one of the test events; the other half (those tested in the Temple laboratory) heard the counterbalanced audio. This design (in addition to the use of the simultaneous trials) allowed us to evaluate whether there was a stimulus salience effect across the laboratories. Furthermore, since the match was to opposite sides in the two labs, we could, if such an effect occurred, conclude that it did not affect the dependent variable. Counterbalancing the linguistic stimulus so that it matched one member of a visual stimulus pair for half of the subjects and the opposite member for the other half also provided another check on stimulus salience. If the results revealed a

Table 4.1
Experiment 1: Video events and accompanying linguistic stimuli the six blocks of trials

	Tape 1	Linguistic stimulus*	Tape 2
1	Woman$_1$ eating a banana	"Hey, she's eating the *banana*!" (cookie)	Woman$_2$ eating a cookie
2	Woman$_1$ kicking a chair	"See, she's kicking the *bag*!" (chair)	Woman$_2$ kicking a bag
3	Woman$_1$ smelling a shoe	"Look, she's smelling the *boat*!" (shoe)	Woman$_2$ smelling a boat
4	Woman$_1$ tickling a phone	"Oh, she's tickling the *phone*!" (book)	Woman$_2$ tickling a book
5	Woman$_1$ kissing a ball	"Look, she's kissing the *ball*!" (keys)	Woman$_2$ kissing a set of keys
6	Woman$_1$ pushing a plant	"Hey, she's pushing the *cup*!" (plant)	Woman$_2$ pushing a cup

* The italicized word was the linguistic stimulus used in the Delaware laboratory; the word in parentheses was used in the counterbalance condition carried out in the Temple laboratory.

visual preference for the matching event, this preference could not be attributed to infants' general preference for that event since the match was a different event for the two halves of the design.

All linguistic stimuli were recorded directly on the videotape by a female experimenter who used child-directed speech. During the sequential and the simultaneous trials, the audio was neutral in that it matched either screen equally well. During the test trials and the intertrial intervals that preceded them, the audio exhorted the infant to find the match (e.g., "Where's she kissing the keys?").

As table 4.1 shows, all but one of the stimuli ("eating the banana/ cookie") portrayed events that are relatively implausible and certainly rare: for example, "tickling the phone/book," which was probably the least likely of the six events. Unusual events were selected on the same rationale that Sachs and Truswell (1978) used (and indeed, some of the stimuli themselves were Sachs and Truswell's): infants could not rely on their extralinguistic knowledge to interpret sentences that described events they had never witnessed. Thus, if infants watched the matching screen more than the nonmatching screen, it could not be because they resorted to watching the most typical event—neither event in a pair was typical (except for "eating the banana/cookie," where both events were typical).

Subjects Thirty-two infants, 16 boys and 16 girls, aged 13 to 15 months (mean age = 14 months), were the subjects in experiment 1. Half of them (8 boys and 8 girls) were tested in the Delaware laboratory; the other half in the Temple laboratory. All but 2 out of 31 infants (1 infant's language data were lost) were producing only single-word speech. According to the Rescorla Language Inventory (1991), which parents filled out in the laboratory, the infants produced an average of 17.5 words. In fact, 26 of the 31 infants (84%) had productive vocabularies of fewer than 25 words.

In order to participate in this study, infants had to be able to comprehend the names of the 12 objects shown on the videotapes (see table 4.1). If infants did not know the names of the objects singly, there would be little chance of revealing any sentence integration skill. During the first phone contact, parents were asked whether their infants understood the 12 nouns in question. Only infants whose parents reported comprehension of 11 of the 12 nouns were invited to participate. The parents of the others were reassured that infants at this age do not often comprehend this many words and were told that we would call them back in a couple of weeks and ask again. If, in the meantime, parents wished to teach these words to their children, that would be fine.

To obtain 16 subjects in the Delaware laboratory, 74 infants were tested. Of the 58 infants who were dropped, 26 were dropped because of fussiness, 14 because of equipment problems, 5 because of experimenter error, 1 for failing to center, and 12 because of center or side preferences. (Chapter 3 describes these reasons for subject loss in more detail.) Retention rates are available only from the Delaware laboratory because the discarded-subject files from Temple were lost in a laboratory move. We believe that subject loss data from this laboratory were comparable.

Subject loss can be attributed to two factors. First, and most prominently, the videotapes used in this experiment were longer than the ones used in subsequent experiments (4.5 minutes, instead of around 3 minutes), containing six rather than the usual four blocks of trials. Second, since this was one of the first studies carried out in this paradigm, a large number of equipment failures and experimenter errors hampered our efforts. A full 26% of the original subjects were discarded for this reason —a number that was much reduced in subsequent experiments.

Procedure   Infants and their parents participated in experiment 1, carried out in our university laboratories, as described in chapter 3. Before participating in the videtape portion of the study, these children were shown the objects they would see in the videos, lying in a random pile on the floor. The experimenter labeled the objects repeatedly for the child during play, although none of the actions to be seen in the videotapes was ever modeled or described. Then, after the parent received the instructions, parent and infant were installed in the testing area and the infant was shown the videotapes.

Results

Calculation of Stimulus Salience from the Simultaneous Trials   Recall that the simultaneous trial, when the test events are seen at the same time on both screens with a neutral audio, allows the relative salience of each member of a pair of stimuli to be calculated. If the events in a pair are indeed equally attractive (as they were designed to be), then attention to these events across 32 subjects should be distributed randomly, approximately 50% of the total looking time during a trial to each event.

Children's attention to each event in a pair of events during the simultaneous trials was compared in an analysis of variance. Each infant's total visual fixation time to both events in each of six pairs of simultaneous trials was entered into a mixed analysis of variance. The between-subjects factors were sex (male vs. female) and laboratory (Temple vs. Delaware). The within-subjects factors were match level ("match" vs. "nonmatch") and stimulus (6 levels). The laboratory factor was also the counterbalance of the linguistic stimulus. That is, for the events of the woman kissing the keys or the ball, the children tested in the Delaware laboratory heard the linguistic match to the "keys" screen; the children tested in the Temple laboratory heard the match to the "ball" screen. The match level factor in the analysis identified which of the pair of events was to be the match (or nonmatch) during the subsequent test trials.

The analysis revealed no overall effect of the match factor ($F(1, 341) = .65, p > .40$). Yet there were three significant interactions: stimulus by match ($F(5, 341) = 2.74, p < .02$); match by laboratory ($F(1, 341) = 18.91, p < .0001$); and stimulus by match by laboratory ($F(5, 341) = 2.52, p < .03$). Table 4.2 presents the means for the simultaneous trials by stimulus, laboratory, and match factor. It is apparent from the table that there was an overall preference for the "match" in the

Table 4.2
Experiment 1: Mean visual fixation time (in seconds) by laboratory and stimulus to the "matching" and "nonmatching" screen during the simultaneous trials

| | Laboratory | | | | | |
| | Delaware ($n = 16$) | | Temple ($n = 16$) | | Mean | |
Stimulus*	Match	Nonmatch	Match	Nonmatch	Match	Nonmatch
1	3.11	1.54	2.01	3.14	2.56	2.34
2	2.65	2.02	1.65	3.32	2.15	2.67
3	2.17	2.21	2.53	2.10	2.35	2.12
4	2.91	1.25	1.71	3.34	2.31	2.30
5	2.04	2.23	1.91	2.70	1.98	2.29
6	3.70	1.36	2.32	1.46	3.01	1.31
Mean	2.76	1.77	2.02	2.68		

*Table 4.1 describes the stimuli in the order in which they appeared.

Delaware laboratory and for the same stimulus in the Temple laboratory (where it served as the "nonmatch"). Notice that this pattern occurs only on four out of six stimuli in both laboratories; this is the probable cause of the interaction with the stimulus factor. Furthermore, post hoc Tukey tests comparing the differences between the "match" and the "nonmatch" for each stimulus in each of the two laboratories revealed that only one of the differences was statistically significant at the .05 level (children watched the "match" more than the "nonmatch" for the last stimulus in the Delaware laboratory; see table 4.2). The general absence of significant differences between the "match" and the "nonmatch" within each stimulus and laboratory may appear to contradict the three-way interaction reported above. Yet the interaction tested differences between any and all means rather than just between the means that are of theoretical interest in this study. Further, examination of the means in the stimulus by laboratory by match interaction reveals that only 6 of the 12 means favor the "match."

If children were to display knowledge of constituent structure in this experiment, those tested at the Delaware laboratory would have had to maintain their preference for the match during the test events. On the other hand, children tested at the Temple laboratory would have had to *overcome* their preference for the nonmatch during the simultaneous trials. Thus, if children retained the preferences found in response to the simultaneous trials, there would be no significant effect of matching screen on the test trials and hence no evidence that children appreciate constituent structure. Alternatively, if children do appreciate constituent structure, we would have expected a main effect of match to emerge in the test trials.

Test Trials   To see if infants overall—and particularly in the Temple laboratory—preferred to watch the matching or nonmatching screen (or neither) during the test trials, the average of each child's total visual fixation time in seconds during the two test trials for each of the six stimulus pairs was entered into a mixed analysis of variance. The between-subjects factors were laboratory (Delaware vs. Temple) and sex (male vs. female); the within-subjects factors were stimulus (6 levels) and match level (match vs. nonmatch). The laboratory factor also contained the counterbalance of the linguistic stimulus. Subjects tested in the Delaware laboratory heard a linguistic stimulus that matched one event of a pair; those tested in the Temple laboratory heard a linguistic stimulus that matched the other event of the pair. The key prediction was that infants would watch the screen that matched the linguistic stimulus significantly more than they watched the screen that did not match that stimulus. No other effects were predicted to reach significance.

Results indicated that these infants, the vast majority of whom (84%) were in the one-word stage of language production, were nonetheless predisposed to organize their input into packages of words that represent relationships. As table 4.3 indicates, the mean visual fixation time in seconds to the match was 2.72 seconds and to the nonmatch, 2.23 seconds. The magnitude of this difference resulted in a main effect of the match factor ($F(1, 341) = 7.97, p < .005$). There were no other significant main effects or interactions. Thus, across laboratories children watched the matching event more than the nonmatching event, indicating a sensitivity to constituent structure. This finding also holds when we compute the number of subjects whose means to the match were greater than their means to the nonmatch: 24 out of 32 subjects (75%) fit this pattern.

Although the match effect was the only significant finding, two other effects approached significance: sex by match ($F(1, 341) = 3.16, p < .08$) and stimulus by match ($F(5, 341) = 1.94, p < .09$). Inspection of the means in table 4.3 indicates that children watched the match more than the nonmatch on five of the six stimuli. Therefore, the stimulus by match interaction may be due to the second stimulus, where the nonmatch was

Table 4.3
Experiment 1: Mean visual fixation time (in seconds) by sex and stimulus to the matching and nonmatching screen during the test trials

Stimulus*	Sex					
	Male ($n = 16$)		Female ($n = 16$)		Mean	
	Match	Nonmatch	Match	Nonmatch	Match	Nonmatch
1	3.15	2.18	3.61	1.76	3.38	1.97
2	2.23	3.04	2.68	2.51	2.46	2.77
3	3.09	2.06	3.13	2.29	3.11	2.18
4	2.41	2.46	2.53	1.99	2.47	2.22
5	2.50	2.44	2.83	2.15	2.66	2.29
6	1.99	2.10	2.55	1.80	2.27	1.94
Mean	2.56	2.38	2.89	2.02	2.72	2.23

*Table 4.1 describes the stimuli in the order in which they appeared.

watched slightly more overall than the match. The more interesting marginal effect is the sex by match interaction. The means in table 4.3 suggest that the match was preferred over the nonmatch only by the girls in the sample. The mean difference between the match and the nonmatch was greater for the girls than for the boys (for girls, 2.89 seconds for the match and 2.02 seconds for the nonmatch; for boys, 2.56 seconds for the match and 2.38 seconds for the nonmatch). To test this conjecture, separate analyses were conducted by sex.

Analysis by Sex   The within-subjects factors were match versus nonmatch (2 levels) and stimulus (6 levels). The between-subjects factor was laboratory. The analysis of the girls' data resulted in a significant main effect of match versus nonmatch ($F(1, 168) = 9.81, p < .002$). There were no other significant main effects or interactions. The match factor did not even approach significance in the boys' data ($F < 1.00$), however. Further, there were no other significant main effects or interactions. Thus, it appears that only the girls watched the match more than the nonmatch. It is clear from these findings that in the overall analysis the main effect of match is carried by the girls' response, though note that 11 of 16 boys (69%) had overall means greater to the match than to the nonmatch.

One reason for the sex difference may be that the girls had significantly more words in their productive vocabularies. According to parental report, the girls' mean vocabulary was 24.73 words, with a range of 0 to 112. The boys' mean was 10.94 words, with a range of 0 to 31. This difference was not, however, significant by t test ($p = .13$).

Discussion

To induce a grammar, the child must be able to identify sequences of words that are "packaged" together to convey some unit of meaning. These results suggest that even some immature speakers (most notably girls in this sample) have taken this step in the language-learning process: they seem to have an operating principle that biases them to look for "packages"—constituents beyond the single word—in the language that they hear. Further, this result occurs if the linguistic stimuli describe events that are implausible in nature. With implausible sentences, infants must rely on the organization of the sentence to decide which event is the match. That is, upon hearing a bizarre sentence such as "She's kissing the keys" and seeing two equally bizarre events of "key kissing" and "ball kissing," the infant must integrate the words in the stimulus sentence in order to find the match. Infants cannot rely on what they know of events to find the match because both key kissing and ball kissing are equally unlikely .

This finding suggests that although infants may often rely on their knowledge of events in comprehending sentences in the world (e.g., see Bever 1970; Chapman and Kohn 1978; Strohner and Nelson 1974; Clark 1994; Golinkoff and Markessini 1980; also see section 7.1, discussion of phase II), they are also capable of using language-specific knowledge like constituent structure. In sum, in this experiment, infants—at least the girls—who were one-word speakers demonstrated a bias to interpret the input as packages of words rather than as single words. They also seemed to know which words went together. For example, had they focused only on "She's kissing," either video depiction would have been appropriate. They clearly showed a preference for one of the videos over the other. They seemed to know that the crucial unit here was the one that comprised the verb phrase—for example, "kissing the keys" versus "kissing the ball."

The fact that the findings seem to be carried by the girls is in line with other studies that use infant attention as the dependent variable. In addition, studies in early language development often find girls ahead of boys (Fenson et al. 1994). As Fenson et al. write:

The large number of analyses of gender effects reported here reveal a remarkably consistent pattern. On nearly all measures, females score on average slightly higher than males, but this difference typically accounts for just 1–2% of the variance. (p. 81)

Perhaps female infants mature slightly faster than their male counterparts (Haywood 1986; Held 1989). Several experiments by Baillargeon (1995) suggest that the boys catch up readily, looking the same as the girls just a month later. Perhaps a slightly older sample of boys tested in this experiment would have responded as the girls did.

Three concerns may be raised about the present data set. The first is the number of subjects who needed to be tested to obtain 32. As described above, there were several reasons why subject loss was high. Even so, it could be argued that the final sample represented the "cream of the crop" of 13- to 15-month-olds—those willing to sit through six repetitive blocks of test trials, continually scanning back and forth between monitors, and clever enough to return to the center light between trials. Although this may be true, it should be noted that the reasons for discarding subjects' data (when we exclude reasons that have nothing to do with the subjects themselves, such as experimenter error) may be relegated to the domain of attention. For example, some children did not wish to remain on their parent's lap once they had seen interesting toys during the period preceding the testing. Further, although an attempt was made to schedule children when, according to their parents, they would be at their best, some children appeared tired and cranky even before testing began. In addition, not all children at this age watched television regularly at home. Thus, it is difficult to disentangle whether children who remained in the sample were truly more linguistically advanced than their peers, or just having a better day! It is the case, however, that there was large variability in the lexical skills of the children who served as subjects. In general in the present paradigm, we have found that there is an inverse relationship between the age of the children in a particular study and the number of children who need to be tested to make up the sample. As in all research on infants using attentional dependent variables, the younger the subject, the more transient state variables intrude on the testing.

A second concern is the apparent stimulus preference effect that emerged in the simultaneous trials. Two factors allay this concern. First, the effect appeared to be ephemeral when analyzed with post hoc tests. Second, because the linguistic stimulus matched both screens, half of the subjects saw the match to the preferred screen and half the match to the nonpreferred screen. Thus, the overall preference for the match in the test trials cannot merely be reflecting stimulus preferences.

A third concern is that although the current results seem convincing, an alternative explanation exists. Perhaps infants solved the task by searching for the video screen in which the object named by the last-mentioned word (in the keys/ball tape, "keys") is being acted upon in what might be construed as the main event, namely, "kissing." This could occur if infants (1) do observe Slobin's (1985a,b) principle "Attend to the last word" and (2) prefer to watch labeled items participating in interactive events. After all, language is often used by individuals in the child's environment to comment on ongoing interactions. Hearing "... keys" and looking for the video in which the keys are involved in a particular action (as opposed to just moving in the foreground) could result in finding the match, but not for the hypothesized reason. That is, infants would *not* be achieving this result by attending to constituent structure. If this counterhypothesis is true and infants can find the match just by hearing a word in sentence-final position, then infants given sentences that ask only for the last item mentioned should also be able to find the match.

If infants are truly integrating individual words heard in sentences, however, an audio like "Where are the keys? Find the keys!" should result in chance performance, with neither screen being preferred. Before discussing the results of experiment 1 further, we will describe experiment 2, which was designed to rule out this simpler alternative.

4.2   Experiment 2: Can Infants Find the Match by Attending Only to the Last-Mentioned Word? A Control Study

The purpose of experiment 2, a control experiment, was to see if infants could still find the match when all they were offered in the linguistic stimulus was the same last noun as in the test trial audio for experiment 1. The subjects, selected in the same way as the subjects for experiment 1, were shown the same tapes as in experiment 1. The linguistic stimuli were still presented in child-directed speech, but here they were reduced to asking for the last item mentioned in the strings in experiment 1—for example, "Where are the keys?" as opposed to the sentence "She's kissing the keys," in which an agent is also mentioned. In this experiment the match was considered the screen on which the woman was acting upon the object the linguistic stimulus asked for (in fact, in this experiment the linguistic stimulus matched both screens, since both displayed (e.g.) keys —keys being kissed, in one case, and keys being waved in the foreground, in the other). If infants solved the task in experiment 1 by attending to constituent structure, they should fail to find the match here since all they are given of the original sentence is the last word. Alternatively, if in the original study infants used a "final-word and item-in-interaction strategy," they should still watch the match here.

Method

Subjects   Since no significant differences emerged in experiment 1 between the Delaware and Temple laboratories, this experiment was carried out only in the Delaware laboratory. Eighteen children (10 boys and 8 girls), who met the same vocabulary criterion as in experiment 1, were tested. To obtain 18 subjects, an extra 26 children were tested. Seven were dropped for fussiness; 2 for parent interference; 1 for experimenter error; 5 for equipment failure; 9 for missing too many trials by the centering criteria; and 2 for side biases. Note that subject loss was much reduced here relative to experiment 1, as we gained experience using the paradigm.

Children's level of lexical development was no different from that of the children in experiment 1. They had a mean productive vocabulary of 22.3 words, with only 2 out of 17 producing word combinations (language data from 1 child were lost). Twelve of the 17 children (71%) had productive vocabularies of fewer than 25 words.

Procedure   The procedure was identical to that used in experiment 1, including the training with the objects whose names were used as lexical items on the videotapes.

Stimuli   The videotapes were the same ones used in experiment 1; only the linguistic stimuli were changed by redubbing the audio onto channel 1 of one of the tapes. The new stimulus sentences merely asked for the item in question, using carrier phrases such as "Where's the . . . ?", "Find the . . . !", "Do you see the . . . ?", and so on. As noted earlier, the "match" was considered the screen on which the woman was acting upon the object named. That is, the "match" for "Where are the keys?" was the screen on which the woman kissed the keys. In fact, the linguistic stimuli matched both screens equally well since both displayed keys.

Table 4.4
Experiment 2: Video events and accompanying linguistic stimuli for the six blocks
of trials

	Tape 1	Linguistic stimulus*	Tape 2
1	Woman$_1$ eating a banana	"Where's the banana?"	Woman$_2$ eating a cookie
2	Woman$_1$ kicking a chair	"Find the bag!"	Woman$_2$ kicking a bag
3	Woman$_1$ smelling a shoe	"Can you find the boat?"	Woman$_2$ smelling a boat
4	Woman$_1$ tickling a phone	"Do you see the phone?"	Woman$_2$ tickling a book
5	Woman$_1$ kissing a ball	"Where's the ball?"	Woman$_2$ kissing a set of keys
6	Woman$_1$ pushing a plant	"Find the cup!"	Woman$_2$ pushing a cup

*Additional sentences with slight variations in the carrier phrases were presented
with each stimulus.

The video events and linguistic stimuli used in experiment 2 are listed in
table 4.4.

Results

Calculation of Stimulus Salience from the Simultaneous Trials As in experiment 1, visual fixation times during the simultaneous trials were compared in a three-way analysis of variance with the between-subjects factor of sex and the within-subjects factors of stimulus and match. The analysis revealed a two-way interaction of stimulus by match ($F(5, 192) = 2.48$, $p < .04$). Post hoc Tukey comparisons between the means of the match and nonmatch for each stimulus indicated that the match for the fourth stimulus (tickling the phone) was preferred to the nonmatch (tickling the book) (mean to match = 3.15 seconds; to nonmatch = 1.45 seconds).

Test Trials A three-way mixed analysis of variance was performed with the factors of sex (2 levels), stimulus (6 levels), and the main variable of interest, match level (match vs. nonmatch). Since experiment 2 was designed to see whether the match was still favored using linguistic stimuli that simply asked for the last lexical item used in the original sentences, the "match" was considered to be the same as the match for the original audio. That is, the "match" was assumed to be the scene where the lexical item in question was being acted on by the woman.

Neither any of the main effects nor any of the interactions were significant (p's > .05). The mean visual fixation times to the match versus the nonmatch for all stimuli did not differ significantly when the control audio was used (mean to the match = 2.77 seconds; to the nonmatch = 2.54 seconds). This lack of significance indicated that the original result from experiment 1 could not be attributed to a strategy of "find-the-screen-where-the-last-item-mentioned-is-being-acted-upon." In addition, out of 18 children only half (9) had overall means that favored the match.

Given that girls and boys responded differently in experiment 1, however, these data were then also analyzed separately by sex. A within-subjects analysis with the factors of stimulus (6 levels) and match versus nonmatch was carried out on the boys' and girls' data. The results were surprising: the boys'—but not the girls'—analysis yielded significant effects. The boys had a borderline significant match effect ($F(1, 84) = 3.87$, $p = .052$) and a match by stimulus interaction ($F(5, 84) = 3.05, p < .025$). T tests on the appropriate comparisons (the mean visual fixation time to the match and nonmatch for each stimulus) revealed that the boys watched the match more than the nonmatch for the first and fourth stimuli (p's < .05) only. For the remaining four stimuli, the boys had no significant preferences for either the match or the nonmatch. Figures 4.1 and 4.2 show how the children in the control experiment compared with the children in the main experiment.

Discussion

This control experiment was conducted to rule out the possibility that infants in the main study were finding the match for a reason other than integration of the words in the sentence: namely, merely by attending to the last word in the test sentence rather than by integrating the verb and its object (e.g., "kissing" and "keys"). The present results indicate that, on the contrary, infants *are* forming a unit between the words "kissing" and "keys" in the main experiment and are then looking toward the video screen that portrays that relationship.

A test sentence that did not encode this relationship between kissing and keys did not inspire children to watch the "matching" event. That is, the linguistic stimulus "Where are the keys?", which asked the child only to find the keys (present on both screens), was not enough to get the child

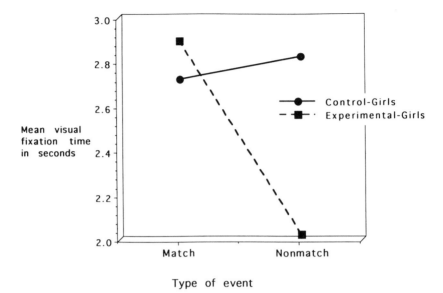

Figure 4.1
Mean visual fixation time to the match and nonmatch by the girls in experiment 1
(the main experiment) and experiment 2 (the control experiment)

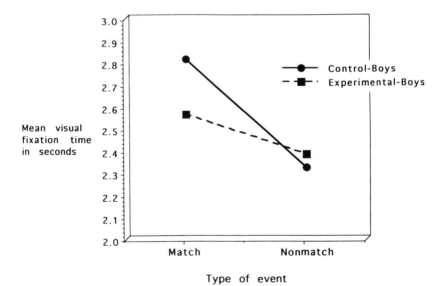

Figure 4.2
Mean visual fixation time to the match and nonmatch by the boys in experiment
1 (the main experiment) and experiment 2 (the control experiment)

to watch the integrated event where the keys were being kissed. The fact that children could not find the "match" in this condition indicates that it is not sufficient for the child to hear the last word to find the match. Apparently, infants attend to the verb (e.g., "kissing"), in addition to its object, and integrate the meaning of these individual words to search for the correlated video event.

4.3 General Discussion

These experiments were designed around three questions.

1. Do preverbal infants know that words "go together" or form units?
2. Do infants know which words in the sentence form units?
3. Do infants understand that words that form units map to specific events in the world? (That is, when do infants have the knowledge that single words, and then groups of words in sentences, refer to specific events and relationships in the world?)

The answer to each of the questions is yes. Months before they begin to spontaneously combine words in their own productions, infants appear to know that words form units. They also seem to know that these word groups specify unique events in the world. We know this because in experiment 1 infants watched the particular event specified by the verb phrase more than an event that depicted the action and the object in a way that did not combine them. Further, infants were capable of integrating word meaning across both plausible and implausible sentences that they had never before encountered. It is highly unlikely, for example, that infants had ever witnessed someone tickling a book or a telephone! Therefore, they could not have relied on their extralinguistic knowledge to solve this task.

   In experiment 2 an alternative explanation for the results of experiment 1 was ruled out. Infants could not have preferentially watched the matching screen simply by attending to the last word they heard and finding the screen on which it was the focus of the action (the match). We can make this claim because when the linguistic stimulus emphasized what was the final word in the original audio, infants' attention to what had been the matching screen was the same as their attention to what had been the nonmatching screen. Thus, in acting as though "Where are the keys?" matched both screens, 13- to 15-month-olds operated presumably as adults would have.

Thus, the results presented here parallel those presented by Sachs and Truswell (1978) and do so with younger children, all of whom were in the one-word stage. As Sachs and Truswell acknowledge, the ability to use constituent structure does not mean that the children are operating with a grammar. Grammatical knowledge involves more than an appreciation of how words are grouped. For example, no amount of grouping or re-grouping will help children to link the words "brother" and "himself" in the sentence "The brother of John washed himself." Grammars are con-structed from the hierarchical (and not serial) organization of sentential constituents. Nonetheless, identifying the constituents is an important and necessary step in language learning.

What about constituent structure do these children really know? The results of the main experiment do not permit us to say any more than that children seem to form a "package" or unit from the verb and its object. We cannot claim that the words have this grammatical status for infants; for them, these words may represent the action word and the name of the object being acted on.

Why do children assume that groups of words are combined into orga-nized structures? Our best guess is that this organization is a loose one imposed by the prosody of the language. There is much evidence to suggest that infant-directed speech exaggerates prosodic markings at con-stituent boundaries, where "prosody" here refers to shifts in fundamental frequency, pausing, and stress (Fernald 1991; Bernstein Ratner 1995). Research has also shown that infants are sensitive to these prosodic boundaries when they listen to speech (see Jusczyk et al. 1992). Thus, in experiment 1, where the sentences were uttered in infant-directed speech, infants might well have exploited unspecified acoustic cues for the unity of the verb phrase. Infants appear to have presumed that words that fell within that acoustically specified verb phrase work together to generate meaning.

One way to assess the role of prosody in this task would be to reduce the magnitude of the prosodic cues by using adult-directed speech and to conduct the experiment again to see whether infants of the same age would continue to respond as if the verb phrase were an integrated unit. Indeed, we are attempting such an experiment, using the original tapes and an adult-directed audio. Already we have experienced extensive sub-ject loss, a fact that is interesting in its own right. In short, the answer to the first question may be that the prosody suggests to children that words operate in tandem.

What do infants know about which words go together? Here again the data are less than clear. First, in the current study all children were pretested for their knowledge of the nouns used, but they were not screened for their knowledge of the verbs used. Perhaps any nonsense word that occurred within the prosodic envelope would be sufficient to guarantee a correct response. For example, would the infants have responded similarly if the voice on the audio had said, "She's blurting the keys (ball). Where is she blurting the keys (ball)?" The role that the verb played in these sentences is an empirical issue that needs to be investigated. Second, it is not clear whether infants are concerned with the internal structure of the verb phrase. That is, were the children attending to the *order* of the verb relative to the direct object? Would they have responded similarly to a sentence that preserved the original prosody but changed the order of the words (e.g., "She's key the kissing. Where is she key the kissing?")? Again, this is an empirical question.

Finally, would children be as facile with longer noun phrase constituents as they seemed to be with verb phrase constituents? Again, evidence from the literature on infant speech perception suggests that they would be (Jusczyk et al. 1992). In Jusczyk et al.'s study, noun phrases that were disrupted by inserting a pause were significantly less preferred than noun phrases that were left intact by placing the pause at the end of the phrase. A large proportion of the English input to young children has no acoustically marked initial noun phrase constituent (Reed and Schreiber 1982). Most of the sentences that begin with pronouns or proper nouns have minimal prosodic cues. It would be interesting to see when infants begin to group together phrase-internal words in the noun phrase.

In sum, the studies reported above suggest that infants are using constituent structure to unite words into a coherent meaning. Much more research needs to be done to demonstrate exactly what infants are relying on to solve this task. The studies also highlight the potential of the intermodal preferential looking paradigm, which permits researchers to look at the ways in which very young children analyze the language that they hear.

Above we suggested that children might be sensitive to constituent structure, but that the task used in experiments 1 and 2 could not discriminate whether the infant subjects were sensitive to the mere acoustics of the language that they heard or to the actual order of the words that they heard within the acoustic envelope (in chapter 7 we will develop this idea further). Word order has been a central focus of many studies in psycholinguistics because it serves as one of the basic grammatical cues to meaning in a number of the world's languages. In chapter 5 we present research that pushes the constituent structure finding one more step, focusing on infants' attention to word order: we examine the import of word order within current grammatical conceptualizations and explore whether infants do attend to this cue in the input stream.

Chapter 5

Single-Word Speakers' Comprehension of Word Order

... order is so essential to human language that an organism unequipped to notice and store sequential information could hardly acquire such systems.
Slobin, "Crosslinguistic Evidence for the Language-Making Capacity"

Thus far we have reviewed research in which young children have shown their capability to detect some of the basic units of language. For grammatical learning to proceed, however, the detection of units must be coupled with the ability to note relationships or patterns between the units. In this chapter we present two experiments (one main experiment and one control study) that investigate children's perception of relational information, specifically, word order relationships in sentences. If children can detect constituents in sentences before they can speak, then they might be able to attend to the order of elements in a string before they produce multiword utterances. As the epigraph indicates, any skeleton for language learning must contain a "bone" dedicated to order perception, lest the child be unprepared for detecting a key factor in the construction of all the world's languages.

The world's languages encode relations between objects and events by relying on two grammatical devices: word order and inflections (affixes on nouns and verbs) (Greenberg 1963; Comrie 1981). Although English may be unusual with respect to its almost exclusive reliance on word order, the great majority of languages can still be characterized as having preferential orderings for basic, active, declarative sentences containing a subject, a verb, and an object (Greenberg 1963; Comrie 1981). Thus, in a sentence like "Brutus killed Caesar," where the typical English subject-verb-object (SVO) order is preserved, the first noun signals the agent of the action whereas the second signals the patient of the action. In fact, reversing the order of the nouns results in a different historical picture.

The other end of the continuum from English is exemplified by languages like Turkish, which have much freer word order but a strong inflectional system. Children acquiring Turkish learn to rely heavily on the endings that are appended to nouns to figure out the "case roles" (or "who-did-what-to-whom"; Fillmore 1969) in the event being described. Interestingly, however, even Turkish-speaking children perform better in a sentence imitation task when the stimuli are in the order noun-noun-verb, which corresponds to the subject-object-verb order of adult Turkish (Slobin and Bever 1982).

Though languages vary in their reliance on word order and inflections, most children must learn how to order nouns with respect to verbs in order to convey the meaning relations they intend.[1] Not surprisingly given the properties of English, word order appears to be among the first formal grammatical devices that English-speaking children employ in their two- and three-word utterances (Bloom 1970; Schlesinger 1971; Brown 1973). (Even this finding is a matter of some dispute, however. See, for example, Howe 1976; Bloom, Capatides, and Tackeff 1981; Golinkoff 1981.)

The question posed here is whether single-word speakers recognize the significance of the word order in the sentences they hear. That is, do young children know that the sentence "Mommy's tickling Baby" describes a different event than the sentence "Baby's tickling Mommy"? The answer to this question has important implications for both families of theories of language acquisition. For example, for the Outside-in theories (Braine 1988; Schlesinger 1971, 1977, 1988; Bowerman 1973; Bloom 1978; Bates and MacWhinney 1987), learning language is a two-step process: (1) mapping case role relations (e.g., agent, location) into utterances, and (2) gradually reorganizing one's grammar on syntactic lines, by noting the diversity of roles that may occupy different positions in a sentence. Detecting order is thus important at both stages of the learning process.

Similarly, Inside-out theorists hypothesize that children attend to ordering relationships in the input to determine how to set their innate parameters. Atkinson (1987) and Berwick (1986), for example, both point out that early in the acquisition process, children must note whether they are learning a "head-initial" or a "head-final" language. That is, they must detect whether the lexical item that gives the phrase its name (its head; e.g., the verb in a verb phrase) occurs first or last in the phrase. Finding head direction in a language gives critical information about how that language works. From the Inside-out perspective, then, attention to word order is required either to determine the order of major constituents (e.g., is my language an SVO or an SOV language?) (Pinker 1984) or to trigger the setting of parameters like the head parameter (Hyams 1986; Lust and Mazuka 1989; Lust, Suñer, and Whitman 1994).

Although these two families of theories make some different assumptions about the importance of word order, both seem to presuppose a learner who is sensitive to word order and to particle order in the input language. Attention to word order appears to be critical for language learning. Nevertheless, there are very few studies in the literature that document early attention to word order cues in the input. Among these are studies by Golinkoff and Markessini (1980) and Roberts (1983). Golinkoff and Markessini investigated whether young children could detect word order in reversible (e.g., "mommy's baby") and nonreversible (e.g., "mommy's face") possessive phrases. These researchers used a picture book reading task in which children (mean length of utterance (MLU) from 1 to 4) pointed to one of two pictures that best represented the phrase they heard. Although it turned out that such phrases are *not* reversible from a child's point of view (i.e., "Mommy's baby" is apparently considered the canonical relation), even the youngest, least linguistically advanced children refused to respond when an anomalous relationship (e.g., "face's mommy") was created by reversing word order. The authors interpreted this response as an indication that children noticed that "the reversed word order created improbable possessive relationships" (p. 132).

Slightly more compelling evidence for attention to word order by young children comes from Roberts (1983). In the task that Roberts devised, children (23 to 31 months of age; MLU between 1 and 2) heard sentences with the reversible actions "hug," "kiss," and "tickle" in the presence of their mother and an older sibling. For example, one sentence was "Can *child's name* tickle *caretaker's name*?" The dependent variable was response latency: did children respond significantly more quickly for sentences where they were the designated agent than for sentences where they were the designated patient of the action? Results indicated that even the youngest, least linguistically advanced children demonstrated some sensitivity to word order in this task.

These two studies stand in contrast to a large literature that reveals little evidence for sensitivity to word order in single-word speakers. In a striking example, Wetstone and Friedlander (1973) found that children (mean MLU = 1.75) responded equally well to scrambled sentences (e.g., "Truck the where is?") and to normal sentences (e.g., "Where is the truck?") when asked to respond to implicit requests for action. They write:

Very young children utilize very little of the multilevel linguistic information available to the experienced listener; in fact, they are able to understand only the barest essentials of what they hear; their comprehension is confined to recognition of familiar words and concrete relationships between those words . . . (p. 739)

Many other researchers have concurred with Wetstone and Friedlander's conclusions. Indeed, some argue that even the consistent production of ordered speech in sentences is not evidence for the understanding of word order (Chapman and Kohn 1978; Chapman and Miller 1975). Children may *appear* to use word order in speech production because the linearity of language compels them to do so and not because they are sensitive to word order constraints. For example, de Villiers and de Villiers (1973) report that children with MLUs of 1 and 1.5 could produce two- and three-word sentences but could not use word order in any of their sentence comprehension tasks. In another demonstration, Chapman and Miller (1975) engaged children with MLUs of 1.8, 2.4, and 2.9 in object manipulation tasks. Though these children adhered to word order constraints in their production, they failed to respect word order in the comprehension tasks—exhibiting great difficulty in carrying out commands in which an inanimate subject was acting on an animate object (e.g., "The boat pushed the boy"):

The semantics of verbs determine the selectional restrictions on noun as subject and object, and the verbs that predominate in early language are those that allow reference to people doing things and inanimate objects being acted upon. (Chapman and Miller 1975, 296)

These authors, along with others (Strohner and Nelson 1974), conclude that when semantics or event probability and word order cues are placed in conflict, word order cues lose out in favor of semantically plausible interpretations. As long as these factors are not in conflict, young speakers appear to be more sophisticated than they really are—placing the noun for the probable agent in the first noun phrase position in the sentence and the noun for the object in the second noun phrase position. Thus, under this view, attention to word order develops relatively late—even after children are using word order in their productive speech.

There is some reason to doubt the pessimistic conclusions reached by most researchers who have addressed the word order question. First, as

Savage-Rumbaugh et al. (1993) note, some of the studies that report the production of word order prior to the comprehension of word order are flawed. In both Chapman and Miller's (1975) and de Villiers and de Villiers's (1973) studies, a different criterion was used for successful comprehension than for successful production. Children were given credit for correct use of word order if they produced a two-word utterance (e.g., SV or VO), but in comprehension they had to successfully interpret *three*-word SVO constructions. Thus, comprehension of word order may come sooner than is reported in these studies. Second, the tasks that were used to investigate word order were those reviewed in chapter 3 that rely on subject compliance as much as on subject knowledge of the construct being studied.

Nonetheless, using attention to word order as a litmus test for measuring syntactic prowess, these authors conclude, as do other investigators (e.g., Bloom 1973) that there is no evidence of any formal syntactic knowledge until children are at least able to use word order knowledge in production. This view is most clearly articulated in Atkinson's (1985) review, where he writes, "... it appears that there are good reasons for withholding formal syntactic notions from an analysis of two-word speech" (p. 300).

Not surprisingly, given his evaluation of two-word speech, Atkinson (1985) is similarly pessimistic about the capabilities of one-word speakers:

The conclusions to which I am drawn are largely negative.... For syntax, I believe that the arguments are convincing and that no case can be made for the one-word child having any access to a system of syntactic representation. (p. 294)

In sum, it has become the established wisdom (but for a few dissenters; e.g., see Pinker 1984; Ihns and Leonard 1988; Bowerman 1988; Bloom 1990) that there is little evidence for syntactic knowledge in one- and two-word speakers. In large part, this impoverished view of the syntactic ability of young children is due to the finding that children with limited production capabilities cannot even note the simplest of relationships between the units of language—namely, that they cannot even detect word order in the language addressed to them.

In this chapter we report on studies that challenged this view by testing for sensitivity to word order comprehension in the intermodal preferential looking paradigm. If the child is sensitive at all to word order relations, we reasoned that this sensitivity would be revealed in this paradigm. Two separate experiments (a main experiment and a control experiment) were conducted with children whose speaking vocabularies were small and who produced mostly single-word utterances. The results of these studies may reopen the debate on the linguistic status of the single-word speaker.

5.1   Experiment 3: Do Infants Comprehend Word Order?

Experiment 3 addressed this question: would children, between the ages of 16 and 18 months, producing mostly single words, comprehend word order in the intermodal preferential looking paradigm?[2] Using this paradigm, Golinkoff et al. (1987) had previously demonstrated word order comprehension with 28- to 30-month-old children already producing word combinations. In that study, Sesame Street characters performed reversible actions, with the agent and patient on one screen engaging in the opposite role relations on the other screen. Children were able to use the word order of the stimulus sentences (e.g., "Where's Big Bird tickling Cookie Monster?") to guide their looking as they watched the monitor that depicted the matching event significantly more than they watched the monitor that depicted the nonmatching event.

Experiment 3 replicates and extends that research, although it differs from it in four important ways: (1) the ages and linguistic competency of the subjects were much reduced; (2) four verbs (rather than two) were used to test for word order comprehension; (3) each subject was tested on all four verbs (each child in the prior study had been tested with only one verb); and (4) the experimental design was altered to reduce carryover from one stimulus to the next (the "win-stay/lose-shift" strategies found in Golinkoff et al.'s (1987) study were eliminated).

The main question addressed here is whether children who produce mostly one word at a time in their own speech can detect and use word order information present in five- or six-word sentences that they hear. There are two possible outcomes. First, children could fail to show evidence of word order sensitivity, perhaps because they do not comprehend the grammatical significance of word order until they themselves produce ordered combinations of words. Second, children could succeed in showing evidence of word order comprehension, suggesting that even before children produce their first two-word utterance, they are already tuning in to at least one important variable in their native language. This in turn would suggest that children may not have been credited with linguistic analyses that they *do* perform prior to language production.

Method

In chapter 3 we describe the intermodal preferential looking paradigm in detail. Here we will describe only those features specific to conducting this experiment.

Procedure   The child was first invited to play with the experimenter, who had a small set of toys. Big Bird and Cookie Monster hand puppets were used to introduce the characters and their names. During this familiarization period the experimenter attempted to gauge informally through little on-the-spot experiments whether the child knew the names of each character.

Subjects   Subjects were 48 infants, 16 to 19 months of age (mean age = 17.5 months). Half of the infants were from the Temple laboratory and half were from the Delaware laboratory. In each sample, half of the infants were boys and half were girls. The infants' mean productive vocabulary as reported by the parent was 67.6 words (range 2–255, figured over $N = 47$, since one subject's language data were lost). Twenty-five infants did not produce word combinations, 9 were just beginning to combine words, and 13 used combinations regularly. Approximately 100 children were tested to obtain the 48 whose data were analyzed. Children's data were eliminated from consideration for the following reasons: computer failure; fretfulness; side preferences to one of the two video screens, defined as 75% or greater visual fixation to one screen; failure to demonstrate knowledge of the characters' names; loss of more than two trials because of failure to return to the center light between trials; or parent's viewing of the tapes from under the visor.

Stimuli

Character Identification Phase   Word order testing was preceded by another set of tapes (see table 5.1 and figure 5.1) that first trained the infant subjects on the characters' names and then tested their comprehension of these names. First, Cookie Monster and Big Bird appeared, one on each monitor, in a set of sequential trials. The linguistic stimulus that accompanied each sequential trial told the infant the character's name—for example, "Oh, see Cookie Monster! There's Cookie Monster." Then both characters appeared, in a simultaneous trial accompanied by the sentence "Here they are!" Finally, both characters appeared in four test trials

Table 5.1
Experiments 3 and 4: Character identification videotapes

Tape 1	Linguistic stimuli	Tape 2
	Sequential trials	
Cookie Monster waving	"Oh, see Cookie Monster? See Cookie Monster?"	Blank screen
Blank screen	{Center light}	Blank screen
Blank screen	"See Big Bird? Where's Big Bird?"	Big Bird waving
	Simultaneous trial	
Blank screen	{Center light} "Here comes Big Bird and Cookie Monster!"	Blank screen
Cookie Monster waving	"Here they are!"	Big Bird waving
	Test trials	
Blank screen	{Center light} "Where's Cookie Monster?"	Blank screen
Cookie Monster waving	"Can you find Cookie Monster?"	Big Bird waving
Blank screen	{Center light} "See Big Bird?"	Blank screen
Cookie Monster waving	"Can you find Big Bird?"	Big Bird waving
Blank screen	{Center light} "Find Big Bird?"	Blank screen
Cookie Monster waving	"Where's Big Bird?"	Big Bird waving
Blank screen	{Center light} "Look, Cookie Monster!"	Blank screen
Cookie Monster waving	"Can you find Cookie Monster?"	Big Bird waving

during which the child was asked to "find" each of them by name. Each character was requested twice; the order of the matches was either right-left-left-right or its mirror image. Each trial on these tapes was 4 seconds long; intertrial intervals were 2 seconds long. In total, these tapes were 54 seconds long.

The criterion for including a child's data was a disjunctive one: either the child watched the match more than the nonmatch on three out of four character identification test trials or the child demonstrated knowledge of the characters' names during the playroom session. Word order compe-

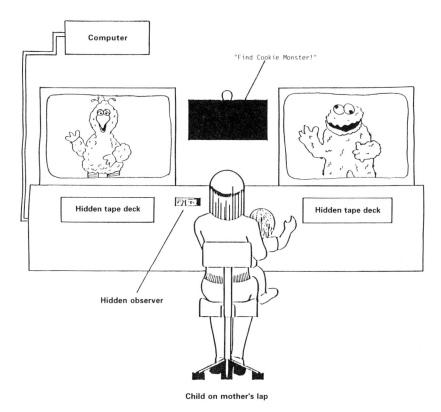

Figure 5.1
Cookie Monster and Big Bird as shown in the character identification tapes for
experiments 3 and 4. Each character appears on only one screen, waving to the
viewer.

tence would be logically impossible to demonstrate if children did not
know the names of the two characters.

Word Order Test   The word order tapes immediately followed the character identification tapes. Table 5.2 shows the sequence of events and accompanying audio for the verb "tickle." Table 5.3 describes the events and
linguistic stimuli for the other three verbs ("feed," "wash," and "hug"),
which were tested in the same format, except for counterbalancing the
side of the appearance of the first sequential trial, the side of the matching
screen, and the side of the screen on which Cookie Monster and Big Bird
appeared. Each trial on this tape was 6 seconds long; intertrial intervals
were 3 seconds long. In total, these tapes were 3 minutes long.

Table 5.2
Experiment 3: The structure of the stimulus videotapes for the verb "tickle"

Tape 1	Linguistic stimuli	Tape 2
	Sequential trials	
Cookie Monster (CM) tickles Big Bird (BB) while Big Bird holds a box full of toys.	"Who's tickling?"	Blank screen
Blank screen	{Center light} "Who's tickling?"	Blank screen
Blank screen	"Who's tickling?"	BB tickles CM while CM holds a box full of toys.
	Simultaneous trial	
Blank screen	{Center light} "They're tickling!"	Blank screen
CM tickles BB ...	"They're tickling!"	BB tickles CM ...
	Test trials	
Blank screen	{Center light} "Look! CM is tickling BB! Where is CM tickling BB?"	Blank screen
CM tickles BB ...	"Look! CM is tickling BB! Where is CM tickling BB?"	BB tickles CM ...
Blank screen	{Center light} "Hey, CM is tickling BB! Find CM tickling BB!"	Blank screen
CM tickles BB ...	"Hey, CM is tickling BB! Find CM tickling BB!"	BB tickles CM ...

Table 5.3
Experiment 3: The video events and linguistic stimuli for the verbs "hug," "wash," and "feed"

Tape 1	Linguistic stimuli	Tape 2
*2. Big Bird (BB) hugs Cookie Monster (CM) as CM wipes his face with a towel.	"See? BB's hugging CM!" or "See? CM's hugging BB!"	CM hugs BB as BB wipes his face with a towel.
3. CM washes BB's face as BB waves him away.	"Oh! BB's washing CM!" or "Oh! CM's washing BB!"	BB washes CM's face as CM waves him away.
4. BB pretends to feed CM from a large wooden spoon. CM motions continually as if to say, "Keep it coming!"	"Wow! BB's feeding CM!" or "Wow! CM's feeding BB!"	CM pretends to feed BB from a large wooden spoon. BB motions continually as if to say, "Keep it coming!"

*The first event, as seen in table 5.2, was tickling. That table also shows the actual structure of the videotapes for the verb "tickle," and by analogy, for each of the other verbs.

Each trial on the word order tapes showed an agent, an action, and a patient of the action; trials differed only in which character played which role. Thus, on each tape Cookie Monster was the agent for two of the verbs and Big Bird was the agent for the other two verbs. Further, both the agent and the patient were in continuous motion so that the child could not locate the agent by merely attending to which character moved or moved first. For example, in the trials that tested the verb "tickle," the character who did the tickling did so while facing the back of the other character. The "ticklee" did not just stand there and receive the tickling, but instead held a box of toys at chest level and moved vigorously in response to the tickling.

The test tapes were designed so that preceding each pair of test trials, there was an exploratory period containing sequential and simultaneous trials (see chapter 3), accompanied by a nondescript audio like "Who's tickling?" The audio for the two test trials that followed matched only one of the video scenes (e.g., "Look, Big Bird is tickling Cookie Monster!"). For each verb, the two test trials asked for the same matching screen.

Results

Calculation of Stimulus Salience from the Simultaneous Trials   The first analysis was done to ensure that the scenes depicted for a given verb pair were equally salient or attractive. Thus, for each verb, the mean visual fixation times during the simultaneous trials were assessed. Recall that a simultaneous trial immediately preceded each pair of test trials and included a linguistic stimulus that did not direct the child to either event (see table 5.2). An analysis of variance—sex (male vs. female) by stimulus (4 levels) by match level (match vs. nonmatch)—was conducted on the data from 46 of the children. (The data from 2 children tested at the Temple laboratory were lost.) There were no significant main effects or interactions, indicating that infants had no preference for one scene over the other for any of the stimulus pairs. Across the stimuli, the mean visual fixation time to the match was 2.11 seconds; to the nonmatch, it was 2.18 seconds.

Test Trials   To see whether infants preferred to watch the matching or nonmatching screen (or neither) during the test trials, the average of each child's total visual fixation time in seconds during the two test trials for each of the four stimulus pairs was entered into a mixed analysis of variance. The between-subjects factors were laboratory (Delaware vs. Temple) and sex (male vs. female); the within-subjects factors were stimulus (four verbs) and match level (match vs. nonmatch). In addition to representing the two different testing sites, the laboratory factor represented two other variables. First, the order in which the four blocks of test trials were presented in one laboratory was the reverse of the order in which they were presented in the other laboratory. That is, in the Delaware laboratory children saw the four verbs in the order shown in tables 5.2 and 5.3; in the Temple laboratory children saw these events in the reverse order, with feeding first. Second, the two laboratories presented counterbalanced linguistic stimuli. For example, whereas the Delaware laboratory used the audio as shown in tables 5.2 and 5.3, the Temple laboratory used the opposite audio, reversing who-did-what-to-whom. If, for some reason, one scene/linguistic stimulus combination of a pair was more salient for infants, this would show up in a stimulus by laboratory by match level interaction. This was not predicted to occur, since a concerted effort was made to balance the visual and linguistic salience of the test events. The key prediction was that infants would watch the screen that matched the linguistic stimulus significantly more than they watched

Table 5.4
Experiment 3: Boys' and girls' mean visual fixation times (in seconds) to the match versus the nonmatch for the four stimuli during the test trials

Sex	Stimuli				
	"Hug"	"Tickle"	"Feed"	"Wash"	Means
Girls					
Match	2.59	3.21	2.57	2.79	2.79
Nonmatch	1.91	1.99	2.15	2.15	2.05
Boys					
Match	2.09	3.23	3.88	2.19	2.85
Nonmatch	2.78	1.82	1.77	2.43	2.20

the screen that did not match that stimulus. No other effects were predicted to reach significance.

There were two main effects of the analysis of variance: (1) laboratory $(F(1, 355) = 5.20, p < .025)$; and (2) the key comparison for word order comprehension, match versus nonmatch $(F(1, 355) = 21.98, p < .001)$. Two interactions were also significant: (1) stimulus by match $(F(3, 355) = 5.69, p < .001)$, and (2) stimulus by match by sex $(F(3, 355) = 5.38, p < .025)$. Table 5.4 presents the mean visual fixation times to the match and nonmatch by stimulus and sex.

The main effect of laboratory was attributable to higher looking times across both the match and the nonmatch in the Temple laboratory (mean = 2.64 seconds) as compared to the Delaware laboratory (mean = 2.30 seconds). (Because the lights were dimmed to a lower level in the Temple laboratory, infants had little else than the screens to look at during the testing.) Note that there was still a significant preference for looking toward the match in both laboratories. Differences in the ambient light merely affect *overall* attention to the screens: less light equals more attention. The absence of a laboratory by match interaction ($p > .54$) indicates that regardless of greater overall looking in the Temple laboratory, children in *both* laboratories watched the match more than the nonmatch.

The significant stimulus by match interaction is superseded by the three-way stimulus by match by sex interaction. Inspection of the means in table 5.4, combined with the sex differences reported in chapter 4, suggested that separate analyses by sex might be of interest. Separate analyses of variance were therefore conducted on the boys' and on the girls' data, with each analysis containing the factors of laboratory, stimulus, and match.

The girls' analysis yielded only a significant effect of match ($F(1, 176) = 12.85, p < .001$), indicating that the girls watched the match more than the nonmatch for each of the four stimuli. Their mean visual fixation time to the match was 2.79 seconds; to the nonmatch, 2.05 seconds. On the other hand, the boys' analysis yielded two significant effects: match ($F(1, 176) = 9.47, p < .003$) and a stimulus by match interaction ($F(3, 176) = 10.42, p < .001$). Dunn's a priori one-tailed t tests indicated that the boys watched the match more than the nonmatch on only the middle two stimuli (t's = 2.41 and 3.60, p's < .05, respectively). As table 5.4 indicates, the boys' mean visual fixation times on both the first and the last stimuli go in the opposite direction, although not significantly so. Interestingly, in the separate analyses by sex, the significant laboratory factor is no longer significant in either analysis ($p > .17$ for boys and $p = .06$ for girls). Thus, the main effect for laboratory in the overall analysis appears to be mainly due to the fact that the *girls* in the Temple laboratory allocated more visual fixation to the task than the girls in the Delaware laboratory.

We next examined the number of children who watched the match more than the nonmatch overall, regardless of sex. The overall visual fixation mean of 36 out of 48 children (or 75%) was greater to the match than to the nonmatch, indicating that the effect was carried by a preponderance of the subjects.

These data confirm the hypothesis that young children can comprehend word order. On the whole, infants were guided by the linguistic stimulus to watch the match more than the nonmatch.

Is There a Relationship between Linguistic Level and Word Order Comprehension?   The above results could conceivably have emerged because the children with relatively greater productive language skills (the two- and three-word speakers) could have carried the data. To investigate this possibility, an analysis of variance was performed, dividing the children in the sample by whether or not they were producing multiword utterances. According to parental report and samples of speech recorded during their laboratory visit, 22 children (out of 48) were producing novel two-word combinations such as "Mommy sock" or "Big truck." If all of the child's two-word combinations were of the type "Bye-bye" or "What's that?", it was assumed that these were unanalyzed units. The analysis of variance contained three of the same factors that were used in the overall analysis above (laboratory, stimulus, and match); the sex factor was omitted. In addition, it included the word combinations factor (no combinations produced vs. combinations produced). If the children who were producing combinations were carrying the effect of the match variable, there would have been an interaction between language level and match. Neither this interaction nor any other interaction with the word combinations factor reached significance; nor was the main effect of word combinations significant. Thus, the more linguistically advanced children were not carrying the match effect. Children's comprehension of word order in this paradigm appears to be independent of their ability to produce word combinations.

Discussion

These results provide the clearest evidence to date that infants who produce limited or no two-word speech can comprehend word order in active reversible sentences. Since discrimination of word order can be considered evidence of early syntactic ability, it appears that 17-month-olds, some with only two words in their productive vocabularies, are sensitive to this piece of the syntactic input.

It is interesting that, as in experiment 1, the girls' performance is slightly ahead of the boys'. The girls watch the match more than the nonmatch for all the stimuli; the boys for only the middle two stimuli. The fact that the boys watch the match for two of the four stimuli, and that these stimuli fall in the middle of the testing sequence, suggests that boys may have required a bit more exposure to the stimuli to warm to the task and then may have disengaged sooner than the girls. Whatever the reason for their poor performance on the first and last stimuli, however, the fact that they were able to watch the match significantly more than the nonmatch for two of the events clearly indicates that they can use the order of mention of the two characters to find the match.

Why, in the face of so much previous research that reached the opposite conclusion, do one- and two-word speakers show word order comprehension in this experiment? Four factors seem to be responsible. First, the intermodal preferential looking paradigm makes minimal demands on subjects. No motor activity (other than ocular), or direction following, or inferring of action from two-dimensional pictures is required. Second, the intermodal preferential looking paradigm taps an ability that is probably prerequisite to language learning. That is, if infants were not compelled to search for the real-world scene that a speaker is describing, they could not begin to uncover the mapping between language and nonlinguistic events. In the realm of single words, infants as young as 13 months of age appear to be capable of mapping a particular word to its referent even in the presence of a foil (Woodward, Markman, and Fitzsimmons 1994).

Third, whereas prior research has tested for word order comprehension using a variety of linguistic stimuli, the vocabulary used in this experiment was very limited. Part of the experimental procedure ensured that subjects could comprehend the names of the two Sesame Street actors. Also, four common transitive verbs were used. If subjects were not previously familiar with these verbs, the sequential and simultaneous trials that preceded the test trials (see table 5.1) served the function of labeling the action without identifying the role relations. For example, the auditory stimulus asked, "Who's *tickling*?"

Fourth, many other procedures employed to test for word order comprehension put word order cues in conflict with semantic cues (e.g., Chapman and Miller 1975). In these procedures the ability to use word order is granted only when reliance on it surpasses reliance on other cues. Experiment 3 tested for word order comprehension while avoiding such conflict; semantic and syntactic cues were not put in competition. When semantic cues are neutralized—as in the present study—reliance on syntactic cues is required.

That young children appear to allocate more attention to events that match the word order they hear than to events that do not match the word order in the linguistic stimulus is an intriguing result that speaks to both families of language acquisition theories. Before we explore these consequences, however, we must eliminate two artifactual explanations for the data. The first concern, evaluated above, is whether the results were carried by the infants who already produced two- and three-word speech. No relationship was found between infants' productive language skills and their performance in the experiment.

The second concern is whether infants are giving the appearance of comprehending word order but in fact are using a simpler strategy to "solve" the task. Perhaps infants only need to attend to the first noun mentioned to guide their search for the match. This artifactual explanation presupposes that when, for example, Cookie Monster is the *agent* of "tickle" (and his name is the first noun mentioned), he is more active than when he is the *patient* of the action (and his name is the last noun mentioned). If this is true, then when infants hear "Where is Cookie

Monster tickling Big Bird?", they merely need to find the tape in which Cookie Monster—whose name is the first-mentioned noun—is the more active.

Experiment 4 tested this hypothesis by shortening the linguistic stimulus to the mention of the first noun only. If the children who participated in experiment 3 had solved the word order task by noting the first name mentioned and looking for the more active of the two actors, then in experiment 4 children should continue to watch the "matching" event. If, on the other hand, children's ability to use word order in experiment 3 requires attention to the order of *both* nouns around the verb, then their performance in experiment 4 should drop to chance. That is, they should watch the original "matching" event no more than they watch the original "nonmatching" event.

We predicted that children's performance would drop to chance in experiment 4 for one reason: experiment 3 had counterbalanced the linguistic stimulus. That is, half the subjects had heard sentences in which one character was named as the agent of the action (say, Cookie Monster), and half had heard sentences in which the other character was so named (Big Bird). Given that the result obtained over both halves of the design, it was unlikely that salience biases, interacting with a minimal linguistic strategy, could be responsible for the effects.

5.2   Experiment 4: Can Children Succeed by Merely Focusing on the First-Mentioned Actor? A Control Study

Method

Stimuli   The same videotapes were used in experiment 4 as in experiment 3 (see tables 5.2 and 5.3). However, the linguistic stimulus of experiment 3 was reduced. Instead of hearing a full agent-action-patient sentence as in experiment 3, children heard a sentence containing only the first noun of the original sentence. For example, they heard either "Where's Cookie Monster?" or "Find Big Bird!", depending on which character was the agent in the original sentences. Thus, for two of the blocks of events the linguistic stimulus requested Big Bird; for the other two blocks, Cookie Monster was requested.

Since there was no actual match or nonmatch for this experiment's control audio, the match and nonmatch were taken to be what would have been the match and the nonmatch had the test sentence continued. Thus, if the child heard "Find Big Bird!", the match was taken to be the side where Big Bird was doing something to Cookie Monster. Had the child been a subject in experiment 3, the sentence would have gone on to ask, "Find Big Bird tickling Cookie Monster!" and the match would have been to the same side—the side where Big Bird was the agent of the named action.

The design counterbalanced all relevant variables, however, as if there had been a true matching screen in each stimulus pair. Thus, half the subjects saw tape 1 in deck 1 and half saw it in deck 2. The linguistic stimulus was also counterbalanced: for any given pair of test trials, half the children heard the audio ask for one of the characters and half heard it ask for the other. Further, the number of "matches" was the same on both monitors (two on a side).

Subjects   Twenty-four children (half boys and half girls) were tested in the Delaware laboratory. Using the same criteria for subject inclusion as those mentioned for experiment 3, 74 potential subjects were tested to obtain 24. Data from potential subjects were discarded for the following reasons: fussiness (21); failing to return to the center light on three or more trials (9); showing no evidence of knowing the names of the characters (9); equipment or experimenter error (9); and side biases (2).

Procedure   The procedure was identical to that employed in experiment 3, including the casual training and assessment of children on the names of the characters during the familiarization period and the use of the character identification tapes.

Results

A three-way mixed analysis of variance was conducted with the between-subjects factor of sex and the within-subjects factors of stimulus (4 levels) and match level (match vs. nonmatch). No significant main effects or interactions emerged. In fact, all F values were less than 1. The mean visual fixation time to the match was 2.38 seconds and to the nonmatch, 2.59 seconds. Only one of the four stimuli had mean visual fixation scores greater to the match than to the nonmatch. Further evidence supporting the absence of an effect is the number of subjects whose overall means to the match were greater than their means to the nonmatch. Out of 24 subjects, 12 favored the match and 12 favored the nonmatch.

Discussion

The purpose of this control experiment was to see whether infants in experiment 3 could have solved the word order task by using a strategy that did not rely on word order comprehension. Perhaps the infants in the original study watched the "correct" screen (the match) by attending only to the first name they heard and finding the screen in which that actor was more salient. For example, upon hearing "Cookie Monster's tickling Big Bird," the child might look for a screen where Cookie Monster is somehow more salient than when he is the object of "tickling." We considered this unlikely for two reasons. First, we attempted to balance the frequency and quality of the movement of the actors on each screen. Both characters were in constant motion from the second the videotapes began. Second, *both* characters acted as agents, albeit one of a transitive action and one of an intransitive action. When Cookie Monster was the agent of the action of tickling and tickled Big Bird from behind, Big Bird was the agent of the action of "carry" or "hold" (holding a box of toys) and "bounce" (in response to the tickling). Nevertheless, although this possibility seemed unlikely to us as adults, we could not view the videotapes through the infants' eyes. Thus, it was important to rule out this alternative explanation.

The results of this experiment, using the same videotapes and reduced linguistic stimuli, were negative. When infants heard a sentence mentioning only one of the characters, they could no longer find the screen that was the match in the original experiment. This inability to find the match is depicted in figure 5.2, which shows the mean visual fixation times of children in the main experiment and in the control experiment. Thus, it is highly unlikely that infants solved the word order task in experiment 3 by resorting to a simpler strategy that did not rely on word order. Further, the negative finding from experiment 4, combined with the positive finding from experiment 3, suggests that in the original study infants were using at least the order of the two nouns, and possibly the verb, to find the match. This would not be surprising given that the videotapes contained high-frequency verbs (e.g., "tickle," "hug") and that experiments 1 and 2 indicate that even younger children are capable of attending to the verb phrase as a whole. Of course, to see whether children were using the verb in addition to the two nouns, the experiment should be carried out again, substituting nonsense verbs (e.g., "gorping") for the real verbs.

The results of this control study, then, suggest that children attend to word order at least in utterances that (1) describe two-character relations in transitive sentence frames and (2) do not contain difficult vocabulary

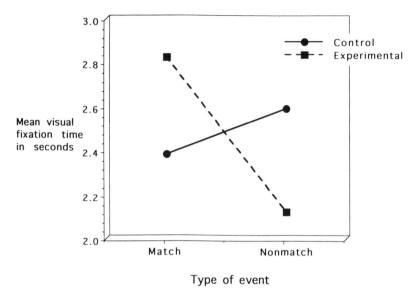

Figure 5.2
Mean visual fixation time to the match and the nonmatch by the children in experiment 3 (the main experiment) and experiment 4 (the control experiment)

items. Whether young children can use word order in other situations is of course an empirical question. That they can use it *at all*, however, adds an important fact to researchers' understanding of the course of language acquisition.

5.3 General Discussion

Two experiments were conducted to assess whether one-word speakers are sensitive to a key feature of language structure, namely, word order. The first experiment showed comprehension of word order by children not yet producing multiword speech. To secure this result, a second, control experiment was conducted, using a shortened linguistic stimulus, to see whether children could have solved the task in the original experiment without using word order. Children could not find the "match" with the shortened linguistic stimulus, indicating that the original result must be attributed to children paying attention to the order of both nouns around the verb.

The finding that word order is comprehended early is interesting from the perspective of both Outside-in and Inside-out theories. Both families of theories require word order analyses (or attention to particle order in agglutinative languages), either for attention to distributional properties of the input or for the setting of internal language parameters. The two families start with different premises, however. The Outside-in theories start with the premise that distributional analyses are carried out over semantic categories like agents and actions; the Inside-out theories with the assumption that children begin to set parameters by noting the order of grammatical categories like nouns and verbs. The findings presented in this chapter cannot address the question of whether children are solving word order problems by accessing syntactic grammatical systems or semantic ones. That is, they do not permit us to determine whether children are carrying out "subject-verb-object" or "agent-action-patient" analyses. Indeed, distinguishing between these explanations of early child grammar has been a major occupation of acquisition theorists (e.g., Pinker 1984; Bowerman 1973).

Though the exact nature of children's grammatical analyses is unclear, the current findings have three important implications. First, the fact that children can show *comprehension* of ordered speech suggests that they may well have the ability to use ordered speech in their *production*. Second, even one-word speakers are capable of performing distributional analyses and of attending to order in the input. Third, if children can attend to the order of the units within an utterance, then arguments for "syntactic bootstrapping" become more plausible. We treat each of these implications below.

The first implication of these data is that English-speaking children's early productions may well, in fact, observe word order (Brown 1973). One opponent of this view (Howe 1976) has argued that in order to assign reliable word order, researchers filter the child's incomplete utterances through their own adult grammatical systems and engage in unlicensed semantic interpretation. In other words, the practice of "rich interpretation" (Bloom 1970) is really overinterpretation. However, when children are shown to discriminate the order of noun arguments around reversible verbs (actions) in comprehension, the claim that children observe word order in their own speech receives support. The word order witnessed in children's productions is apparently not due solely to adult interpretation, but rather is due to the children's own sensitivity to word order relationships.

The second theoretical implication is that if children are attuned to features like word order that are crucial for later grammatical learning, as the present data suggest, they may also be equipped to perform the distributional analyses that are a central ingredient of many language acquisition theories; in other words, they are able to form linguistic generalizations and classes by observing the way words or inflections are used in the input. Two language acquisition theories have distributional analyses at their core.

In the first theory, Maratsos and Chalkley (1980) attempt to account for the acquisition of form classes such as "noun" and "verb." They reject two popular hypotheses: that these classes are given innately (e.g., Chomsky 1965) and that these classes arise from the semantic similarities of their members (Slobin 1966). Instead, they support an account that falls between these semantically and syntactically based theories, positing that children construct form classes by a combination of semantic and distributional analyses. To construct the category "verb," for example, the child conducts both a distributional analysis, noting the sequential arrangement of linguistic elements (e.g., verbs appear before inflections such as "ed" and after "do"-forms), and a semantic analysis, noting that verbs enter into certain types of meaning-based relations such as "past occurrence of event." The data generated in this study suggest that children are capable of conducting sequential analyses of some types of sentences. Whether or not Maratsos and Chalkley's account is correct (see Gleitman and Wanner 1988; Pinker 1984 for critiques), at least infants appear to use precedence relations in their analysis of input.

A second Outside-in language acquisition theory that relies on the use of order information is the Competition Model of Bates and MacWhinney (1987). These theorists also accept the view that the child must detect correlations across linguistic usages. They claim that in deciding what to correlate with what, the child is guided by two principles: "semantic connectedness" and "positional patterning." Their theory presupposes that the child is constrained to notice order over the infinite number of other features that could be noticed in the input. Some argue, however, that even this theory is not specific enough, failing to indicate which of the many potential orderings are important (Gibson 1992 offers a critique of this view).

In both of these Outside-in theories, attention to word or particle order is presumed to be a function of the child's general cognitive processing capabilities. The research presented here indicates that infants may indeed be conducting semantic-distributional analyses very early in language acquisition and that they may be using word order cues to construct their grammar in comprehension before the appearance of ordered speech in production (see also Savage-Rumbaugh et al. 1993 for a relevant discussion of this point).

It is important to realize that a form of distributional, word order analysis is equally important for the Inside-out, syntactically based theories that grant the child considerably more innate linguistic knowledge. A key claim of this family of theories is that all languages can be described by a finite set of universal parameters. Whether the parameter choices are fixed word order versus free word order, head-initial versus head-final (Atkinson 1987; Mazuka 1995), or pro-drop versus non-pro-drop (Hyams 1986), these parameters require the analysis of positional information— information that infants appear to be sensitive to well before they themselves begin to speak.

In sum, then, whether one endorses the Outside-in or the Inside-out theory, attention to word or particle order in the input is central for the acquisition of grammar. The research reported here suggests that sensitivity to word order is in place to assist language learning as early as the one-word stage of language production. The developmental course of language learning is thus not as concentrated as had previously been believed. Some of the sensitivities that emerge in production appear much earlier in the course of language comprehension.

The third theoretical consequence is that to the extent that infants are using some grammatical devices in the one-word stage, our findings also have bearing on the viability of the "syntactic bootstrapping hypothesis" proposed by Landau and Gleitman (1985; see also Naigles, Gleitman, and Gleitman 1993; Gleitman 1990). Syntactic bootstrapping occurs when syntactic patterns in the input are used by the learner to make inferences about the meaning of linguistic items. For example, English-speaking children may learn that a verb is likely to be a causative when it appears in a transitive sentence structure, with a noun on either side; a verb that has only one noun argument, which moreover precedes it, is likely to be noncausative or intransitive. Children acquire this correspondence between syntax and semantics by noting the mapping between language and events, as both Bloom (1970) and Jackendoff (1983) suggest. Under the syntactic bootstrapping account, on the presumption that the learner can identify which item is the verb in a string, the learner uses these cor-relations between syntax and semantics to deduce aspects of a new verb's meaning.

The research presented here provides a kind of baseline for the syntactic bootstrapping process. It demonstrates clearly that infants in the begin-ning stages of language learning can attend to syntactic cues and that they can use these cues to distinguish between two relatively similar scenes in their environment.

In sum, then, as focus shifts from language production to language comprehension, a new picture of language development begins to emerge. The study reported here demands a new look at the linguistic capabilities of children who are not yet combining words in their own speech. These one-word speakers appear to be five- or six-word listeners. Further, they are capable of imposing organization on what they hear through the use of word order information. The use of word order cues (and other posi-tional information) can take learners a long way toward the acquisition of grammar. To date, it is not clear whether children are born with a predis-position to note order in linguistic strings or whether attention to order develops as a more general tendency to process sequential information. Whatever the case, it is clear that by 17 months of age, in the one-word stage, language learners attend to one kind of cue, word order, that will significantly help them in learning the grammar of their language.

Chapter 6

Young Children's Use of Syntactic Frames to Derive Meaning

With Letitia Naigles

In prior chapters we have reported on research that investigated whether infants can detect sentence units (chapter 4) and whether they use the order of these units to derive meaning (chapter 5). In this chapter we focus on both units and relations: on units, because the general question posed is how children learn about verbs; and on relations, because we are concerned with whether children can use a verb's argument structure to derive information about the meaning of that verb.[1] Specifically, then, we discuss how children learn a type of language unit—verbs—that many have considered the cornerstone of the sentence (e.g., see Bloom 1978; Chafe 1971; Chomsky 1981; Bresnan 1978). The larger issue that we address is whether children *can* use syntactic information, combined with observation of the world, to make conjectures about meaning.

Consider the distinction between transitive and intransitive verbs as one example of how grammatical information can be used to predict semantic information. In English a *transitive* verb must be associated with two noun phrases (arguments), one describing the agent of the action and the other describing the patient of the action, as in "Jordan gorps Benjamin." An *intransitive* verb requires no patient: "Allison and Michael blick" is perfectly acceptable. The very fact that there are two arguments in the transitive sentence leads the reader to assume that the first actor must be affecting the second actor. That is, Jordan is either *making* Benjamin do something or *contacting* Benjamin in some way. The reader does not assume such a relation with the intransitive sentence, "Allison and Michael blick," because Allison and Michael make up a conjoined, single argument for the verb "blick." Here, Allison and Michael are presumed to be doing something *together*. No contact or causation is implied. The question that we will address in this chapter is whether learners can capitalize on this relationship between form and meaning to assist them in the learning of verbs, that is, whether they can capitalize on the subcategorization frames that surround a verb to derive some of the verb's meaning.

How *do* children learn verbs? As Quine (1960) points out, logically a given word might have any of an infinite number of possible meanings. For example, consider a child who hears "Daddy's dancing." She sees her father raising his legs repetitively, smiling, flapping his arms, and moving in a circle. To which aspect of the event—including possibly the event as a whole—does the verb refer? Although the indeterminacy of reference is a general problem for all word learning, many argue that verbs pose a special problem for the learner (Golinkoff et al. 1995; Golinkoff, Jacquet, and Hirsh-Pasek 1994; Tomasello and Merriman 1995). Gentner (1983) entertains a number of hypotheses about why verbs appear to be more difficult to acquire than nouns (but see Bloom, Tinker, and Margulis, in press; Tardif 1994). Although most nouns that appear in early vocabularies label concrete objects that are relatively permanent and tangible, verbs label actions that are often relational by definition, ephemeral in nature, and performed by different actors. Furthermore, languages conflate different aspects of meaning into their verbs. For example, manner is part of the verb in English (as in "hammered on the door" versus "knocked on the door"), whereas in Spanish the manner in which the action is performed is not part of the verb but requires a separate adverb.

One way in which the child might "break into" the verb system is through observation. For example, upon hearing the verb "wash," the child sees a "washer" and a "washee" (perhaps a body part or an inanimate object), but upon hearing the verb "run," the child sees a single individual performing an action. That the first verbs are learned from pairing words with actions is embedded in a position known as the "semantic bootstrapping hypothesis" (Grimshaw 1981; Pinker 1984, 1987). The problem is that children need to learn how the language that they hear maps onto their internal grammar. Under the bootstrapping view, the first basic discoveries about their grammar come when children pair concrete objects with the grammatical category of nouns and actions with the category of verbs. Thus, although semantic bootstrapping is not formally a theory of how children learn verb meanings, the theory posits that they will learn their first verbs by "lifting themselves up by their bootstraps," by pairing actions that they see in situational contexts (meanings) with syntax (forms). It is only after this initial insight that young children come to use the syntactic frame in concert with observation to inform noun or verb meaning.

An alternative view of initial verb learning posits that even at the outset, observation taken alone offers inconclusive cues to verb identification. Children need to attend to a verb's arguments to deduce its meaning. Gleitman and Gillette (1995) have made the strongest case for this position. They showed adults videotapes of mothers and young children interacting. Every time the mother said the target verb, a beep was substituted for the word. The adults' task was to guess what verb the mother was saying at that moment. Even though adults apparently limited their choice of verbs given the age of the addressee (e.g., they offered "think" rather than "ponder"), they failed dismally in being able to predict the correct verb. In short, although situational context can perhaps reduce the range of what a verb might refer to, observation of the situational context is clearly not sufficient for verb learning. Thus, with only situational observation available, verb learning might be impossible.

Situational observation is surely an important component of verb learning. For example, seeing two individuals involved in a physical altercation can rule out a vast number of candidate meanings for the verbs "fight." Yet Gleitman and Gillette's study indicates that the number of candidate meanings for a potential verb is still too large to be of much use to the child. As Gleitman (1990) writes:

I think the problem is that words don't describe events *simpliciter*. If that's all words did, we wouldn't have to talk. We could just point to what's happening, grunting all the while. But instead, or in addition, the verbs seem to describe specific perspectives taken on those events by the speaker, perspectives that are not "in the events" in any direct way.... Since verbs represent not only events but the intents, beliefs, and perspective of the speakers on those events, the meanings of the verbs can't be extracted solely by observing the events. (p. 17)

As an example of how the same event can be accurately described using different verbs, consider an event in which a dog is chasing a fox. The fox is *running*, but it is also being *chased*. Though "is running" and "is being chased" are equally plausible descriptors of the event, the sentence "The fox is running from the dog" focuses attention on the fox, whereas the sentence "The dog is chasing the fox" highlights the dog's role in the event. Note that the two verbs participate in distinct syntactic environments. "Run" can take the preposition "from"; "chase" cannot.

The difficulty of learning verbs through observation alone gave rise to a view of verb learning first suggested by Landau and Gleitman (1985) as the syntactic bootstrapping hypothesis. Under this hypothesis, the child inspects not only the world, but also the syntactic contexts in which a verb is used, to make predictions about its meaning. The syntactic context in which a verb participates acts like a "zoom lens" (Gleitman 1990) that focuses the listener on one aspect or another of the action that is witnessed (in the present case, the chasing or the running).

In contrast to the semantic bootstrapping hypothesis, the syntactic bootstrapping hypothesis *is* a theory of verb learning. It presupposes that children analyze events into predicate-argument structures, and that they link sentences to the event structure that they parse. Children hearing a sentence can map the nouns onto the arguments that they observe. Given this sensitivity to noun-argument linkages, children find the verb (the predicate) through the process of elimination. They then deduce the verb's meaning through the joint contribution of the syntactic context in which the verb is embedded and observation of the extralinguistic scene (Gleitman and Gillette 1995). For example, the child could know that the action of *giving* is being described if she observes an object being transferred and hears the sentence "John is giving a present to Mary." Under this view, the child knows (1) that "John," "present," and "Mary" are nouns in her lexicon and elements in the scene; (2) that John is the agent of the observed action (see Mandler 1992) and that agents typically become sentence subjects (these are "linking rules"; see Pinker 1989; Jackendoff 1972); (3) that the preposition "to" implies directionality. Through the process of elimination the child deduces that the word "giving," the only unspecified part of the sentence, must represent the predicate and hence the verb. Thus, the first part of the syntactic bootstrapping hypothesis allows the child to find the verb. The second part allows the child to deduce the meaning of the verb by noting the arrangement and number of the verb arguments. Upon hearing the verb "give" with its three arguments ("X is giving a Y to Z"), a "to" phrase, and an agent "John" as subject, the child can deduce that the action of transfer is being described from the perspective of the agent. This makes the child likely to interpret the verb as having the meaning associated with "give" rather than the meaning associated with "receive."

The syntactic bootstrapping hypothesis rests on the assumption that the presence of certain syntactic frames roughly correlates with meanings. In a series of experiments in English and Italian, Fisher, Gleitman, and Gleitman (1991) showed that there are strong and reliable parallels between the structural and semantic properties of verbs. That is, verbs that were judged to share certain syntactic properties were also judged to be similar in meaning. For example, verbs that take three arguments, like "give" and "receive," were rated as more similar to each other in meaning (both have to do with transfer of an object) than verbs that do not share this structural property. These results have been replicated in Hebrew (Geyer, Gleitman, and Gleitman 1995) and Mandarin (Li, Gleitman, and Gleitman 1994). With this as evidence, the syntactic bootstrapping hypothesis holds that young children could potentially deduce part of the meaning of the verb by noting the sentence structure—particularly, the number and arrangement of the verb arguments in the sentence.

In sum, different theories have been advanced about how children might come to learn the meaning of verbs. Among these theories, semantic bootstrapping and syntactic bootstrapping are often seen as rival hypotheses. For the semantic bootstrapper, observation of the situational context is the key to entering the grammatical system. The same action observed in multiple contexts provides the basis for the mapping between a verb and its meaning. For the syntactic bootstrapper, although observation is important, verb meaning is not *learned* through observation. Rather, verb meaning is *informed* by observation in conjunction with knowledge of the noun arguments in the sentence frame. The child who can decipher the configuration of noun arguments in the sentence can then figure out not only where the verb must be, but also what the verb is likely to mean. As the child hears a verb used in multiple language frames, the meaning of the verb becomes even more refined.

Although semantic bootstrapping and syntactic bootstrapping have their differences, they also share many similarities. First and foremost, both credit the language learner with a rich, innate linguistic base that must be "linked" to a given language as the learner hears language used in context. Second, both assume that after the initial breakthrough— whether it be through observation as in semantic bootstrapping or syntax as in syntactic bootstrapping—syntax and semantics create a dialectic that allows the child to pair form with meaning and meaning with form. That is, although they have different starting points, both theories hypothesize a learner who is sensitive not only to observational and contextual cues, but also to syntactic information in the input. The question that must be addressed—and the focus of this chapter—is whether young children who have just begun to produce two-word utterances themselves are even capable of attending to argument structure configurations in the speech that they hear.

To explore whether children can exploit the syntactic frames in which verbs are embedded to make inductions about verb meanings, children were presented with contrasting sentences that used either transitive or intransitive sentence frames. Research suggests that there exists a strong, though not perfect, correlation between transitive frames and causal action and between nontransitive frames and noncausal action (at least within the class of motion verbs). If children capitalize on this correlation, then they should, upon hearing a transitive sentence like "Where's Big Bird bending Cookie Monster?", look significantly more at a scene in which Big Bird is causing Cookie Monster to bend than at a scene in which Big Bird and Cookie Monster are both bending. Similarly, children hearing the intransitive sentence "Find Cookie Monster and Big Bird bending" should choose to watch the noncausal alternative in which the two characters are bending together. If children are sensitive to verb subcategorization frames, then they should attribute different meanings to the same verb (here, "bend") when it is used in one sentence frame as opposed to another.

Prior research indicates that young children can attend to verb syntax. For example, children presented with an enactment task were willing to alter the meaning of a familiar verb to conform to the frame in which it was encountered—a "frame-compliant" response. The younger the children, the more frame-compliant (as opposed to "verb-compliant") responses they gave. Using a Noah's ark model and toy wooden animals, Naigles, Gleitman, and Gleitman (1992) presented 2-, 3-, and 4-year-old children with transitive verbs used intransitively (e.g., *"The zebra brings") and intransitive verbs used transitively (e.g., *"The elephant comes the giraffe"). The younger subjects acted out these novel sentences—sentences that really have no right or wrong interpretation—in accord with the demands of the frame, changing the meaning of the verb. So, for example, for the sentence *"The elephant comes the giraffe," a frame-compliant response was scored if the child acted the sentence out by having the elephant make the giraffe move somewhere, as if the verb "come" had become causal. What Naigles, Gleitman, and Gleitman's results show, therefore, is that young children are capable of using verb syntax or, in other words, using the forms in which verbs occur to predict something of their meaning.

In their study Naigles, Gleitman, and Gleitman used children no younger than 30 months because of the demands of enactment tasks. They also used only familiar verbs. The intermodal preferential looking paradigm enabled us to follow up on their results with even younger children and with both familiar and unfamiliar verbs. Would younger children, who are in the throes of verb learning, give frame-compliant responses with both familiar and unfamiliar verbs? Would even younger children show causal interpretations of verbs that appeared in transitive frames and noncausal interpretations of verbs that appeared in intransitive frames?

In part, then, the studies to be reported in this chapter were undertaken to test the assumption that children are sensitive to verb syntax as would be required by both the semantic (Grimshaw 1981; Pinker 1984, 1994) and syntactic bootstrapping hypotheses (Landau and Gleitman 1985; Gleitman 1990). More specifically, these experiments focus on the role that attention to syntactic frames might play in verb interpretation. To investigate this question in the intermodal preferential looking paradigm, children were shown a causal and a noncausal version of the same action. For example, either Big Bird was seen causing Cookie Monster to bend or Big Bird and Cookie Monster were seen bending together in synchrony. Without accompanying language stimuli, there should be no inherent preference for either of these scenes. Both events have the same characters and both show variants of the same action. If children recognize the link between syntactic forms and meaning, however, the introduction of language stimuli should drive a looking preference for one of these scenes over the other.

To test this hypothesis, four experiments were conducted with children in three different age groups, using known and unknown verbs and several different transitive and intransitive sentence frames. The first (and main) experiment, here called experiment 5, employed a cross-sectional design in which children from 18 to 30 months heard either transitive or intransitive stimulus sentences with known and unknown verbs. Positive results were obtained, but mostly with the older children and only with the transitive sentence frames. Experiment 6 presented four nonsense verbs in transitive sentences to replicate and secure the findings of experiment 5. Finally, by using intransitive frames that gave subjects additional linguistic cues to an intransitive sentence interpretation, experiments 7 and 8 attempted to determine why only the transitive sentences supported the hypothesis in experiment 5. Experiment 7 used intransitive sentence frames in which the oblique marker "with" signaled the intransitive interpretation (e.g., "Big Bird is squatting *with* Cookie Monster!"). Experiment 8 used the auxiliary "are" to buttress the intransitive interpretation of joint, though not causal, action (e.g., "Big Bird and Cookie Monster *are* squatting!").

6.1   Experiment 5: Do Young Children Interpret Verb Meanings According to Their Syntactic Frames? A Cross-Sectional Study of Frame Compliance

Experiment 5 was designed to investigate when children at different ages attend to and use a verb's subcategorization frames to predict meaning. For example, if children are given a transitive sentence frame with an argument on either side of the verb, are they likely to think that the sentence implies a causal relation between the entities referred to by the arguments of the verb? On the other hand, if children hear only a single argument preceding the verb, will they give the verb an intransitive or noncausal interpretation? Children who are aware of the link between syntactic frame structure and meaning should watch a causal scene when they hear a transitive motion verb and a noncausal scene when they hear an intransitive verb.

Another goal of this study was to explore whether children were equally capable of using syntactic frames to guide their semantic interpretations for known ("bend" and "turn") versus unknown verbs ("squat" and "flex"). Both "turn" and "bend" can be used in both transitive and intransitive frames, for example, "She's bending the pipe" and "She's bending (herself)." If children assign different meanings to a known verb (such as "bend") when it appears in a transitive versus an intransitive sentence frame, they may be sensitive to these subcategorization frames and to the meanings with which they correlate. Alternatively, children could have memorized the relation between the frames and the meanings for known verbs. Thus, even if children can look to the correct screen for known verbs, this still leaves open the question of whether they can use sentence frames to predict something of the meaning of what are, for them, novel verbs. If children use syntactic frames to assign different meanings to unknown verbs (such as "squat"), they must be doing so by a general rule that unites syntactic form and meaning. Therefore, a result indicating frame-compliant interpretations with unknown verbs would provide stronger evidence that toddlers can use syntax to predict verb meaning. In addition, the two unknown verbs selected ("flex" and "squat") can actually only be used intransitively. The ability to predict the meaning of these verbs from transitive sentence frames would support the argument that children do not know these verbs and that they are using the subcategorization frames to infer their meaning.

Another possibility, however, and a persistent problem for language studies, is that the meaning of unknown verbs could be assigned by analogy to the meaning of known verbs. That is, children may hear a novel verb (say, "squat") with two arguments and assume, by analogy with the known verb "bend," that it must refer to the event in which one character is making the other character act. This possibility cannot be eliminated, since analogy is one of the mechanisms children use to learn language (MacWhinney 1978). Nonetheless, even if children are using analogy, it could be argued that if they are capable of responding correctly to unknown verbs, they must have made some broader generalizations based on the relations between syntactic surface form and semantic information.

Method
The paradigm used in all experiments was the intermodal preferential looking paradigm as described in chapter 3.

Design of the Video Events   The same video events were used in all four experiments; only the linguistic stimuli paired with the events differed. For this reason, the video events are described only for experiment 5; the description is not repeated for experiments 6–8.

Table 6.1 shows the layout of the tapes for the verb "squat" and the linguistic stimuli for experiment 5. Figure 6.1 shows the visual events for the verb "squat," with the causal event on the left. As table 6.2 indicates, the other three verbs used in experiments 5, 7, and 8 were "turn," "bend," and "flex." These were presented in exactly the same format as displayed in table 6.1. The stimuli were chosen as examples of known ("turn," "bend") and unknown verbs ("flex," "squat")—a categorization reaffirmed by all parents when they were questioned about their child's comprehension vocabulary in the laboratory. The verbs were also chosen so that they could be equally well portrayed as transitive or intransitive events. For example, in the transitive version of "squats," Big Bird caused Cookie Monster to squat by pushing him down. In the intransitive version, Cookie Monster and Big Bird each squatted independently in synchrony.

The transitive and intransitive stimulus tapes were identical in structure down to the number of frames per episode and the 3-second intertrial intervals. Further, the two tapes portrayed an equal number of "squat" actions. Because of this level of precision, the two tapes could begin

Table 6.1
Experiment 5: Video events and accompanying transitive linguistic stimuli for the verb "squat"

Tape 1	Linguistic stimuli	Tape 2
	Sequential trials	
Big Bird (BB) pushes Cookie Monster (CM) into a squatting position.	"See, squatting!"	Blank screen
Blank screen	{Center light} "See, squatting!"	Blank screen
Blank screen	"Look, squatting!"	BB and CM squat side by side.
	Simultaneous trial	
Blank screen	{Center light} "See, squatting!"	Blank screen
BB pushes CM into a squatting position.	"See, squatting!"	BB and CM squat side by side.
	Test trials	
Blank screen	{Center light} "Find BB squatting CM!"	Blank screen
BB pushes CM into a squatting position.	"Find BB squatting CM!"	BB and CM squat side by side.
Blank screen	{Center light} "Look at BB squatting CM!"	Blank screen
BB pushes CM into a squatting position.	"Look at BB squatting CM!"	BB and CM squat side by side.

at exactly the same frame and could remain in synchrony trial for trial; moreover, at any given time the same amount of action appeared on both screens.

As is evident in table 6.1, and as was the case in the other studies reported here, children were given an opportunity to visually examine the events on the tapes before the test trials began. The first sequential trial, for example, allowed children 6 seconds to look at the causal event that would later be accompanied by the transitive audio. This exploration trial was accompanied by a nondescript audio that was neither transitive nor intransitive: "Squatting! See, squatting!" The second sequential trial, accompanied by the same nondescript audio, showed the intransitive or

Figure 6.1
A sample stimulus set showing Cookie Monster causing Big Bird to squat on the
left panel and Cookie Monster and Big Bird squatting together on the right panel

Table 6.2
Experiment 5: The video events and linguistic stimuli for the verbs "turn,"
"bend," and "flex"

Causal events	Linguistic stimuli*	Noncausal events
1. Cookie Monster (CM) stands still and turns Big Bird (BB) around in tight circles.	TR: "Look at CM turning BB!" IN: "Look at CM and BB turning!"	CM and BB turn side by side in tight circles.
*3. BB holds CM's shoulders and makes CM bend at the waist.	TR: "See BB bending CM?" IN: "See BB and CM bending?"	BB and CM bend side by side from the waist.
4. CM makes BB do a deep knee-bend as BB's arms come forward.	TR: "Watch CM flexing BB!" IN: "Watch CM and BB flex!"	CM and BB do deep knee-bends side by side.

*TR = transitive; IN = intransitive
**The second event, as seen in table 6.1, was squatting. That table also shows the
actual structure of the videotapes for the verb "squat," and by analogy, for each
of the other verbs.

noncausal event on the opposite screen. During the simultaneous trial, children saw both the causal and the noncausal scenes again, this time side by side and with the neutral audio. Finally, children saw the two test trials. Here, the video scenes were displayed simultaneously and the accompanying linguistic stimulus was either transitive (for half of the children) or intransitive (for the other half). The transitive audio was "See Big Bird bending Cookie Monster!"; the parallel intransitive audio was "See Big Bird and Cookie Monster bending!" Thus, this experiment had a between-subjects design.

The independent variables were (1) the form of the linguistic stimuli (transitive vs. intransitive), (2) verb type (known vs. unknown), (3) age (18–22 months, 23–25 months, and 27–30 months), and (4) sex (male vs. female). The dependent variable was the total amount of visual fixation time allocated to the matching and nonmatching screens across each pair of test trials. Four variables were counterbalanced. First, the order of mention of the two characters on the sequential trials was counterbalanced. On half of the trials, Cookie Monster was mentioned first; on the other half, Big Bird was mentioned first. Second, the screen side of the match was counterbalanced by showing half of the children tape 1 in deck 1 and half of the children tape 1 in deck 2. Third, the match occurred an equal number of times on the left and right screens. Fourth, the side of the appearance of the first sequential trial was counterbalanced.

Subjects   Ninety-six toddlers, half boys and half girls, participated in experiment 5, which was conducted exclusively in the Temple laboratory. The children were equally distributed among three age groups: 18–22 months (mean age = 19.28 months), 23–25 months (mean age = 24.15 months), and 27–30 months (mean age = 28.3 months). Their average productive vocabularies were 102 words, 230 words, and 315 words, respectively, as assessed on the Rescorla Language Inventory (1991). According to parental report, the average number of words per sentence was 1.6 for the youngest group, 3.0 for the middle group, and 3.8 for the oldest group.

Subjects were contacted as described in chapter 3. To obtain the final sample of 96 subjects ($n = 32$ at each of 3 ages), 90 additional children were tested. Subject loss distributed itself approximately equally in each age group (youngest, 30 subjects dropped; middle, 31 dropped; oldest, 29 dropped) and condition (intransitive group, 44 dropped; transitive group, 46 dropped). Of those whose data were discarded, 25 had shown a side bias (75% or greater looking preference to either the right or left screen during the test); 32 failed to return to the center light before four or more of the intertrial intervals; 15 were too fussy and did not complete the experiment; 14 were discarded because of technical error; and 4 showed language delay (that is, they were tested by mistake, having been identified as delayed for the purposes of another study).

Results and Discussion

Calculation of Stimulus Salience from the Simultaneous Trials   Recall that the audio during the simultaneous trials did not direct the children to watch either the causal or the noncausal events. When inspection of the means indicated the possibility of a "match" level by age interaction, three separate analyses of variance, one on the data from the simultaneous trials for each age group, were performed. Each analysis of variance contained the two between-subjects factors of sex (male vs. female) and type of linguistic stimulus (transitive vs. intransitive), and one within-subjects factor—"match" level (match vs. nonmatch). Thus, for half of the children in each age group, the "matching" event during a simultaneous trial (which actually contained neutral audio) was the *causal* event; children were to hear transitive sentences describing this event during the test trials but had not yet been exposed to the transitive audio. For the other half of the children, the "match" was the *noncausal* event, accompanied by neutral audio during the simultaneous trials and by the intransitive audio during the test trials. Children's mean visual fixation times to the four simultaneous trials that preceded each of the four sets of test trials were entered into the three-way analyses of variance. It was predicted that since pains were taken to balance these events for stimulus salience, neither the causal nor the noncausal screen would receive more attention from either linguistic stimulus group.

For the children in the youngest group—the 19-month-olds—none of the main effects or interactions were significant. The mean visual fixation time to the match and nonmatch in the causal scenes during the simultaneous trials was 2.38 seconds; to the match and nonmatch in the noncausal scenes, the mean was 2.83 seconds $(F > .15)$. For the 24-month-olds, there was a significant main effect of "match" $(F(1, 28) = 3.90, p = .05)$ and no other significant effects. This means that the middle group preferred to watch the noncausal event during the simultaneous trials. The mean visual fixation time to the causal event was 2.34 seconds; to the noncausal event, 2.83 seconds. Any significant findings in the main analysis with this age group will need to be interpreted in light of this unexplained preference for the noncausal event. The analysis of the 28-month-old children's visual fixation times indicated that there were no significant effects or interactions.

In summary, a preference for the noncausal event was found for the 24-month-olds during the simultaneous trials. Neither of the other age groups showed any preference for either type of event.

Test Trials   Two separate four-way mixed analyses of variance were conducted on the data from each linguistic condition (transitive vs. intransitive). The two between-subjects factors were age (19-, 24-, and 28-month-olds) and sex. The two within-subjects factors were verb type (known vs. unknown) and match level (match vs. nonmatch).

The Transitive Sentence Group   For children hearing the transitive audio, the only main effect was that of the match variable ($F(1, 42) = 7.95$, $p < .007$). Children in this group preferred to watch the match (the causal scene) significantly more than the nonmatch (the noncausal scene). The mean visual fixation time to the match was 2.92 seconds; to the nonmatch, 2.42 seconds. Two significant interactions, however, indicated that these results were not carried by all age groups. A match by age interaction ($F(2, 42) = 6.01$, $p < .006$) that collapsed across the two types of verb (known and unknown) was superseded by an age by verb type by match interaction ($F(2, 42) = 5.78$, $p < .007$). The interactions were tested with a priori one-tailed t tests since in all cases we predicted that the match would be watched more than the nonmatch. Further, not all means were tested against all other means; only those that made sense theoretically were compared. Table 6.3 gives the mean visual fixation times to the match and the nonmatch by age and type of verb.

The t tests revealed that the youngest group showed no preference for the match for either the known or the unknown verbs. The middle group watched the match (mean = 3.48 seconds) more than the nonmatch (mean = 2.05 seconds) for the known verbs ($t(42) = 3.20, p < .05$). The difference between match and nonmatch for the unknown verbs was not significant and in the wrong direction (nonmatch mean = 2.91 seconds; match mean = 2.06 seconds). Thus, the 24-month-olds were able to find the match only for the verbs they were acquainted with ("turn" and "bend") and could not use the syntactic frame in which the verb appeared to help them solve the task for novel verbs. This pattern must also be

Table 6.3
Experiment 5: Mean visual fixation time (in seconds) for each age and sex group to the matching and nonmatching screen for known and unknown verbs during the test trials in the transitive sentence condition

Age (in months)	Sex	Verb type			
		Known*		Unknown	
		Match	Nonmatch	Match	Nonmatch
19	Male	2.73	2.74	2.44	2.54
	Female	2.50	2.28	2.16	2.97
	Mean	2.62	2.51	2.30	2.76
24	Male	3.16	2.70	2.17	2.87
	Female	3.80	1.39	1.94	2.64
	Mean	3.48	2.05	2.06	2.91
28	Male	3.51	2.15	3.80	3.01
	Female	3.14	2.77	3.80	2.03
	Mean	3.32	2.50	3.80	2.02
Overall mean		3.14	2.35	2.72	2.56

*The known verbs were "turn" and "bend"; the unknown verbs were "squat" and "flex."

interpreted in light of the 24-month-olds' preference for the noncausal event during the simultaneous trials. The 24-month-olds maintained the pattern of looking more toward the noncausal event when presented with unknown verbs during the test trials. They were, however, able to overcome this preference for the noncausal event in the case of the known verbs. This suggests that for known verbs, the structure of the linguistic stimulus (a transitive sentence frame) had a powerful effect. The linguistic stimulus could have influenced children to move only to a "neutral" position, with attention to the causal and noncausal stimuli about equal. Instead, it influenced children not only to abandon their preference for the noncausal event, but in fact to prefer the causal event (the match) significantly more than the noncausal event (the nonmatch).

By the time children reached 28 months of age, just about 4 months later, they had no difficulty using the linguistic stimulus to guide their watching even for the unknown verbs. Further, unlike the 24-month-olds, this group did not have to overcome any preference for either event during the simultaneous trials. These children watched the match more than the nonmatch for both known and unknown verbs. This group's mean visual fixation times for the known verbs were 3.32 seconds for the match and 2.46 seconds for the nonmatch ($t(42) = 1.90, p < .05$). For the unknown verbs, this group's means were 3.80 seconds for the match and 2.02 seconds for the nonmatch ($t(42) = 3.96, p < .05$).

To see if individual subjects' results would match the overall results from the analysis of variance, we next counted how many children in each age group had mean visual fixation times greater to the match than to the nonmatch. In line with the analysis of variance results, 13 of the 16 children in the oldest group preferred to look at the matching screen rather than the nonmatching screen. In the middle group, 11 of 16 children preferred the matching screen, and in the youngest group, only 8 of 16 children, or half, preferred to look at the matching screen.

Analyses by Sex   Although the present analysis failed to turn up any significant main effects of or interactions with the sex factor (all *p*'s > .20), inspection of the means in table 6.3 indicated that the boys and the girls in some age groups responded differently to the transitive test sentences. In order to evaluate the effects of the sex factor more closely, two two-way analyses of variance were conducted within each age group, one for boys and one for girls. The factors in these analyses were verb type (known vs. unknown) and match level (match vs. nonmatch).

In the youngest group, as the prior analysis indicated, neither boys nor girls watched the match more than the nonmatch, regardless of whether the verbs were known or unknown. In the middle group, the boys responded like the children in the youngest group, failing to watch the match more than the nonmatch regardless of the verb type. The girls, however, showed a marginally significant effect of match ($F(1, 7) = 4.37$, $p < .08$) and a marginally significant verb type by match interaction ($F(1, 7) = 5.28, p < .054$), which indicated that the match was watched more than the nonmatch *only* for the known verbs (mean to match = 3.80 seconds; to nonmatch = 1.39 seconds) (see table 6.3). When the two key theoretical comparisons (match vs. nonmatch for known and unknown verbs, respectively) were analyzed with an a priori one-tailed *t* test, only the difference between match and nonmatch for the known verbs was significant ($t(7) = 2.51, p < .05$). Indeed, comparing the mean visual fixation time to the match and nonmatch overall, 7 of the 8 24-month-old girls demonstrated preference for the matching screen in the transitive condition with known verbs. The boys' responses were considerably weaker: only 4 out of 8 showed overall means to the match greater than to the nonmatch with known verbs. Thus, the result described above for the middle group was really a result carried by the girls alone. The 24-month-old boys functioned much like the 19-month-old children on this task, only 4 out of 8 having overall means in favor of the matching screen.

However, in the 28-month-old group the boys watched the match significantly more than the nonmatch, regardless of verb type ($F(1, 7) = 26.27, p < .002$) (mean to match = 3.66 seconds; to nonmatch = 2.08 seconds). The girls, on the other hand, did not show a main effect of match but did show a significant match by verb type interaction ($F(1, 7) = 17.30, p < .005$). Although their means favored the match for both verb types, the difference between the means was about twice as large for the unknown as for the known verbs. For the known verbs, their means were 3.14 seconds for the match and 2.77 seconds for the non-match, which misses significance. For the unknown verbs, their means were 3.80 seconds for the match and 2.03 seconds for the nonmatch ($t(7) = 7.42, p < .05$). Thus, in the oldest group, both sexes watched the match more than the nonmatch for the unknown verbs but only the boys watched the match more than the nonmatch for the known verbs.

Summary of the Transitive Sentence Group   In general, then, by the age of 28 months, children who have productive vocabularies of approximately 315 words and who are speaking in 4-word sentences can use a verb's argument structure to predict verb meaning. In fact, these $2\frac{1}{2}$-year-olds did better (considering the girls' nonsignificant performance on the known verbs) with unknown verbs than with known verbs! Thus, by this age, children can use subcategorization cues to partially derive a new verb's meaning. It appears that they can also predict which meaning of a known verb is being offered, although the girls' means failed to reach significance.

The 24-month-old children were not as sophisticated. At 2 years of age, the girls showed a propensity to relate syntax to meaning only in the case of the known verbs.

The youngest children demonstrated no evidence of frame compliance, whether the verbs were known or unknown. Only 8 of the 16 youngest children who heard the transitive audio paired it with the causal scene. It appears, then, that children begin to notice the position and number of a verb's arguments at around 2 years of age and that they can recognize appropriate situations for the use of these verbs. With development, they are able to generalize this knowledge from known to unknown verbs, at least with transitive sentence frames.

Table 6.4
Experiment 5: Mean visual fixation time (in seconds) for each age and sex group to the matching and nonmatching screen for known and unknown verbs during the test trials in the intransitive sentence condition

| Age (in months) | Sex | Verb type | | | |
| | | Known* | | Unknown | |
		Match	Nonmatch	Match	Nonmatch
19	Male	2.58	2.62	2.74	2.29
	Female	3.28	2.52	2.94	1.94
	Mean	2.93	2.57	2.84	2.12
24	Male	2.59	2.62	2.09	2.32
	Female	2.30	2.96	3.32	2.44
	Mean	2.45	2.79	2.71	2.38
28	Male	2.69	3.41	3.12	1.88
	Female	3.23	2.78	3.12	2.79
	Mean	2.97	3.09	3.12	2.33
Overall mean		2.78	2.82	2.89	2.28

*The known verbs were "turn" and "bend"; the unknown verbs were "squat" and "flex."

The Intransitive Sentence Group   The results for children who heard the intransitive audio are very different from those for children who heard the transitive audio (see table 6.4). There were no results on any analyses. Across ages, only 24 of the 48 children looked longer at the noncausal scene when hearing the intransitive sentences. Even children in the oldest group responded randomly in this condition, with only 7 of 16 children looking more to the matching than the nonmatching screen. Although the trends were often in the right direction, they did not reach significance.

Although the children did not use the argument structure of the intransitive verbs presented to glean something of their meaning, their uniform failure on these sentence types does illustrate that they could discriminate one- from two-argument verbs. This in itself is an interesting finding since it shows that the stimulus sentences in the transitive condition were clearly driving children's visual fixation. This finding alone makes the results with the transitive verbs seem more valid, since if an artifact was operating, it should have influenced these results as well.

General Summary

The results of experiment 5 suggest that children have some knowledge of the significance of the transitive verb form and its implications within the class of motion verbs. By $2\frac{1}{2}$ years of age, children seem to comprehend that verbs in transitive sentences often refer to causal relations between the referents. Children do not seem to conclude the reverse—that intransitive frames are related to noncausal scenes. The distinction found between known and unknown verbs in the study also points to a developmental path in the young child's knowledge of the relationship between syntactic structure and meaning. It appears that 24-month-olds (at least, girls) enter a verb in the lexicon with its surrounding syntax. When they have memorized enough verbs in context, children can then generalize across similar frames, eventually using the frame itself to derive something about an unknown verb's meaning. That is, children may use analogy to begin solving the verb-learning problem.

Although these results are interesting, they leave much unexplored. Were the older children in the transitive condition overly influenced by the presence of the known verbs? For example, did they use their answers with the known verbs to influence their responses with the unknown verbs? Did the children in the intransitive condition really fail to understand the implications of the intransitive sentence frame or was there something about the particular intransitive frame used in the experiment that proved problematic? Are 24-month-old boys truly less sensitive to syntactic frames (like the 19-month-olds) or was this just an unusual sample? These questions provided the grist for three follow-up experiments.

6.2   Experiment 6: Do Young Children Exhibit Frame Compliance with Unknown Transitive Verbs?

As noted above, the older children may have responded correctly to the unknown verbs in experiment 5 because they used their knowledge of form-meaning pairings with known verbs to predict where to look when they heard unknown verbs. That is, the solution to the "unknown" verb problem was found by *analogy* to known verbs.

One could argue that exposure to the known verbs caused the children to always look toward the causal scenes and to ignore the noncausal scenes. In addition, perhaps children thought the known verbs were always causal. The data, however, do not bear this out. Children distributed their attention randomly to the causal and noncausal scenes when there was no directive audio during the simultaneous trial. Further, the 24-month-old group responded correctly to the known verbs, but not to the unknown verbs.

Even though the interpretation that invokes analogy is unlikely, it must be conclusively ruled out. For this reason, experiment 6 was conducted, using four unknown verbs and a new pool of subjects from the oldest age group.

Method

Subjects   Sixteen children were tested in the Yale University laboratory of Letitia Naigles, and 20 were tested in the Delaware laboratory. In each laboratory, half the subjects were boys and half were girls. The children were 27 to 30 months of age (mean age = 29;0) and had an average vocabulary of 312 words. To obtain results from 36 children, 61 children were tested. Potential subjects were dropped for the following reasons: 5 because they failed to return to the center light during intertrial intervals on more than four test trials; 4 because of fussiness; 8 because of equipment failure or experimenter error; 4 because of side bias; 3 because the parent watched the videotapes; and 1 because the child did not know the characters' names.

Stimuli   The video events were the same as those used in experiment 5 (see tables 6.1 and 6.2). All of the test sentences were transitive and followed the syntax shown in table 6.2. The only difference was that instead of actual English words, four nonsense words—"glorp," "blick," "dax," and "krad"—served as the verbs.

Results and Discussion

Calculation of Stimulus Salience from the Simultaneous Trials   As in experiment 5, the simultaneous trial data showed that without any directive linguistic stimuli, children look randomly toward the causal and noncausal scenes. The mean visual fixation time to the causal scenes (averaged over the four verbs) was 2.40 seconds; to the noncausal scenes, 2.60 seconds.

Table 6.5
Experiment 6: Mean visual fixation time (in seconds) to the matching and nonmatching screen for nonsense verbs in transitive sentences ($n = 20$; mean age = 29;0)

Stimulus*	Mean visual fixation time		Mean**
	Match	Nonmatch	
1	3.07	2.04	2.56
2	2.64	2.64	2.64
3	2.79	2.31	2.55
4	2.65	2.00	2.33
Mean	2.79	2.25	

*A description of the stimuli and the order in which they appeared is found in table 6.2.
**A main effect of stimulus was due to the difference between stimulus 2 and stimulus 4.

Test Trials   The data were tested in a three-way mixed analysis of variance with the between-subjects factor of sex (male vs. female) and the within-subjects factors of match level (match vs. nonmatch) and stimulus (the four verbs). The analysis revealed two main effects—match level ($F(1, 34) = 6.64$, $p < .02$) and stimulus ($F(3, 102) = 3.34$, $p < .03$)—and no significant interactions. The match level main effect occurred because children watched the match significantly more than the nonmatch (mean to the match = 2.79 seconds; to the nonmatch = 2.25 seconds) (see table 6.5). Thus, the results of this experiment parallel and secure the results of the transitive condition in experiment 5 (compare the means in tables 6.3 and 6.4). By 29 months children are able to use a verb's arguments to derive a causal interpretation of that verb—whether it is known or completely novel. That is, they are able to make frame-compliant responses to the transitive sentences that they hear.

The main effect of stimulus was due (according to Tukey tests) to the difference between the second stimulus and the fourth. The mean visual fixation times to these stimuli were 2.64 seconds and 2.33 seconds, respectively. This fall-off of approximately one-third of a second is probably attributable to the fact that children became a bit bored with the videotapes by the fourth block of trials. Although no stimulus by match level interaction emerged, the means in table 6.5 show that for the second stimulus event, the match was watched for exactly the same amount of time as the nonmatch.

The important finding is that children watched the match more than the nonmatch for three completely novel verbs that they could not have heard prior to this experiment. In short, then, these results replicate and secure the findings of experiment 5: children were capable of using a novel verb's argument structure to predict that it had a causal component conflated in its meaning. They watched the causal event significantly longer than they watched the noncausal event in the presence of a linguistic stimulus that used the nonsense verb in a transitive sentence frame. Furthermore, this result is not attributable to an overall preference for the causal event; children did not watch the causal event more when it was accompanied by a neutral audio during the simultaneous trials.

The next experiment reexamines a previously nonsignificant finding, namely, why children hearing intransitive sentence frames in experiment 5 failed to watch the noncausal event significantly more than the causal event.

6.3   Experiment 7: Do Children Know the Noncausal Implications of Intransitive Sentence Frames Containing the Grammatical Marker "With"?

There are several reasons why the children who participated in experiment 5 might have failed to watch the matching screen when they heard the intransitive stimuli. First, children of this age may in general be incapable of responding to intransitive frames. That is, they may master the meaning implications of transitive sentence frames before they master the meaning implications of intransitive sentence frames.

Second, the children may not have understood the *particular* frame chosen in experiment 5 to test for comprehension of intransitivity. The frame selected was quite bare, containing only a conjoined subject whose two parts were linked by an unstressed "and" (e.g., "See Big Bird and Cookie Monster glorping"). Children did not even hear a plural auxiliary verb (as in "See, Big Bird and Cookie Monster *are* glorping!") to buttress the interpretation that the sentence contained a conjoined subject. If the children did not process or comprehend the significance of the "and" in creating a complex noun phrase, they might well fail to interpret the sentence as an intransitive. Thus, the conjoined subject might have confused them. Unsure of what it signaled, children might have watched the causal and noncausal events approximately the same amount since both named characters were shown on both screens.

To see whether children could show understanding of the meaning implications of intransitive frames, two more experiments were conducted that gave additional grammatical cues for an intransitive interpretation. Experiment 7 signaled the intransitive frame with a prepositional phrase (e.g., "Where's Cookie Monster turning with Big Bird?"); experiment 8 introduced a plural auxiliary verb to underscore the conjoined subject.

For experiment 7, the inclusion of "with" should block the interpretation of "Big Bird" as a direct object of the verb if children appreciate the function of the preposition. That is, children should not construe the sentence "Where's Cookie Monster turning with Big Bird?" as though it was "Cookie Monster is turning Big Bird!" If children do not attend to the function of the prepositional phrase "... with Big Bird," they will derive the wrong interpretation: under that scenario, children should interpret the sentence as a transitive and watch the causal scene more than the noncausal scene.

Method

Subjects The subjects were 32 children (half boys and half girls), all tested in the Temple laboratory. Subjects were very close in age to the two older age groups tested in experiment 5. There were 16 children from 22 to 25 months of age (mean = 23; 20 months), with a mean vocabulary (as indicated on the Rescorla Language Inventory (1991)) of 235 words. There were also 16 children from 26 to 30 months (mean = 28.5 months), with an average productive vocabulary of 300 words. To obtain a final sample of 32 subjects, 41 children were tested. Children's data were eliminated for the following reasons: 2 for side bias; 3 for failing to center on four or more trials; 3 for fussiness; and 1 for technical problems.

Stimuli The stimulus videotapes were the same ones used in experiment 5 (see tables 6.1 and 6.2). Here, however, the linguistic stimuli for the intransitive test sentences were on the order of "Find Cookie Monster turning with Big Bird!", for all four of the original verbs ("turn," "bend," "squat," and "flex").

Results

Calculation of Stimulus Salience from the Simultaneous Trials A two-way analysis of variance with the between-subjects factor of age (2 levels) and the within-subjects factor of "match" (noncausal vs. causal) was first conducted. No main effects or interactions resulted. Thus, there was no preference for the causal over the noncausal scene during the simultaneous trials for either age group. The mean visual fixation time to the causal scene (averaged across all four verbs) was 2.69 seconds; to the noncausal scene, the mean was 2.94 seconds.

Test Trials A four-way mixed analysis of variance with age (23 vs. 28 months), sex (male vs. female), verb type (known vs. unknown), and match level (match vs. nonmatch) was conducted. Table 6.6 presents the results. The only significant effect was an interaction of age by sex by match ($F(1, 28) = 3.96, p < .03$).

A priori one-tailed t tests performed on the means to the match and nonmatch within each age and sex group revealed the following pattern of results. In the older group only the boys watched the match significantly more than the nonmatch (mean to match = 3.01 seconds; to nonmatch = 2.24 seconds) ($t(28) = 1.86, p < .05$). Although the girls' means were in the right direction, they failed to reach significance (mean to match = 3.07 seconds; to nonmatch = 2.45 seconds). However, despite the failure of the girls' mean difference to reach significance, overall, 15 of the 16 older

Table 6.6
Experiment 7: Mean visual fixation time (in seconds) for each age and sex group to the matching and nonmatching screen during the test trials in the intransitive "with" condition

Age (in months)	Sex	Mean visual fixation time	
		Match	Nonmatch
23	Male	2.26	3.21
	Female	3.07	2.45
	Mean	2.67	2.83
28	Male	3.01	2.24
	Female	3.22	2.37
	Mean	3.12	2.31
Overall mean		2.89	2.57

children had higher visual fixation times to the matching than to the nonmatching screen.

The picture was different with the 23-month-olds. Here, the girls outperformed the boys. The girls' means were 3.22 seconds to the match and 2.37 seconds to the nonmatch ($t(28) = 2.05, p < .05$). Further, of the 8 girls tested, 6 had overall means in favor of the match. The boys' means indicated that they preferred to watch the nonmatch over the match (mean to match = 2.26 seconds; to nonmatch = 3.21 seconds). In fact, the overall means for 7 of the 8 boys indicated that they watched the nonmatch more than the match! Ironically, had we performed one-tailed t tests in the *opposite* direction (i.e., predicting that the mean to the nonmatch would be greater than the mean to the match), the difference between the boys' means would have been significant ($t(28) = -2.29$, $p < .05$). This finding means that the 23-month-old boys treated the intransitive "with" sentences as though they were active sentences, either ignoring "with" or failing to understand its function in the sentence. Thus, an intransitive sentence signaled by the use of a prepositional phrase (e.g., "See? Big Bird is bending *with* Cookie Monster!") was interpreted by the boys as though it were a transitive sentence ("See? Big Bird is bending Cookie Monster!"). These boys watched the causal event far more than the noncausal event.

Discussion

By contrast to the result for the intransitive condition in experiment 5, here the older group and the girls in the 23-month-old group showed a significant preference for the matching (noncausal) scene when the intransitive frame was created with the use of a prepositional phrase. This experiment revealed that children were able to comprehend the noncausal implications of *some* intransitive sentence frames. When intransitivity was signaled by the preposition "with," at least the 28-month-olds and the 23-month-old girls were able to find the matching screen.

The outcome of experiment 7 suggests the following conclusions about, and possible explanations for, children's failure in experiment 5. First, because of the 23- and 28-month-olds' success in experiment 7 we can rule out the possibility that children are simply unable to comprehend intransitive sentences. Second, children may understand intransitive sentences, but the presence of a conjoined subject in experiment 5 may have confused them. That is, in the intransitive frame used in experiment 5 ("See

Cookie Monster and Big Bird turning"), Cookie Monster and Big Bird "shared" the subject slot. Yet children may not have understood the function of the conjunction "and." Thus, upon hearing the conjoined subject, they may have thought that since both screens depicted both of the mentioned characters, either screen could be a match for the sentence. Third, as will be discussed further under experiment 8, the intransitive frame used in experiment 5 was bare of any additional cues to intransitivity.

In experiment 7 the conjoined subject was not a problem, since it was omitted. Instead, only the name of the first-mentioned character was the subject of the sentence; the name of the second-mentioned character became the object of a prepositional phrase signaled by "with" (e.g., "See Cookie Monster turning with Big Bird"). Thus, children had to discriminate between Cookie Monster turning *with* Big Bird on one screen and Cookie Monster turning by himself on the other screen, where the causal action was taking place (i.e., on the screen where Big Bird was seen making Cookie Monster turn).

Impressively, the 28-month-old boys and the 23-month-old girls appear to be sensitive to the preposition "with" used in this experiment. If they had attended only to the predicate, the arguments, and word order, then they would have given the opposite, incorrect response, treating the sentence as an active. In fact, this may be what the 23-month-old boys did, since their mean visual fixation times were clearly in favor of the nonmatch. These younger boys may not yet have gone beyond the simpler "semantic" strategy of noting the order of actor, agent, and actor. This result is interesting in light of the findings from experiment 5. There, even for known verbs, the boys in the transitive condition looked more to the causal scene but not significantly so.

The 23-month-old girls and the 28-month-old boys appear to have gone on to a more "syntactic" strategy, focusing on unstressed oblique markers in the sentence frame. (The older girls' means favored the match, although the difference in visual fixation times did not reach significance.) This developing syntactic sophistication permits them to notice even subtle differences in sentence frames and to give frame-compliant responses in this task.

6.4   Experiment 8: Do Children Know the Noncausal Implications of Intransitive Sentence Frames Containing the Auxiliary "Are"?

The results of experiment 7 suggest that children as young as $2\frac{1}{2}$ years are capable of using intransitive argument structure to derive sentence meaning. Conjoined subjects (like the ones in the stimuli for experiment 5) appear to be a source of difficulty for children: once conjoined subjects were removed in experiment 7 and "with" was added, some children did use the intransitive frame. Another earlier-mentioned interpretation of the failure to achieve expected results in experiment 5 is a bit more complicated. Although the conjoined subjects may indeed have caused difficulty, the problem may have been compounded by the paucity of other grammatical cues to intransitivity. For example, the form of the verb used (a gerund such as "squatting") was unmarked for number and certainly did not provide the child with any cue to the fact that the sentence subject was in the plural. Further, the sentence frame did not include an auxiliary verb (such as "is" or "are") marked for number.

Experiment 8 assessed the hypothesis that if an auxiliary verb marked for number (e.g., "are") were included in the test sentences, children would be able to find the scene that matched the intransitive sentence. Whereas in experiment 5 the audio was "See Cookie Monster and Big Bird turning," in experiment 8 it was "See, Cookie Monster and Big Bird *are* turning." If children do *not* attend to the plural auxiliary, then their responses should look like those of the group tested in the intransitive condition of experiment 5; that is, there should be no difference in visual fixation time between the matching and nonmatching screens. If, in contrast, the children are assisted by the addition of the plural auxiliary, then they should prefer to look at the noncausal scene.

Method

Subjects   The subjects were 47 children tested in the Delaware and Temple laboratories. Sixteen children (8 boys and 8 girls) were from 23 to 25 months of age, with a mean age of 24; 12 and a mean productive vocabulary of 276 words. Thirty-one children (17 boys and 14 girls) were from 28 to 30 months of age, with a mean age of 29; 13 and a mean productive vocabulary of 305.33 words.

To obtain 47 children, 70 were tested. Children's data were eliminated for the following reasons: 1 for side bias; 7 for failing to center on four or more trials; 11 for experimenter error or technical problems; and 4 for fussiness.

Stimuli   Again, the video stimuli were as presented in tables 6.1 and 6.2. The linguistic stimuli, however, were constructed to include the auxiliary "are." Thus, for all four verbs, the test sentences were of the type, "See? Cookie Monster and Big Bird are turning!"

Results and Discussion

Calculation of Stimulus Salience from the Simultaneous Trials   Two separate one-way analyses of variance, one for each age group, were conducted on the amount of time children watched the causal (taken to be the nonmatch) and noncausal (taken to be the match) scenes during the simultaneous trials that preceded the test events. The results indicated that there was no preference for the causal or the noncausal scene in the simultaneous trials. That is, the factor of match was not significant in either analysis ($F(1, 250) = 1.93, p > .16$ for the younger children; $F(1, 250) = 1.61, p > .21$ for the older children). Across ages, the mean visual fixation time to the causal scene was 2.61 seconds; to the noncausal scene it was 2.32 seconds. Since there was no preference for either type of event during the simultaneous trials, any difference between visual fixation times on the test trials can only be a result of the linguistic stimulus drawing children's attention to one or the other of these types of events.

Test Trials   The results for the test trials are presented in table 6.7. A four-way mixed analysis of variance was conducted with the between-subjects factors of age (24 vs. 29 months) and sex (male vs. female) and the within-subjects factors of verb (known vs. unknown) and match level

Table 6.7
Experiment 8: Mean visual fixation time (in seconds) for each age and sex group to the matching and nonmatching screen during the test trials in the intransitive "and-are" condition

Age (in months)	Sex	Mean visual fixation time	
		Match	Nonmatch
24	Male	3.46	2.82
	Female	2.83	1.55
	Mean	3.15	2.19
29	Male	2.62	2.58
	Female	2.84	2.47
	Mean	2.73	2.53
Overall mean		2.94	2.36

(match vs. nonmatch). The only two significant effects were a main effect of match and an age by match interaction ($F(1, 43) = 13.88, p < .001$; $F(1, 43) = 5.51, p < .03$, respectively). Each age group's mean visual fixation times to the match versus the nonmatch were tested with a priori t tests, given our hypotheses. These tests yielded a surprising result: the match was preferred to the nonmatch only by the 24-month-old subjects. Their mean visual fixation time to the match was 3.07 seconds; to the nonmatch, 1.82 seconds ($t(43) = 3.76, p < .05$). For the 29-month-old group, the mean visual fixation time to the match was 2.77 seconds; to the nonmatch, 2.49 seconds. This result does not approach significance.

The fact that 24-month-olds can comprehend the semantic implications of intransitive sentences when the sentences include an auxiliary verb replicates the results of Naigles (1990).[2] At 25 months of age, Naigles's subjects, hearing intransitive sentences with the same structure as the sentences heard by the children in this experiment, watched the matching screen significantly more than the nonmatching screen. In addition, Naigles's subjects heard only nonsense verbs—more difficult linguistic stimuli than were used in the present experiment. Thus, there are two studies securing the result that by 24 months of age, children can use the meaning implications of some kinds of intransitive sentence frames (in particular, a frame that includes an auxiliary verb) to watch noncausal events more than causal events.

Why should the younger children appear to do better than the older children? By our rudimentary assessment of their linguistic capabilities (i.e., size of productive vocabulary and length of word combinations), the older children who participated in experiment 8 do not appear to differ from the older children tested in experiments 5, 6, and 7. Nor do the 24-month-olds appear to be particularly accelerated. It may be that the 29-month-old boys are the source of this noneffect, although a sex by age by match interaction does not show up in the main analysis.

What do the present findings say about children's inability to comprehend the semantic implications of the intransitive sentences in experiment 5? The bare intransitive sentence frame used in experiment 5, which was not marked for number and was marked for intransitivity only by the lack of a direct object, may have been misunderstood by the children. They may have been uncertain about how to interpret the conjunction ("and") in the absence of additional information about subject number. They appear to have watched both the causal and noncausal scenes to the same degree, perhaps guided by the fact that each scene showed both named characters. With the addition of the plural auxiliary in the linguistic stimuli of experiment 8, children were able to overcome the difficulty and to render a noncausal interpretation of the intransitive. Thus, these children seem to be looking for syntactic cues in the input—and even for subtle, unstressed syntactic cues—to make responses that comply with the syntactic frame.

6.5 General Discussion

In this chapter we have presented four experiments designed to test how children learn about verb meaning. The arguments presented here turned on the position that one significant route to the learning of verb meanings is through attending to sentential relations. That is, the present studies tested the hypothesis that by noting a verb's arguments, in addition to the situational cues, the learner can glean important information about verb meaning.

The present studies specifically examined the correlations between semantics and syntax for transitive and intransitive motion verbs. Transitive sentence frames, which include direct objects, are canonically (although not invariably) associated with expressing a causal relationship between the entities to which the arguments refer. Intransitive sentence frames, which omit direct objects, do not usually imply causation. The question addressed by these experiments was whether young children, at an early point in language acquisition, are capable of exploiting such regularities to watch causal events when they hear transitive verbs and noncausal events when they hear intransitive verbs. Children in three different age ranges (discussed here in terms of each group's mean age) were selected for study. Eighteen-month-olds, just beginning to combine words and shown in chapter 5 to be sensitive to at least the order of constituents in sentences, made up the youngest group. Twenty-four-month-olds, typically speaking in two- and three-word sentences and utilizing the rudiments of grammar, constituted the middle group. Twenty-nine-month-olds, typically using much longer sentences and capable of at least comprehending sentences that contain hierarchical structure (see chapter 7), made up the oldest group. Since both syntactic and semantic bootstrapping rest on children's ability to parse sentences into different units, and on their having had at least some experience with the semantics-syntax correlations implied by the bootstrapping construct, it was important to investigate at what point in their linguistic development children are capable of attending to verb syntax in the language that they hear.

Summary of the Results of Experiments 5–8
Experiment 5 asked whether children could, hearing two known and two unknown verbs, use transitive and intransitive sentence frames to show a looking preference for causal and noncausal events, respectively. Except for the 18-month-olds, children watched causal events when they heard transitive sentences. All age groups failed to watch noncausal events when they heard intransitive sentences.

Experiment 6, using transitive sentences only, explored whether children could watch the causal event if they heard sentences containing nonsense verbs (i.e., verbs they had never heard before). A positive result would be evidence for the claim that children can use syntactic frames to learn something of the meaning of new verbs. The data from 29-month-olds indicated that novel verbs posed no problem; children watched the causal more than the noncausal event. This finding replicates the work of Naigles (1990), who used nonsense verbs with 25-month-olds.

Experiments 7 and 8 probed the null finding with intransitive sentences from experiment 5. The hypothesis underlying both studies was that the syntactic frame signaling the intransitive in experiment 5 may have been too bare for young children. Experiment 7, using a different intransitive construction (where the intransitive was accompanied by a prepositional phrase), found that the children in the two older groups (except for the 24-month-old boys) were now able to use the sentence frame to watch the noncausal more than the causal event. Thus, without the conjoined subject used in the bare sentence frame of experiment 5, these children could even override a straight word order strategy to interpret the intransitive. However, the 24-month-old boys did interpret these intransitive sentences as though they were transitives, watching the causal event significantly longer than the noncausal event. Finally, in experiment 8, where the only change in the linguistic stimulus relative to experiment 5 was the inclusion of a plural auxiliary verb ("are"), 24-month-old children showed their ability to use the new sentence to watch the noncausal event. This finding also replicates the work of Naigles (1990), who used this sentence frame with novel verbs. The 29-month-old group's visual fixation means surprisingly did not reach significance.

How Did the Children Represent the Stimulus Sentences?
The ability of children in the two older groups to watch the causal or noncausal events in response to transitive or intransitive sentence frames suggests that, at a minimum, these children were able to identify which character was which and to find the agents and patients in the sentences they heard. However, these data suggest that in addition to parsing and performing a semantic analysis, children were performing syntactic analyses. This is most forcefully suggested by experiment 7, where children heard sentences of the type "Big Bird is squatting with Cookie Monster," with the subject (the name of one intransitive actor) at the beginning and the object of the preposition (the name of the other intransitive actor) at the end. The simplest (but incorrect) sentence analysis would have been to ignore "with" and treat the sentence as though it were transitive (as in "Big Bird is squatting Cookie Monster"—that is, causing Cookie Monster to squat). In fact, this appears to have been just the analysis performed by the 23-month-old boys. That the majority of the children did not make this mistake suggests that in this experiment, and possibly in the others as well, children may have been computing syntactic relations such as subject and predicate of the sentence. Regardless of the particular nature of children's representation of the sentences used in these experiments, however, the fact that children consistently watch the screen that matches the sentence frame they hear indicates that children can use these frames to partially derive verb meaning.

What exactly is the meaning children derive from these sentences? This, too, is somewhat indeterminate despite the fact that children were able to watch the matching screen. As Naigles (1990) points out, children could have assumed that the transitive frames they heard were implicating not causal events but "unergative" transitives (Perlmutter 1978; Levin 1985). In an unergative transitive the entity whose name is in subject position acts as an experiencer and the entity whose name is in direct object position acts as the patient. For example, in the transitive sentence "Adam eats the fish" or "Mary sees John," no causation is implied. If children in the present studies interpreted the transitive sentences as unergatives, they could have thought that "Cookie Monster is daxing Big Bird" meant something like 'Cookie Monster is holding Big Bird while Big Bird waves his arm'. That is, the explicit causal component would be absent, and Cookie Monster's role would be reduced to that of helper or accompanist rather than the cause of Big Bird's action.

A similar argument can be made about the intransitive sentences used here (see Naigles 1990 for a lengthier discussion). Not all intransitives express noncausal meanings. It is therefore possible that "Big Bird and Cookie Monster are daxing" could be interpreted as 'Big Bird is performing a symmetric action with someone using his arm', an interpretation that is not specifically noncausal. To determine which interpretation children in our experiments made requires further research. In particular, it requires presenting children with scenes that pit these interpretations against each other and seeing which they choose to watch in the presence of certain sentence frames. As an example of this kind of work, Naigles and Kako (1993) conducted a set of experiments to determine whether children (1) can interpret transitive frames as referring to contact events (e.g., "pat"), and (2) prefer to assign causal or contact interpretations to transitive sentences. To answer these questions, they presented videotapes to 27-month-olds in the intermodal preferential looking paradigm. Their second experiment indicated that toddlers were indeed capable of learning a new contact verb when they heard a transitive sentence frame. More important for the present point is the result of their third experiment. When they pitted a contact event against a causal event, children preferred to watch the causal event without a linguistic stimulus, a preference that continued once an audio using a transitive sentence frame was introduced. Naigles and Kako concluded that children interpret transitive frames as mapping to both causation and contact—in other words, as a more general notion of object affectedness (see Gropen et al. 1991). Clearly, then, it would appear that children in the present experiments who heard transitive frames were at minimum interpreting them in terms of an affected object instead of merely in terms of one character accompanying another while the first carried out an action (e.g., Big Bird simply being there while Cookie Monster performed an action).

Another reason to attribute causal and noncausal interpretations to children for the sentence frames used here stems from the results of Fisher et al. (1994) with 3- and 4-year-old children. When children were shown a videotaped scene that could be interpreted either causally or noncausally, they reliably used the sentence context that accompanied the scene to give it either a causal or a noncausal interpretation. For example, these children were shown a rabbit feeding an elephant, who ate. They then heard either "The bunny is nading the elephant" or "The elephant is nading." The former sentence led children to interpret the verb causally; the latter sentence led them interpret it noncausally. The nature of the dependent variables used in Fisher et al.'s study increases our confidence in the inference that children in the experiments reported here made causal and noncausal interpretations, even though Fisher et al.'s subjects were older than ours. In that study, children were asked to paraphrase the test sentences (a task not possible for the younger children in our experiments to perform): their paraphrases were something like "The bunny is feeding the elephant" and "The elephant is eating."

In sum, Naigles and Kako's (1993) results in the intermodal preferential looking paradigm and Fisher et al.'s (1994) results, using a different dependent variable with older children, suggest that subjects in experiments 7 and 8 may well have made causal and noncausal interpretations of the stimulus sentences.

The Developmental Picture That Emerges from the Experimental Data
The data from experiments 5–8 paint a picture consistent with that sketched above of young children exploiting sentence frames and the known nouns contained therein, as well as their observation of real-world scenes, to interpret the meaning of novel verbs and of familiar verbs with more than one possible reading (e.g., "turn" can be both causal and noncausal). However, children may not start the process of language learning using formal structural information—even when they are familiar with the meaning of the noun arguments that verbs take. The 18-month-old children in experiment 5 showed little ability to use either the transitive or the intransitive frames they were offered despite recognizing Big Bird and Cookie Monster and despite observing videotaped scenes. By 24 months of age, and certainly by 28 months, many children have become sensitive to the phrase-structural implications of transitive sentence frames for describing causal events (experiments 5 and 6), although there is a suggestion that they are more so with known than with unknown verbs. Children were able to use the syntax as a guide to meaning even when the scenes were accompanied by sentences that did not contain an auxiliary verb but only the main verb surrounded by the two noun arguments (e.g., "Find Big Bird bending Cookie Monster!").

For intransitive sentences, bare sentence frames apparently do not work quite as well. For intransitive sentence frames, experiments 5, 7, and 8 clearly suggest a developmental progression for exploiting ever more subtle nuances of syntactic frames. None of the children in these studies could use intransitive frames with a conjoined subject and a verb that failed to mark subject number (experiment 5) (e.g., "Find Big Bird and Cookie Monster bending!"). Once structural information was added to the intransitive frame, however, both older age groups began to show their ability to use syntax to predict meaning. For example, experiment 7 separated the noun arguments, thereby eliminating the conjoined subject, and added the preposition "with." The boys in the 24-month-old group continued to interpret these sentences as though they were active declarative sentences. Whether their failure was due to unfamiliarity with the preposition "with" or an inability to exploit an intransitive sentence frame for meaning is unclear. However, the 24-month-old girls were able to use these frames to look for noncausal events. Furthermore, some children at this age are capable of understanding the function of a conjoined subject when they hear a sentence in which an auxiliary verb marked for number is also provided (experiment 8) (e.g., "See, Cookie Monster and Big Bird are bending!"). Surprisingly, the oldest group did not show a clear effect in experiment 8.

Thus, the intermodal preferential looking paradigm has revealed that children—at least by 23 months of age—are sensitive to phrase-structural information and can use it to predict verb meaning. Transitive constructions seem easier than some intransitive constructions. When additional syntactic information is added to intransitive frames, however, children use them to look for noncausal events.

There are several caveats we should raise before attempting to extrapolate these findings to the way in which children approach verb learning in the real world. First, in the real world, children are not given two scenes from which to choose. Instead, they are usually observing a single scene whose beginning and end may not be clearly demarcated and that may contain overlapping elements from other events. In other words, the paradigm used in these experiments may make it easier for children to decide which aspects of the scene are important for word learning. Second, the studies reported here use absolutely minimal vocabulary, requiring only that children know the videotaped characters' names. In the real world, children probably hear sentences all the time in which both the nouns and the verb are unfamiliar to them. As Gleitman and Gillette (1995) have shown, it is much easier to predict noun meaning from scene observation than it is to predict verb meaning. Still, we have made it easier for children to reveal their ability to use phrase-structural information by so severely limiting the stimulus nouns. Third, not all subjects who are tested in this paradigm produce usable data. This paradigm may work best with children who have longer attention spans relative to their peers.

What these three factors add up to is the possibility that it may take children a bit longer to manifest the skills they show here in real-world language learning.[3] However, whether children use syntactic frames in real life a month or two after they show their ability to do so in the intermodal preferential looking paradigm is not as important as the fact that they can exploit form to learn something of meaning. Further, by the age of 30 months, the earlier-mentioned work of Naigles, Gleitman, and Gleitman (1992) bolsters the present findings on children's sensitivity to syntactic information for determining verb meaning. Their research used a different paradigm—an enactment task with standard verbs like "come" and "bring" embedded in noncanonical constructions.

Additional research must continue to disentangle exactly what aspects of the structural information available to young children in the sentence frames they hear are being exploited by them. Also, input studies must be conducted to examine the range of frames available to the language-learning child (for one such study, see Naigles and Hoff-Ginsberg 1992). In theory, syntactic bootstrapping is most effective as a means of verb learning when several different frames, each giving unique syntactic information about the permissible range of uses of a verb, are available to the child.

Chapter 7

A Coalition Model of Language Comprehension

We began this book by suggesting that language learning is possible only because infants *selectively* attune to certain properties of the language input and because they use a *coalition of cues* available in the input to help them "crack" the syntactic code.[1] In chapters 4–6 we focused on this issue of selectivity by examining children's ability to comprehend sentence constituents, to use word order in comprehension, and to attend to the semantic implications of verb argument structure. In this chapter we return to issues raised in chapters 1 and 2 by synthesizing current research (including the research presented here) in an effort to flesh out the coalition model.

Using a broad brush, we considered in chapter 2 how contemporary theories of language acquisition answer three questions about that process: (1) What is present when language learning begins?, (2) What mechanisms are used in language learning?, and (3) What inputs drive the system forward? We concluded that differences among the theories are more apparent than real. In the end, in fact, it became clear that differences among the theories are less about mechanism and more about what constitutes input to the language-learning system. In the context of the coalition model, answers to these questions demand an *eclectic* approach that allows us to incorporate the foci of the different theories into a developmental story. Nonetheless, an eclectic and dynamic approach to language acquisition does not incorporate all aspects of all theories.

In this chapter we develop new answers to the above questions in the context of language comprehension. We select comprehension as our vehicle for two reasons: first, the research reported here shows that children are clearly capable of more linguistic analysis than they reveal in language production; and second, since language comprehension is at the cutting edge of the child's linguistic knowledge, it seems appropriate to grant comprehension a central role in the child's construction of language and the world. Thus, in section 7.1 we formulate both a new definition and a model of language comprehension. In section 7.2 we focus on why, given this model, comprehension should be expected to come before production. This leads to a discussion of why the intermodal preferential looking paradigm seems to be successful in revealing children's knowledge of language processing and structure. In section 7.3 we suggest new directions for research that are inspired by this approach to comprehension.

7.1 The Definition and the Framework: What Is Language Comprehension?

Our working definition of language comprehension is one that subordinates the goal of language comprehension to the broader end of cognitive development. In particular, we believe that language comprehension plays a significant role in constructing mental models. As Johnson-Laird (1983) writes in defining his view of mental models:

Mental models play a central and unifying role in representing objects, states of affairs, sequences of events, the way the world is, and the social and psychological actions of daily life. They enable individuals to make inferences and predictions, to understand phenomena, to decide what action to take and to control its execution, and above all to experience events by proxy ... (p. 397)

Similarly, Fauconnier (1985) describes the notion of "mental spaces" as the representations "that we set up as we talk or listen and that we structure with elements, roles, strategies, and relations" (p. 1). And Bloom (1993), in interpreting Fauconnier 1985, writes:

Intentional states are momentary beliefs, desires, and feelings 'about something'; they are states of mind directed at an object, event or set of circumstances in the world. (p. 224) ... Language expresses and articulates these representations in acts of expression and sets up such representations in acts of interpretation. (p. 226)

Johnson-Laird, Fauconnier, and Bloom all emphasize the role that mental models or intentional states play in the ability to use language. However, these mental models themselves represent an enormous achievement; they are not constructed overnight. The construction of such elaborate representations and perspectives about events *is* the process of cognitive development (Bloom 1993, 1994). Before children can, in Johnson-Laird's words, "make inferences and predictions" and "experience events by proxy," they will have perceived and categorized the outcomes and variations of many first-hand events. By the same token, before children can structure what Fauconnier refers to as "elements, roles, strategies, and relations," they must come to see the world in terms of these elements and relations. What Johnson-Laird and Fauconnier describe is already the *product* of much development, development along the lines of what Mandler (1992) has described as infants' burgeoning ability to construct first, image-schemas, and second, propositions about their world.

In our view, language comprehension, and a more primitive use of language we refer to below as "acoustic packaging," may partially assist children in constructing these primary representations. They are what allows children to eventually move away from being able to think only about what they experience. The idea that primitive forms of language comprehension in the form of acoustic packaging might assist children in carving up the world is a radical departure from prior discussions of language comprehension and of early representation. Before children can build a mental model and *interpret* the world's events, they must first *internalize* the events that they witness. Thus, in development, language comprehension evolves through phases that begin with acoustic packaging and progresses to syntactic understanding. Language comprehension, then, is one vehicle for the construction of more sophisticated mental models.

Internalization Followed by Interpretation

An analogy from the world of filmmaking is useful in characterizing the difference between internalization and interpretation as they are used here. The *internalization* process is like the film genre called "cinema verité." Ongoing events are captured as they occur, with little or no interpretation by the director. The camera is simply set on a tripod to record the movements and relationships in view, and no directorial perspective is added. Although this analogy feels starkly perceptual, our view goes beyond perception. Cinema verité incorporates objects and animate beings rather than mere shapes. It also shows more than vectors and trajectories. Indeed, the child-as-cinema-verité director is equipped with primitive meanings like those of causality, animacy, and containment that emerge in what Mandler (1992) calls the "image-schematic" format. The earliest characterization of language comprehension, then, is one in which the child operates like a cinema verité director, using the language (or more specifically the surface properties of language, in the form of acoustic parameters) to represent objects, animate beings, and relations in the world. That is, infants may first extract unanalyzed "chunks" from the linguistic stream (chunks defined through a prosodic envelope) that come to be associated with specific persons or events (see Peters 1985). Seen in this way, the acoustic properties of language may also serve to assist the child in parsing the world's ebb and flow into units like objects, actions, or events. This view presupposes that parents often talk about the "here-and-now" when addressing their children directly (as in Western culture) or when describing their infants' actions (as in some non-Western cultures; e.g., the Kaluli culture of Papua New Guinea (Schieffelin 1990)).

The *interpretation* component of language adds another dimension—that of *perspective*. Returning to our film analogy, we can equate the interpretation process with the approach of a film director who does not use the cinema verité genre. Utilizing the techniques of a skilled cinematographer, this director guides viewers toward a particular focus or interpretation of events. Occasionally, for example, the director may employ a zoom lens,[2] zeroing in on actors' faces to suggest how they feel; or the director may focus on only one of the actors in an event, foregrounding that person's actions and emotions relative to the others. Language comprehension comes to serve this function only after the child has engaged in much internalization. That is, before one can gain a perspective on the world's events, one must be able to analyze and represent those events.

As children create a mental analogue of the world via the process of internalization, they move away from cinema verité and start to become talented film interpreters who bring with them knowledge of how to "read" the angles and how to "feel" the scenes. The mental model becomes annotated with personal experience via the process of interpretation. Thus, quite early in development, each child's model bears some "family resemblance" to, but is not a carbon copy of, the events that that child has witnessed (see Bloom 1993, 1994).

Some have argued that this move toward sophisticated mental models that involve both internalization and interpretation of physical events was one of the evolutionary forces behind the creation of language itself. For example, Miller (1990) contends that language evolved from the twin pressures for efficient communication about the world and sophisticated representation of it. Bloom (1993) suggests that for the child, the drive toward more sophisticated mental representations and the need for communication about them provide the incentive for language growth. As mental models become more discrepant from the perceptual world (i.e., move from internalization to interpretation, in our terminology), children seek to share the contents of their minds with others. Communication, first through affect and then through the propositions of language (Bloom 1994), is therefore born from the need to talk about the increasingly complex contents of the mind:

Children will acquire words and grammar of a language as representations in intentional states become increasingly discrepant from the data of perception. In earliest infancy, what young infants are seeing is, to a large extent, what they are thinking. With developments in the capacity for representation and in procedures for retrieval and recall, infants come to access objects and events from memory that do not match the data of perception. This recall of past events is needed for interpreting what others do and, eventually, what they say. (p. 225)

Overview of a Model of the Development of Language Comprehension
How might language comprehension assist the young child in internalizing and interpreting events? Inspired by the work of Gernsbacher (1988, 1990), we propose that the development of language comprehension goes through the following three phases. First, language assists the child in segmenting the *nonlinguistic events* to be internalized and roughly interpreted. At this point language may not even be processed qua language. That is, it may be processed more acoustically (or visually for signers) than linguistically. This first "internalization" phase (phase I—lasting roughly from 0 to 9 months)[3] involves Peters's (1985) process of *extraction* but goes much beyond it to involve what we call *acoustic packaging*. That is, children use perceived acoustic units as a guide to segmenting and unitizing nonlinguistic events. In the second, interpretation phase (phase II—from approximately 9 to 24 months), children begin to analyze *within* the acoustic units extracted in phase I and to map the resulting products (words and phrases) onto their corresponding representations of objects and events. Children make these mappings in ways compatible with the semantics of their native language. When the cues from the semantic, prosodic, contextual, and syntactic systems are redundantly correlated, children show evidence of sentence comprehension (Hirsh-Pasek and Golinkoff 1993) before they produce two-word utterances. For phase III children (roughly 24–36 months), reliance on correlated cues in the input declines as their ability to perform relatively unsupported syntactic analyses increases. Now sentence comprehension can occur more often in the absence of the events being described, and children can perform interclausal linguistic analysis to gain meaning. Hence, phase III is referred to as "complex syntactic analysis"—an advanced phase of language interpretation.

Table 7.1
A three-phase model of language comprehension. (Ages are only approximate.)

Dominant process	Form of representation		Language comprehension	Language production
Phase I: Extraction and acoustic packaging (0–9 months)				
Internalization	Acoustic correlates of linguistic structure	Image-schemas (not propositional)	Some words	Few, if any, words
Phase II: Segmentation and linguistic mapping (9–24 months)				
Internalization and interpretation	Words, some early grammar	Propositions; cuts becoming language dependent	Syntactic, when redundant cues from context, semantics, and prosody coincide	Prototypical transitive and intransitive sentences; often incomplete
Phase III: Complex syntactic analysis (24–36 months)				
Interpretation	Hierarchical representation of linguistic structure	Propositions; language dependent in nature	Syntactic, even when redundant cues fail to coincide; can compute interclausal relations	Complete sentences, variety of structures

In sum, for this speculative model of comprehension to succeed, it must be the case that children (1) attempt to construct mental models of their world, and (2) use language as a vehicle to assist in the construction of these models. With respect to the latter point, children must recognize early on that language maps onto perceived relationships (see chapter 4). Otherwise, they would have no obvious motivation to access the information available (at a number of levels) in the stream of speech. What follows is a review of selected literature on language comprehension that bolsters the case for the three phases described above. Table 7.1 summarizes our claims about these phases.

We offer this framework for three reasons. First, it begins to answer the three questions raised in chapter 2. For example, we will argue that what the child brings to the language-learning task is the ability to analyze input in multiple ways, with a bias for focusing on prosodic information in phase I, semantic information in phase II, and syntactic information in phase III. Thus, we take seriously the oft-stated but rarely researched claim that different language systems (prosody, semantics, and syntax) and environmental influences (e.g., social relations) interact in a kind of coalition in the development of language comprehension. Second, this framework provides a new way of organizing existing data on the language-learning process. Third, although this point is not the main focus of the current chapter, this perspective allows us to view language comprehension as a tool for studying cognitive development in the context of mental model building.

Phase I: Internalization: Acoustic Packaging of Nonlinguistic Events (Approximately 0 to 9 Months)

Imagine that you are watching a movie made in Japan and have no knowledge of Japanese. Would you gain a firmer grasp of the significant events in the movie if you watched it with the accompanying language rather than in silence? We contend that you would. Beyond affording information about the emotional valence (Fernald 1991) of a scene, the narrative may assist in "packaging" or segmenting the flow of events and in focusing attention. For one thing, you unconsciously assume that the language you hear somehow relates to the events you observe. In addition, the language helps you to divide a sequence of events into units. For example, you may see someone performing several actions (opening a closet, removing a coat, putting it on, and leaving). If you hear what sounds like a sentence over the part where the person puts on the coat, you will probably remember that event better than the events that did not have a linguistic overlay. By contrast, if language overlaps the entire sequence, you may think of the subparts as a single event, rather than as four separate events. Thus, without knowing Japanese, you may use the language to help you focus on and unitize the observed events.

Now let us consider infants, who bring no preconceived notions about events like "leave-taking" to their observation of the world. Acoustic accompaniments to events should influence infants' perception even more profoundly than a language overlay influences the perception of adults watching a foreign film. At this level, language (or the acoustic equivalent from the child's point of view) helps to set up the boundaries for real-world events. To be able to use acoustic packaging, however, phase I infants need three abilities. First, they must refine their analysis of the world's *nonlinguistic* events. Second, they must attend to the acoustic information in the incoming language stream. Third—and this is a prerequisite of a different sort—they must assume that contemporaneously heard language maps onto the events being witnessed. Acoustic packaging therefore is a precursor to linguistic mapping. In acoustic packaging, infants use acoustic information to help them segment complex nonlinguistic events into what will be linguistically relevant units at the next phase.

There is some evidence, though much more will be needed, that addresses the phase I infant's navigation through these tasks.

Prerequisite 1: Infants Must Form Image-Schemas of the World's Events
Infants construct mental models based on their representations of the perceived world of objects, actions, and events; they do not merely react to the flow of sensory input (see also Bloom 1974). Indeed, even infrahuman species must have this capability to function in the world. Based on a review of research on infant perception, Mandler (1992) proposes that infants parse the events in their world into a set of "image-schemas" such as PATH, LINK, and CONTAINMENT. These are constructed from infants' analysis of movement trajectories (e.g., self-initiated and contingent movement), and they in turn are the basis for constructing broader categories such as ANIMACY, CAUSALITY, and AGENCY.

Work on infants' ability to find hidden objects provides one piece of evidence for these image-schemas. By 9 months of age, infants can use spatiotemporal cues along with perceptual cues to find a hidden object when their own perspective has been shifted (Acredolo 1978, 1980; Acredolo and Evans 1980; Landau and Spelke 1988). To do this, infants must develop an internal working model of the spatial environment that is transformable. Work on early recall also suggests that infants internalize and encode events (Rovee-Collier and Hayne 1987; Haith, Hazen, and Goodman 1988). Finally, imitation studies by Meltzoff (1990) speak to the infant's ability to internalize and process observed events.

Prerequisite 2: Infants Must Extract Acoustic Correlates of Linguistic Units from the Speech Stream   As Peters (1985) writes, "The child's first problem is to get hold of something to work with linguistically" (p. 1033). A new line of research suggests that even before infants understand the semantics of sentences—let alone their syntactic composition—they may attend to the acoustic information in the speech (see Gerken 1994; Hirsh-

Pasek et al. 1987). Indeed, infants may even possess the ability to locate the acoustic correlates of phrasal and clausal units (Hirsh-Pasek and Golinkoff 1993). Hirsh-Pasek, Jusczyk, Kemler Nelson, and their colleagues (Hirsh-Pasek et al. 1987; Jusczyk et al. 1992; Kemler Nelson et al. 1989) have found that 6-month-old infants prefer to listen to speech in which the integrity of the clausal boundaries is maintained rather than to speech in which the integrity of these boundaries is disturbed. That is, natural infant-directed speech contains pauses approximately 1 second long between clauses. Infants prefer to listen to speech in which pauses occur at the clausal boundaries rather than to speech in which pauses are artificially inserted inside the clauses. A little later in development (by 9 months) infants seem to be sensitive to the acoustic markers that segment major phrasal units such as noun phrases and verb phrases (Jusczyk et al. 1992). In addition, using a preferential listening paradigm, Jusczyk and Aslin (in press) have shown that by 6 months infants recognize their own name and that by 7.5 months they can recognize a word repeatedly presented in a story. With increasing age, infants become capable of discriminating between smaller and smaller constituents in the speech stream. Peters (1985) likens this to a "figure-ground" phenomenon: after an element (e.g., the phrase "shut the door") has been extracted as a single unit and hence stands out as a figure in the speech stream, it becomes the ground from which a new figure (e.g., a single word—"door") emerges.

Prerequisite 3: Language Input Must Describe Ongoing Events   Prerequisites 1 and 2 are psychological preconditions in the child. Prerequisite 3 instead concerns the input that the child hears. This prerequisite stipulates that infants must hear a preponderance of talk (possibly infant-directed speech) about events occurring in the "here-and-now." That is, if the child is to come out of phase I having formed rough acoustic mappings between elements of the speech stream and events, the correlations between language and events must be present to be mined. At least in Western society, mothers of year-old infants *do* talk about objects, actions, and events that are in the infant's focus (Messer 1983; Harris, Jones, and Grant 1983, 1984; Harris et al. 1986; Harris 1992). Adamson (1995) reviews much research that has focused on how infants and mothers set up episodes of joint attention to objects (see also Tomasello and Farrar 1986). Further, she suggests that mothers build "scaffolds" for their infants and act like "narrators of the world surrounding them and their infants" (p. 146). Even in a society where mothers do not address their children directly, like the non-Western Kaluli society (Schieffelin 1990), they talk about what their children are doing.

The Outcome of Phase I: Linking Acoustics and Events   Once children have formed image-schematic representations of events and can isolate acoustic chunks in the language stream, they are ready to form "acoustic packages." To do this, they must assume that the speech stream is somehow "hooked up" to cooccurring events. (This is, in a way, a primitive, nonlinguistic version of the mapping that will occur between linguistic units and events in phase II.) The internalization process involving acoustic packages from the language stream and events can then take two forms. In the minimal case, the acoustic information can be an inseparable part of the whole event. In the maximal case, it is at least conceivable (and empirically testable) that the acoustic information may assist in defining the event. Let us briefly review each of these possibilities.

The minimal role for acoustic packages is noncontroversial and has been commented upon by prior researchers. Acoustic packages are formed when some acoustic chunk is repeated often enough in conjunction with a particular event (e.g., "peek-a-boo" said with a particular intonation by a particular caretaker) that the infant begins to map this chunk onto the same sort of event, often called a "routine" (Peters 1985) or a "format" (Bruner 1975). The child has not analyzed the interior of the particular acoustic chunk and just responds (somewhat like a trained seal) by putting his hands over his eyes. Here the acoustic string is part of the event; the event never occurs without it. The sound-event mapping need not even involve language. For example, a child may become accustomed to seeing a mobile move and hearing its music; when the music stops, so does the mobile.

The maximal role acoustic packaging may play in infants' perception of events is to assist them in fusing the flow of separate events into meaningful macroevents. That is, an acoustic overlay might help infants to see that the subcomponents of a diapering routine, for example, go together and that they are separable from the following "clean-up" event. As a first step in this argument, we should find evidence that language has some effect on infant attention to the environment. Research has shown that infants pay more attention to visual events when they are accompanied by language (Horowitz 1974) and that they play more with an object that has been labeled repeatedly than with one that has not (Baldwin and

Markman 1989). Thus, it is established (at least in a preliminary way) that language (and perhaps other coincident acoustic stimuli) can heighten visual attention. Research would also need to demonstrate that acoustic packages serve an even broader role than that of focusing attention—namely, helping children define the boundaries of an event in the first place. Such a claim calls for language—here in larger chunks like conversations—that overlaps with events. This is partially established (see the discussion of prerequisite 3).

As an example of acoustic packaging, imagine a mother who provides a running narrative while changing her baby's diapers. Diapering consists of a number of separate actions—picking the baby up, undressing the baby, removing the old diaper, and so on. When the mother provides a continuous narrative or a linguistic overlay for this whole event, she may help the child structure or find the boundaries of the event. Here language (or acoustics) may help the child to view many disparate actions as a unit. For some children, throwing the dirty diaper in the bin might be part of the diaper routine. For others, the diaper routine is finished when the clothes are back on and the child is off the changing table; throwing the diaper in the trash represents the beginning of the next event—clean-up.

That the role of prosody, along with other cues such as the infant's repeated participation in the event, helps the child carve up events is speculative at best. Yet it is empirically testable. One could, for example, show an infant a novel multicomponent event such as a basketball game. The event would be accompanied either by a continuous acoustic stimulus (language, music) or by silence. After the child had been repeatedly exposed to this first event, a second event would be superimposed on it, much as in an experiment by Neisser and Becklen (1975) in which two pairs of hands playing a hand-slapping game were superimposed on a basketball scene. If an acoustic overlay helps children to unitize the original event, then children in the acoustic condition should be less likely to notice the hand-slapping game when it appears. In the silent condition, children's attention should be drawn to the hand-slapping game since these children would not have had the help of the acoustic overlay in forming a unit of the original event. To test this claim, the two events would next be separated and viewed in silence in a novelty preference paradigm with the hand-slapping game on one screen and the basketball scene on the other. Infants who were in the acoustic condition should look longer at the hand-slapping game than should those who were in the silent condition because for them, the hand-slapping game is predicted to be more novel. Thus, in this experiment and any number of others, one can put the strong version of acoustic packaging to a test, assessing whether acoustic packaging serves not just as an accompaniment or "attention getter" for the witnessed events, but also as one of many "carving knives" that assist children in making inferences about the components and flow of the events in their environment.

Of course, if the three-phase framework we offer here is to be upheld, research must examine the disconfirmable predictions that phase I offers by examining how language (as compared to, say, music or silence) influences 6- to 9-month-old infants' perception and memory for events. At present, however, little direct evidence exists on how acoustic packaging might work.

Summary of Phase I   Before infants can engage in linguistic analysis and try to understand the mappings between language and events, they must recognize the link between elements of the acoustic stream and events. This prerequisite to language acquisition has, by and large, been presupposed in prior treatments of language acquisition. In phase I, then, infants hear the acoustic aspects of language that accompany events and use them to direct their attention to these events and possibly to "package" or segment them. These acoustically framed units contribute to the infants' *internalization* of information about events, building the foundation for future interpretations.

The phase I child is largely (though not exclusively) a perceptual child looking for correlations between various inputs as a first step in building mental models. At this stage children bring to the task a way of primitively analyzing multiple inputs—from the construction of image-schemas, through perceptual analyses that help them to define animacy and causality, to early social interactions that allow them to participate in and delineate routines, to prosodic analyses that enable them to form acoustic packages from the conversational melodies that they hear. As children selectively attend to aspects of events, people, and sounds, they internalize correlated blocks of input that can later be interpreted. Of course, on-line internalization is not adequate for understanding the roles and relationships that are witnessed in the world. Image-schemas become slowly infused with memory (past experiences), feelings, and desires. The world of phase I "internalization" quickly becomes one of phase II "interpretation."

What mechanism moves the child from phase I to phase II? As a partial answer, we borrow Bloom's (1993) Principle of Discrepancy (quoted above). As the contents of consciousness become different from the data of perception, Bloom argues that infants are motivated to discover more about the grammar of their language so they can express their more complex ideas. In other words, as infants fail in their attempts to communicate their thoughts (see Golinkoff 1983, 1986, 1993), they are presumably encouraged to acquire additional linguistic tools.

In sum, infants' incentive for continued progress in learning language is to enrich and express their mental models. If infants only internalized what they saw, they could never comprehend novel relations between objects, nor could they create and communicate about novel combinations of objects or scenes from their mental world. As infants leave phase I and enter phase II, they have internalized some of the basic units of event structure and of language (even though the motivation for linguistic internalization here was solely acoustic). Their job now becomes one of preliminary linguistic mapping at the level of individual words and grammar.

Phase II: Segmentation and Linguistic Mapping (Approximately 9 to 24 Months)

In phase II, infants move beyond acoustic packaging to linguistic mapping. They also move from a dominant reliance on prosodic cues to a dominant reliance on semantic cues. The key to this phase of development lies in the infant's ability to note redundancy among the prosodic, syntactic, social, and semantic inputs as guides both to units and relations within events and to language structure. For example, in phase I *any* extracted acoustic package (language or music) can map to an aspect of an event. In phase II the child begins to associate particular acoustic packages with particular objects, events, or actions in the world. The products of phase I become inputs for phase II as the child begins to segment these previously extracted acoustic packages and to perform more fine-grained linguistic analysis (Peters 1985). In this phase the child begins to map individual words to their referents (be they actions, objects, or properties of objects and events). By the end of the latter part of this phase (between about 16 to about 24 months), linguistic mappings will occur at the level of *relations* as the child comprehends and produces strings of utterances.

From the start of this phase, children are influenced by the particular language they are learning. As Slobin (1985a) writes:

I propose that OP [Operating Principle]: Functions begin by mapping acoustically salient, uninterpreted speech segments onto scenes as a whole, or onto focused elements of scenes. Using such mappings as an anchor, scenes can gradually be analyzed into those particular notions that are grammaticized in the particular language. (p. 1176)

Slobin (1985a) claims that children first map language onto prototypical transitive activity scenes (as when an animate being acts on an inanimate object). In contrast, Bowerman (1985) and Choi and Bowerman (1991) argue that children approach the language-learning task less rigidly constrained about what they will choose to talk about and even more influenced by the particular language of their environment than Slobin considers them to be. In either event, during phase II the child's task is to map acoustic units into linguistic units and to learn the relationships that map sound to meaning. This occurs through development at many levels—from the word to sentential relations.

Linguistic Mapping: Individual Words   As phase I ends and phase II begins, infants begin to comprehend words. Upon reexamining a study by Benedict (1979), Ingram (1989) noted two important points about early word learning. First, comprehension of lexical items seems to begin about 4 months before production. Second, early words are acquired twice as fast in comprehension as in production (see also Nelson 1973). Benedict (1979) followed early vocabulary acquisition longitudinally and found that according to parental report, by 11 months the 8 children in her sample comprehended 20 words, some of which were embedded in routines (such as "Show me your nose"). Oviatt (1980) similarly reported early comprehension of nouns.

Some researchers (in addition to Slobin (1985a)) have suggested that there may be a set of principles that guide the initial mapping of individual words to their referents. Although outside the scope of this book, this has become an active research area. Suffice it to say that children may approach the word-learning task with some heuristics or principles that can be used in mapping between words and their referents (for reviews, see Clark 1994; Markman 1989; Merriman and Bowman 1989; Golinkoff, Mervis, and Hirsh-Pasek 1994).

To comprehend a sentence, however, infants must go beyond just finding the referents of words and must assign words to open-class or closed-class membership. (Recall that open-class words bear content (e.g., "chair," "red"); closed-class words often indicate grammatical relations (e.g., "with" and "and").) Morgan, Shi, and Allopenna (1995) have argued that these classes may be acoustically distinguishable by the end of phase I. By around 2 years of age (but see Radford 1990), these word classes seem to be identified on linguistic grounds, although items from the closed class are not among the first to appear in production. Evidence that toddlers note closed-class items comes, for example, from the finding that sentence comprehension and sentence memory are adversely affected when closed-class items are omitted or replaced with nonsense words having the same rhythmic properties (Shipley, Smith, and Gleitman 1969; Gerken, Landau, and Remez 1990; Gerken and McIntosh 1993). Data reported in chapter 6 also speak to children's comprehension of closed-class items. In experiments described there, the 24-month-old girls' and the 28-month-old boys' comprehension of intransitive sentences hinged on their appreciation of the closed-class item "with."

Children must also be able to assign open-class words to the correct part-of-speech category; knowing a word's class is central to learning how that word can be expected to function syntactically. Valian (1986) found that by $2\frac{1}{2}$ years of age children use most of the standard form classes in their own speech. Therefore, it is probably the case that this is a phase II achievement manifested first in comprehension. We suggest that during both comprehension and production children have access to a variety of cues in the input that enable them to assign new words to the different word classes—markers that distinguish, say, between open- and closed-class items or between word classes like nouns and verbs. In English, for example, nouns tend to have more syllables than verbs, and nouns receive first-syllable stress (e.g., "REcord" is the noun; "reCORD," the verb) (Kelly 1992; Cutler 1993).

Linguistic Mapping: Beyond Individual Words One could imagine that an infant might know a few words that map to objects or events in the world, but still not realize that *strings* of words, in sentences, also map to events. Recall that in phase I, phrasal and clausal units that cooccur with events are interchangeable from the infant's perspective since mainly acoustic analyses are being conducted. In phase II the child is more attuned to semantics, and to some extent, syntax. When do infants realize that the meaning of a string is greater than the individual meanings of its parts? In other words, when do infants know that strings of words come in "packages" or constituents that form a unit to comment on witnessed events?

In chapter 4 we reported that at least by 13 to 14 months, infants in our study expected strings of words to map to complex events—even though these infants had, on average, fewer than 25 words in their productive vocabularies. We contend that these infants could not have gone beyond individual words to solve the task they faced in that study were a coalition of cues not available for them to exploit.[4] For example, the fact that the stimulus sentences were produced with the exaggerated prosody of infant-directed speech probably helped children recognize the units that the words formed. This ability to recognize that language units map to events in a complex manner may therefore rest on the prior phase of acoustic packaging, when infants discern that elements in the acoustic stream punctuate and highlight different parts of events.

Having learned by 13 or 14 months that strings of words form units (of some type), children are poised to engage in more detailed, clause-internal analyses. As noted in chapter 2, sentences comprise (1) units at a number of levels (e.g., words, phrases, and clauses); (2) relations or ways of arranging these units to express meanings; and (3) hierarchical organization (units at one level, such as words or phrases, build units at a higher level, such as the sentence). Any account of children's sentence comprehension must describe how children become sensitive to the types of units and relations found in sentences.

In sum, to comprehend novel sentences, children must first find the units that compose these sentences. In phase I, infants appear to be sensitive to the acoustic correlates of some syntactic units and may even be able to use acoustic information to distinguish between open- and closed-class words in their language (Morgan, Shi, and Allopenna 1995). By phase II, infants have gone beyond purely acoustic analyses and can recognize individual words and assign them to the correct form class. They also recognize which words form meaningful units that map to specific events in the world.

Finding Sentential Relations   Comprehending sentences involves more than just finding the units that make up the sentence at a number of levels. It also requires that infants note the relations between those units. The development of children's sensitivity to sentential relations has been a controversial topic since the 1970s (see, e.g., Bloom 1970; Bowerman 1973; Braine 1976; Brown 1973; Pinker 1984; Hirsh-Pasek and Golinkoff 1993). Although the experiments on constituent structure presented in chapter 4 begin to address this issue, the word order studies presented in chapter 5 provide an even more pointed example of how the phase II child begins to segment within an acoustic unit and to note grammatically relevant word order relationships. Since we cannot treat young children's sensitivity to all possible sentential relations in any depth here, we will continue to use order relations as our primary example.

Comprehension of Word Order   As noted earlier, word order is one mechanism by which the world's languages convey meaning relations (Greenberg 1963; Comrie 1981). The mental representation that is created for the sentence "Brutus killed Caesar" preserves history; the representation created for the sentence "Caesar killed Brutus" violates it. Given the importance of word order cues to mental model building and to theories of language acquisition (see chapter 5), it is little wonder that questions about the young child's sensitivity to word order have figured prominently in debates regarding syntactic competence.

In the main study reported in chapter 5, infants (mean age 17.5 months), most of whom were producing only single words, demonstrated a significant looking preference for a screen portraying an event that matched the order of the arguments in the linguistic stimulus. However, these results do not determine whether children solve the word order problem by accessing a syntactically based or a semantically based grammatical system. That is, it was not clear whether children were performing a subject-verb-object or an agent-action-patient analysis. Indeed, it is this very ambiguity in the interpretation of the results of experiment 3 that becomes the focus when discussing the phase II child.

Under our theory, the phase II child can comprehend word order relations only when the prosodic, social, semantic, and syntactic systems act in concert. This child, still a bit shaky on syntax, relies on the *redundant* cues available in these domains. "Redundant" is the operative word here, since if any of these systems is disrupted, sentence comprehension will suffer. There is evidence that the phase II child needs to have the "moons in alignment," as it were, to comprehend sentences. For example, Strohner and Nelson (1974) disrupted 36-month-old children's comprehension of active declarative sentences by giving them sentences such as "The mouse chased the elephant." When they gave children toys to act out these sentences, the children made the elephant chase the mouse rather than making the mouse chase the elephant. Children at this age seem to place more weight on the semantic system than on syntax, relying on event probability to act out such sentences.

Comprehension of Passive Sentences Children's fragile knowledge of syntax is also revealed in the comprehension of what are called reversible passive sentences. A reversible sentence is one in which either what is named by the word that is the subject or what is named by the word that is the object could in theory serve as the agent of the action. Thus, the sentence "The dog chased the cat" is reversible because either of the animals could serve the thematic role of agent in a sentence involving chasing: cats are as likely to chase dogs as dogs are to chase cats. Such sentences are to be distinguished from sentences like "John ate a banana," which are nonreversible—it is not plausible for the banana to eat John.

Children hearing nonreversible passive sentences such as "The banana was eaten by John" tend to interpret them correctly, giving the false impression that they understand the passive construction. Their weakness can be exposed by asking them to interpret a reversible passive like "The cat was chased by the dog." Indeed, many researchers have used just such tasks and have discovered that when semantic probability is equal, children show little evidence of understanding the passive construction. Given a "chasing" sentence, children appear to assume that the first creature mentioned is the chaser and the second creature mentioned is the chased (e.g., Bever 1970; Strohner and Nelson 1974). For the phase II English-speaking child, word order is a powerful cue, whereas other grammatical elements are often downplayed or ignored.

Knowledge of the passive can thus be used to reveal the fragility of syntactic processing in the phase II child. In the face of ambiguous or conflicting information, the phase II child's syntactic system appears to break down. In this framework, children move from a period (phase II) of relying heavily on redundant semantic, prosodic, and social information to a period (phase III) in which they can comprehend sentences using syntactic structures in the face of conflicting cues from these other systems. That is, in phase II the comprehension system requires support from multiple sources of input: from a coalition of cues. The phase II child shows "fragile" rather than "resilient" comprehension. By phase III, the child's syntactic knowledge is sufficiently robust that comprehension can occur even when the child is presented with conflicting information from different sources in the input.

Summary of Phase II Development in phase II involves the further segmentation of the speech stream, the preliminary mapping of speech to the child's representation of nonlinguistic events, the noting of correlations that are useful for identifying the parts of speech, and the use of relatively regular and redundant mappings between prosodic, semantic, and syntactic units to comprehend words and sentences.

With respect to what inputs drive the system forward, we believe that the child begins the task of comprehending sentences in phase II in a relatively benevolent world where the semantic, prosodic, and syntactic systems are more often in alignment in the input than not. As Bloom (1973) writes:

> Children's utterances are redundant with respect to the context in which they occur.... [M]others' speech to children is no less redundant, and indeed, language learning probably depends on the fact that mothers will not typically discuss finances or an argument with a friend when they talk to their children. (p. 302)

Indeed, two studies found that children whose mothers provided them with input redundant with the nonlinguistic context had more extensive language than children whose mothers did not describe the available context as often (Harris et al. 1986; Harris et al. 1988; Menyuk, Liebergott, and Schultz 1995). However, although children can exploit redundancy among language systems successfully as a first resort, such a strategy is doomed to failure in the long run. Syntax would not be required if it were merely a system that was redundant with acoustics and semantics. Thus, semantics and acoustics can provide only a toehold (or bootstrap) for linguistic mastery. The phase II child does not realize the full computational power of the grammar for mental model building. Note that the operative phrase here is "full computational power." We are not suggesting that the child has no syntax in phase II. Evidence for early sensitivity to syntax has been reported here as well as in the work of Bloom (1990) and others. Rather, we claim that in the face of conflicting input between syntax and other systems, syntax will not win out and errors of interpretation will be made: when redundant cues are not available, the child in phase II will rely on semantics over syntax.

What mechanism propels the child forward, and what prompts the child in phase II to abandon the strong assumption that syntax, semantics, prosody, and aspects of the social scene map redundantly to each other? To answer these questions, we again turn to the view that language is acquired in service to mental model building. Increasingly complex mental representations motivate the child to acquire a more syntactically complex grammar (Bloom 1993). The shift to phase III in our model is prompted by Bloom's (1993) Principle of Elaboration:

The consequence of learning more about the world is that the contents represented in consciousness have become increasingly elaborated. The more elements and relations between them in these representations, the more the child will need to know of the words and structures of language to express them [and comprehend them].... Two-year-olds progress from saying simple sentences, which express a single proposition, to acquiring the syntax of complex sentences, which require a child to hold in mind two propositions and the relation between them.... [T]o keep up with such changes in mental meanings, a child's knowledge of semantics and syntax must necessarily change. (pp. 29–30)

Several concurrent developments force children to question the assumption that syntax is redundant with other systems like prosody, context, and semantics. First, children hear input that is inconsistent with the redundancy assumption; for example, English passive sentences, although not that frequent in the input, mention the patient of the action in what is typically the subject position. Unless children abandon the redundancy assumption, they will fail to reconcile what they interpret with what is being communicated. They also need grammatical tools for going beyond single-clause analyses so that they can compute relations between clauses. To comprehend a sentence describing an event that they did not witness, such as "Before he left, Big Bird ate the cookie," children must be sensitive to the rules for coreference within and across clauses. Failure to interpret sentences correctly will hinder children's construction of veridical mental models. Second, as children represent more complex propositions about which they wish to communicate, they need greater grammatical capacity to do so (this is Bloom's (1993) Principle of Elaboration, cited earlier). When children are impelled to learn more grammar, they enter phase III.

Phase III: Complex Syntactic Analysis (Beginning at Approximately 24 Months)

By the time they enter phase III, children have come a long way. In phase I, children are able to isolate the acoustic correlates of various linguistic units; they also use the acoustic stream to package events in the world and note the correlations between language and events prerequisite to linguistic mapping. In *phase II*, children discover many important principles about how language works. They master linguistic mapping at the level of the individual word, abstract a set of lexical principles for how these mappings work, and can categorize words into word classes. They also note that language maps onto events in regular, language-specific ways (Slobin 1985a; Bowerman 1985; Choi and Bowerman 1991).

Then children enter phase III. At this point they appear to be working on complex sentential relations that are a degree of abstraction removed from what is witnessed. Children cannot hope to rely on redundancies between social factors, prosody, environmental context, semantics, and syntax to save the day in comprehending sentences whose internal properties alone determine their interpretation. For children to be able to comprehend these more complex sentences, their knowledge of language must ratchet up a notch; they must become aware of interclausal relations within the sentence. It is thus in phase III that children come to appreciate, for example, the grammatical relations that hold in passive constructions, the semantic implications of a verb's subcategorization frames, and the hierarchical relations in what is referred to as binding theory. Each will be briefly reviewed below.

Passive As stated earlier, the passive is an important construction to assess since it is likely that children who can comprehend the passive in reversible sentences are using a syntactic grammar, as opposed to a semantic one. This is because passive sentences violate the agent-action-patient sequence of the English subject-verb-object pattern. To comprehend reversible passive sentences, the child must be operating with the *syntactic* relations of subject and object. Comprehension of the passive also requires that the child notice and understand the function of the closed-class word "by" (as in "The dog is being chased by the girl") as well as closed class inflectional morphology (the ending "-ed" on "chased"). Since early speech is notorious for the absence of closed-class items (Brown 1973), and since theories of adult parsing (e.g., Wanner and Maratsos 1978; Marcus 1980) require exploitation of the closed class, comprehension of the passive takes on great interest.

Linguists in the generative tradition have offered two general accounts of the passive. Under one account (Chomsky 1957, 1965), the passive was created by a transformation that moved the logical object to what was ordinarily the logical subject's position. In addition, a past-participial ending was added to the verb, an auxiliary verb was inserted, and the "by" phrase was introduced. On the derivational complexity theory of sentence processing (see Hayes 1970), constructions like the passive whose creation involved transformations should be more difficult to comprehend than constructions (like the active declarative) whose creation did not involve transformations. This prediction received ample confirmation (e.g., Bever 1970; Strohner and Nelson 1974; Beilin 1975) in studies of children's comprehension of reversible passive versus reversible active sentences.

Under the Government-Binding analysis (Chomsky 1981; Jaeggli 1986), in passives a coindexed trace of the object NP remains after that NP is moved to subject position. The movement and the resulting "argument chain" (Allison$_i$, e$_i$) are shown in (1).

(1) a. Josh chased Allison.

   b. Allison$_i$ was chased e$_i$ by Josh.

The passive morpheme (here realized as "ed") absorbs the external theta role, which can be assigned to the oblique object ("Josh"). The subject position (occupied by "Allison") now receives nominative case. On this view, because of the movement and the case changes, the passive should also be a difficult construction to acquire. Indeed, it emerges in English-speaking children's sentences around late age 3 (Bowerman 1979).

Regardless of which theory is used to describe passive sentences, it is clear that if children are to interpret this structure correctly, they must go beyond expecting prototypical active sentences where the first-mentioned noun is always the agent (Slobin and Bever 1982). That is, to understand the passive, children must be budding grammarians who note structural dependencies within clauses, detect closed-class markers like the "by" phrase, and understand the significance of this marker. Research with the passive construction has proven useful not only in illuminating just when children detect grammatical features in the input, but also in highlighting how semantic variables constrain the application of the passive. Early on, semantic variables seem to control interpretation of passive sentences (in phase II); this explains some of the misinterpretations noted by Strohner and Nelson (1974). By phase III, the child, equipped with an understanding of the significance of the grammatical markers, can interpret these sentences correctly.

Comprehension of the Semantic Implications of Subcategorization Frames
The explanation offered for interpretation of the passive data carries over to interpretation of the subcategorization data presented in chapter 6. Analogous to the phase II child who interprets reversible passives as actives, the child who does not know the significance of the grammatical marker "with" will err by assuming that the sentences "Cookie Monster turns *with* Big Bird" and "Cookie Monster turns Big Bird" are the same. Given the account of burgeoning grammatical competence offered here,

we would expect that phase II children would interpret the first sentence incorrectly—often ignoring "with" and assuming that the order of the noun arguments rules the day. In experiment 7 (chapter 6), we found that 24-month-old boys indeed appeared to ignore "with," apparently interpreting the intransitive sentence as though it were transitive (i.e., "Cookie Monster turns Big Bird"). By contrast, the 24-month-old girls and the 28-month-old boys did detect and use "with" to derive an intransitive interpretation.

Comprehension of Binding Principles   Examination of the constructs found in binding theory provides a final example showing that phase III children have internalized the fact that language has a complex, syntactic structure.

Binding, as it is defined by linguists, is a key concept for the complex sentence analysis performed in phase III. Because it is so central to theories of grammar and serves as a diagnostic that children are performing syntactic (as opposed to semantic) analyses, we will digress briefly to explain it and to point out its relevance to phase III model building.

Binding theory, proposed by Chomsky (1981), deals with restrictions on the coreference between elements such as pronouns and anaphors and the traces left by movement. Thus, in order to understand binding, children must know both about *movement* (as with passive sentences) and about *relationships within the hierarchical structure of sentences*.

One case covered by the binding theory is shown in (2).

(2) After Josh$_i$ arrived, Benjie hugged him$_i$.

In sentence (2) the pronoun "him" refers to Josh; this coreference is indicated by the matching subscripts on "him" and "Josh." "Him" can also refer to an as yet unnamed person, as in (3), where the nonmatching subscripts indicate noncoreference.

(3) After Josh$_i$ arrived, Benjie hugged him$_j$.

As we will show, the binding theory rules out a third possible interpretation, on which "Benjie" and "him" corefer (where * indicates ungrammaticality).

(4) *After Josh arrived, Benjie$_i$ hugged him$_i$.

Binding theory also covers cases like (5).

(5) After Josh arrived, Benjie$_i$ hugged himself$_i$.

Here the only legitimate interpretation is the one indicated by the matching subscripts—namely, "himself" refers to Benjie. Binding theory again rules out the other possible interpretation, on which "Josh" and "himself" corefer.

(6) *After Josh$_i$ arrived, Benjie hugged himself$_i$.

Interpretations (4) and (6) are ruled out because of a hierarchical-structure constraint on the interpretation of pronouns.

Briefly, in sentence (2) "him" can refer only to Josh, not to Benjie, because in the tree structure representation of the sentence (or phrase marker), "Josh" bears no particular structural relationship to "him" (see figure 7.1). On the other hand, "Benjie" is higher in the tree than "him," and these lexical items share a common mother node (the S node). That is, "Benjie" and "him" are in a relation known as "c-command" (short

Tree 1: Principle A

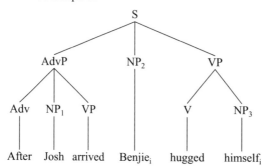

Tree 2: Principle B

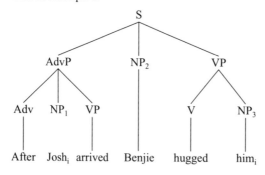

Figure 7.1
Sample trees for sentences exemplifying Principles A and B of the binding theory

for constituent-command): a pronoun may not corefer with a noun that is structurally superior to (or c-commands) it. (Of course, "him" may refer outside the sentence altogether to some third male person who is present in the context, as in (3).)

The situation we have just described is captured by one of the binding principles (Principle B). Binding theory reduces to three principles, of which we will focus on the first two.

Principle A: An anaphor must be bound in its local domain.

Principle B: A pronominal must be free in its local domain.

Principle C: An R-expression must be free.

Anaphors are reflexive words like "himself" or "themselves"; pronouns are words like "he" and "her"; and R-expressions are referring expressions like "John" or noun phrases like "the state government." A domain is the space in which the principles operate, namely, the S (sentence) node immediately above the pronoun or anaphor. To say that an element is "bound" means that it is coindexed with (has the same subscript as) another element in the sentence. Binding can occur only between elements that are at the same height or higher in the sentence tree. That is, binding can occur only when one element c-commands another element.

What do children around the world understand of these sentence-internal relationships? In general, the research so far has suggested that Principle A is understood earlier than Principle B (see Atkinson 1992; Lust, Hermon, and Kornfilt 1994). In some studies children as young as 3 years show sensitivity to the c-commanding relation of reflexives (Deutsch, Koster, and Koster 1986; Jakubowicz 1984; Wexler and Chien 1985; Chien and Wexler 1987; Grimshaw and Rosen 1990; Kaufman 1994). That is, children appear to bind the reflexive to the noun phrase that c-commands it (see figure 7.1, tree 1). Children will do this even when there are other potential referents for the reflexive in the same sentence that are physically closer to the reflexive (as in "The brother of *Piet* washes *himself*"). Such performance suggests that children are not conducting a simple linear analysis of the sentence. Instead, they appear to be sensitive to the hierarchical relations that encode the sentence's meaning relations.

Much more can be said about the nature of the syntactic analysis the child is undertaking and about research in binding theory. Suffice it to say, however, that studies have demonstrated that by 3 to 5 years of age, children show evidence of comprehending complex syntactic relationships within the language that they hear. Children who can achieve this are surely little linguists who have resilient rather than fragile reliance on the internal, hierarchical syntactic structure of the sentence.

To further explore children's sensitivity to binding theory in comprehension, Hirsh-Pasek et al. (1995) presented (in the intermodal preferential looking paradigm) the same videotapes that were used in the subcategorization experiments reported in chapter 6. Children were shown either an event in which Cookie Monster made Big Bird turn, or an event in which Cookie Monster and Big Bird turned in synchrony together. Children heard either "Oh, look! Cookie Monster is turning him" (Principle B) or "Cookie Monster turns himself" (Principle A). Preliminary results suggest that children just around 3 years of age reliably distinguish between these sentences and watch the matching screen. These children thus seem to be able to attend to the relations that differentially govern the binding of anaphors and pronouns.

Summary of Phase III   Recapitulating the story thus far, then, the phase II child had discovered linguistic units in the input (not just acoustic units as had the phase I child) and was able roughly to map those units onto event structure. Whether by using semantic or syntactic rules, the nascent linguist of phase II could comprehend strings of words. This child, however, was at a disadvantage when the linguistic units did not correspond one to one with the structure of the event (as in agent-action-patient word order in English) and when events not present in the immediate context were described. For example, passive sentences (patient-action-agent word order) or sentence frames with "with" markers that violate standard English word order (e.g., "Big Bird squatted with Cookie Monster," where both actors are agents) were misinterpreted.

In contrast to the phase II child, the phase III child recognizes that sentential relations are mapped in even more complex fashion to events (both witnessed and not witnessed) and are consistently governed by structure-dependent rules. The child now recognizes that sentences that mimic active declaratives in their structure need not be active declaratives. Given a set of linguistic rules, and an appreciation of function words such as "with," children can go beyond surface similarities to analyze the actual structure of sentences.

In phase III, children have gone well beyond assumptions about redundant mappings between language and events to deeper insights about the grammar. These children appreciate that canonical word order in the language(s) they are learning does not signal event relationships in the passive and in certain subcategorization frames and that language-internal structure determines coreference in binding constructions. These children are on the threshold of discourse analysis, which requires the comprehension of cross-clausal syntactic relations. They can now rely on syntactic information to build their mental models and to glean sophisticated interpretations from language input.

General Summary and Commentary: The Coalition-of-Cues Model of Language Comprehension

Data from comprehension experiments have provided information about the process of language acquisition that cannot be gained from an exclusive focus on language production. With the case secure for the accessibility and utility of data from language comprehension, we tackled the question, "What is language comprehension?" Inspired by the work of Gernsbacher (1988, 1990) and Bloom (1974, 1993), we introduced the rudiments of a new framework for thinking about language comprehension; namely, as a way to use language in the service of building mental representations of the world. One premise of this view, consonant with Bloom's (1993, 1994) theoretical treatment of early language, is that children are driven to build mental models of the events and relations they observe (or imagine) in their world.

On this account, children go through three phrases in the development of language comprehension. Figure 7.2 depicts the coalition model of comprehension and how different cues are differentially weighted in the three phases. In phase I, children have access to input from the entire coalition of cues but are biased to focus on the cues from *prosody*. They use the acoustic properties of language to accomplish two purposes: to find the acoustic correlates of the units of language and to *internalize* events. This phase is characterized by the phenomena of *extraction* and *acoustic packaging*; acoustic events are extracted and come to be linked with environmental events. At this point the child can be likened to a filmmaker using the technique of cinema verité.

In phase II, children begin to analyze the units they have extracted and to engage in *linguistic mapping*, with a bias toward *semantic* analysis (see figure 7.2). Here children find clause-internal propositions and map language onto objects, actions, and events. Thus, in this phase children are beginning to use language not just for the internalization of their mental

A: Phase 1

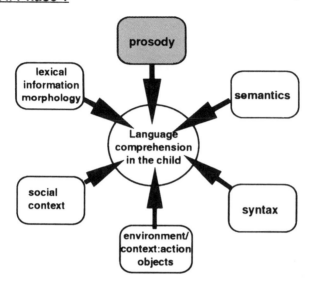

B: Phase 2

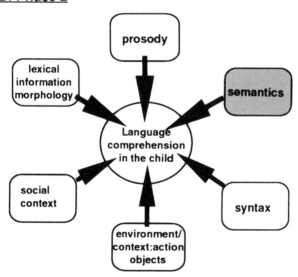

Figure 7.2
A coalition model of language comprehension. Different cues are differentially weighted (as indicated by shading) during the course of development.

C: Phase 3

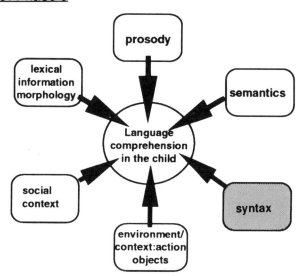

Figure 7.2 (contd.)

models but for perspective or *interpretation* as well. Phase II children already have the ability to parse the speech signal into phrasal and clausal units and to carve the observed world into event sequences. These children rely heavily (though not exclusively) on redundant cues from the coalition as they learn the linguistic tools that will eventually enable them to interpret the world from the perspective of the skilled cinematographer. When the cues in the coalition conflict, phase II children resolve the conflict by relying on semantic probability.

Finally, in phase III, children learn to comprehend and produce language to represent more complex events that they may not have even witnessed, as well as multipropositional cross-clause constructions. Here, as figure 7.2 shows, children are biased to rely on *syntactic* cues (although other aspects of the coalition still influence their interpretation of what they hear). With increased capacity to hold more than one event in mind, they are motivated to learn about specific linguistic properties in their language—properties that expand their power to express and comprehend. Further, by phase III, children are constructing complex meanings from even longer stretches of text, as they comprehend stories and conversations that often presuppose a great deal of knowledge, knowledge partly gained from the continual refinement of the mental models constructed through language.

The coalition model of language comprehension developed here is built upon information of very different types—from sounds, social cues, contextual analyses, and syntax. Yet each of these sources of information represents a coalition of cues in itself. Thus, even the complex model offered here is but the tip of the iceberg. That another coalition of cues is nested within each domain in the coalition has been discussed by Morgan, Shi, and Allopenna (1995) and by Hirsh-Pasek, Tucker, and Golinkoff (1995) for the prosodic domain. In discussing how infants may assign words to open- or closed-class membership, Morgan, Shi, and Allopenna describe how a constellation of cues in the way words in these categories are pronounced allows accurate assignment of the words in over 90% of the cases. When each cue (e.g., reduced vowels in initial syllables of function words; lower stress on function words) is used alone to assign a word to category membership, accurate assignment is not as high. As Morgan, Shi, and Allopenna write:

None of the individual cues we measured has particularly high validity with respect to this distinction [open- vs. closed-class word assignment]; taken together, however, these cues suffice in principle to allow a naive learner lacking any feedback to assign words to these rudimentary categories with very high accuracy. (p. 20 ms.)

A similar argument can be made for all other domains in the coalition. Thus, full discussion of a coalition model of comprehension would require a description of these microsystems in addition to the macrosystem analysis provided here.

A model that presupposes that children rely on a coalition of cues to discover language structure requires a sophisticated learner. This learner must be able to use selected cues in combination, cues that are weighted differentially throughout development. On the surface this may appear to be a tall order for the young child. However, there exists some evidence— both from linguistic development and from the formation of visual categories—to suggest that infants can indeed rely upon correlated cues (Younger and Cohen 1983, 1986; Morgan and Saffran, in press). In section 7.3 we suggest strategies for examining which cues children actually use and how each cue is weighted across development.

Even though a complete description of the coalition view will require considerably more research, this view already provides preliminary answers to the three questions first raised in chapter 2. Regarding what children bring to the language-learning task, we believe (as has been apparent throughout) that even phase I infants are capable and highly selective learners. Within the language domain, infants are biased to attend to prosodic information and to find mappings at the acoustic level between language and cooccurring events. They also bring a burgeoning capability to analyze the world's events, first on image-schematic lines and later as propositions. Finally, they are primed to participate in various social interactions (Messer 1994), interactions that will help them to appreciate the cultural significance of the linguistic forms they will learn in phase II.

With respect to the mechanisms used in language learning, our model deals chiefly with the mechanisms that motivate the transition between the phases. As the mechanism that causes children to move from phase I to phase II, we appeal to Bloom's Principle of Discrepancy; as the mechanism that causes them to move from phase II to phase III, we appeal to her Principle of Elaboration. However, we have suggested that the mechanism for progress within each phase is guided distributional analysis. That is, first the child is primed to selectively attend to certain information *within* each domain that forms the coalition (e.g., prosody, syntax). Second, the child mines these selected inputs *across* domains to construct an interpretation of the linguistic stream and to build mental models. The internalization that characterizes phase I allows the infant to construct the foundation upon which to build mental models of the sort Fauconnier (1985), Bloom (1994), and Johnson-Laird (1983) describe, models that enable individuals to make inferences and predictions (i.e., to carry out what we have called "interpretation"). In most of this book we have concentrated on young children's sensitivity to information in the syntactic domain. Examining sensitivities within domains is the first step toward fleshing out the guided distributional analyses that operate across domains.

The question of what inputs drive the system forward has been answered by positing the existence of a coalition of cues. These cues are *available* to the child at all times; however, they are not equally *accessible* to the child at different points in development. Figure 7.2 (and the accompanying discussion) tells this story.

In sum, this coalition model of language comprehension has much in common with prior discussions of development from a rationalist-constructivist perspective (Gelman 1991). As Karmiloff-Smith (1992) has written:

The skeletal outline [of the mind] involves attention biases toward particular inputs and a certain number of principled predispositions constraining the computation of those inputs. (p. 15)

However, in emphasizing the role of learning, she goes on to say:

[T]he flourishing new domain of cognitive science needs to go beyond the traditional nativist-empiricist dichotomy that permeates much of the field, in favor of an epistemology that embraces both innate predispositions and constructivism. (p. 193)

The framework we have presented here attempts to meet this challenge. We have argued that although children are primed to selectively attend to certain kinds of inputs, language comprehension does not come for free. Children must learn to exploit the correlations that exist across (as well as within) domains to construct linguistic interpretations.

This framework for considering language comprehension raises many more questions than it answers. Continuing in the present spirit of speculation, we next address two of these questions: (1) why should comprehension precede production? and (2) how can we test this framework?

7.2 Why Should Comprehension Precede Production?

The relationship between comprehension and production has long been a topic of debate. There are many reasons to predict that comprehension should precede production. Some of the oft-cited rationales for this prediction are that (1) comprehension involves more recognition memory than recall memory and thus should be easier for the child; (2) comprehension involves relating what is said to an existing schema whereas production involves constructing a schema (Piaget and Inhelder 1971); (3) in language comprehension the input is organized for the listener whereas in production the language must be organized and assembled by the speaker (Golinkoff and Hirsh-Pasek 1995); and (4) the context is more supportive and relevant for the comprehender than it is for the speaker (Bloom 1974). Summing across these various rationales, Bloom (1974) writes:

The memory load for saying a sentence is presumably greater than for understanding, inasmuch as the individual needs to recall the necessary words and their connections to say them, but these linguistic facts are immediately available to him when he hears them spoken by someone else. (p. 300)

Despite the intuition that comprehension ought to appear before production, the literature provides a conflicting picture of the evidence. Some studies demonstrate that comprehension precedes production (Lovell and Dixon 1967). Others find that comprehension occurs contemporaneously with production (Bloom 1973). Still others argue that the comprehension of syntactic structures follows the production of those structures (Chapman and Miller 1975; Strohner and Nelson 1974); these investigators suggest that although children may understand isolated sentences in the language that contain a particular structure, they do not comprehend the language rule or principle in a general sense until after they have used it.

The framework suggested in this chapter provides a principled way to interpret these conflicting and often counterintuitive claims. According to the present model, the comprehension of any particular linguistic structure lies on a continuum. At one end of the continuum (phase II), comprehension of the structure is *fragile*. It will only be evidenced in tasks in which children can use the coalition of redundant language cues to support their immature knowledge of linguistic structure. If the coalition of input sources is fragmented, comprehension will be disrupted. At the other end of the continuum (phase III), comprehension is *resilient* and will be evidenced even in the face of competing cues. When fragile comprehension is revealed, it will occur in advance of production. When only resilient comprehension is tested, then comprehension and production might occur more contemporaneously.

An example of the distinction between fragile and resilient comprehension is seen in a study by Fernald, McRoberts, and Herrera (in press) with 15-month-olds. Using an adaptation of the intermodal preferential looking paradigm, these authors found that children's comprehension of known words "disappeared" when the words were presented in adult-directed speech, although comprehension was evidenced when the words were presented in infant-directed speech. The fact that comprehension was lost under adult-directed prosody shows that these young word learners had only fragile knowledge of these words. These findings further suggest that at least early in phase II, prosody is a major player in the coalition of cues that allows children to reveal their fragile comprehension. Older infants, however, identified these words whether they were presented in infant-directed or adult-directed speech. These older children were resilient comprehenders and needed no extra support from the language input to assist them in the identification task. An experiment by

Golinkoff et al. (1992), also conducted in the intermodal preferential looking paradigm, offers similar evidence for the learning of novel words. When 21-month-old children were taught novel nouns paired with unfamiliar objects, their comprehension of these words was more compelling in the infant-directed-speech condition than in the adult-directed-speech condition. Furthermore, significantly more children were lost as subjects in the adult-directed than in the infant-directed condition, indicating that —at least for these English-speaking children—the prosodic modifications of infant-directed speech are a crucial part of the coalition of cues. In addition, Golinkoff and Alioto (in press) have shown that even adults utilize infant-directed prosody in learning novel words in a nonnative language.

A final example of fragile versus resilient comprehension comes from an experiment by Golinkoff and Markessini (1980). This example turns on how comprehension can be disrupted when linguistic stimuli describe improbable events. These researchers were interested in the comprehension of possessive phrases such as "Mommy's sock." When Golinkoff and Markessini presented children with sentences that conflicted with semantically probable sentences from the child's vantage point such as "Point to the baby's mommy," children refused to respond. Even fragile comprehension was not evident. In contrast, sentences that did not fragment the coalition and were probable from the child's viewpoint, such as "Point to the mommy's baby," were comprehended by children who were not yet using two-word speech. Here, fragile comprehension, at the cutting edge of what the child is capable of, was revealed. Sentences like "Point to the baby's mommy" put word order into conflict with real-world knowledge, disrupting the natural coalition of language input sources (see also Strohner and Nelson 1974; Chapman and Kohn 1978).

Of what consequence is the distinction between fragile and resilient knowledge for the comprehension-production debate? In fact, it helps to explain the very source of this debate. Competing views of the relationship between comprehension and production have arisen for two reasons. The first reason is that the properties of the particular language structure under examination may lend themselves *differentially* to fragile versus resilient comprehension. Any syntactic form in which the thematic roles violate the canonical order that children expect in their language should prove more difficult to comprehend (e.g., passives). Further, any syntactic form that requires complex sentential analysis (e.g., analyses of proforms such as "he" and anaphors such as "himself") should require resilient comprehension. Finally, any language form in which the child is unable to recover thematic roles from the situation (e.g., "Daddy will be home for dinner tonight") mandates resilient comprehension. If extralinguistic sources of information that buttress the interpretation of such forms are absent, comprehension should not appear in advance of production. Thus, comprehension of the passive, of subcategorization frames of the sort addressed in experiment 7 in chapter 6, and of the binding principles should not appear far in advance of the child's use of these forms. These language forms require resilient comprehension by their very nature.

The second potential reason for the complex relationship between comprehension and production is that various methods of testing language comprehension may differentially tap fragile or resilient language comprehension. Methods like the intermodal preferential looking paradigm, for example, require only a looking response and keep the coalition of language input largely intact. These methods reveal fragile, phase II language comprehension, with comprehension generally occurring in advance of production. In contrast, methods that put members of the coalition into conflict, perhaps by not providing appropriate discourse contexts (e.g., Grimshaw and Rosen 1990), by presenting semantically improbable sentences (e.g., Golinkoff and Markessini 1980), or by requiring metalinguistic sentence judgments (Kaufman 1994), tap only resilient, phase III language comprehension. These methods ought to provide data that show production either in tandem with or in advance of comprehension.

This view of comprehension, then, makes two testable predictions, which we will discuss in turn. First, comprehension should precede production for those syntactic structures that, relatively speaking, "coincide" with redundant cues in the input (i.e., in the environmental context, prosody, etc.) and require relatively less sentence-internal analysis. Second, comprehension should be found in advance of production only when assessment methods are used that permit the child to capitalize on the correlated cues in the input. An extremely idealized version of this argument is presented in figure 7.3. The vertical axis represents the complexity of a particular syntactic structure (from high to low),[5] whereas the horizontal axis represents the degree to which a comprehension assessment method provides the child with support by not fragmenting the natural coalition of cues that often accompany sentences directed at young children.

We argued earlier that certain syntactic structures, like the passive in English, violate English speakers' expectations. As children acquire

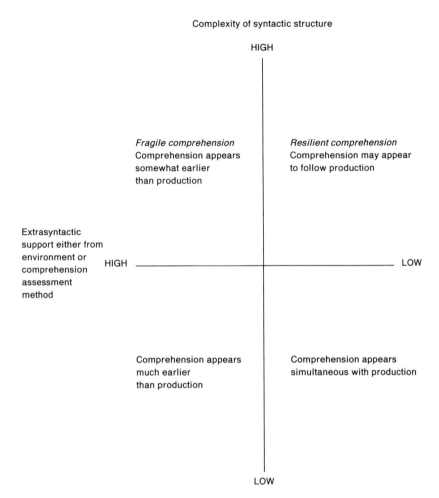

Complexity of syntactic structure

HIGH

Fragile comprehension
Comprehension appears
somewhat earlier
than production

Resilient comprehension
Comprehension may appear
to follow production

Extrasyntactic
support either from
environment or
comprehension
assessment
method

HIGH

LOW

Comprehension appears
much earlier
than production

Comprehension appears
simultaneous with production

LOW

Figure 7.3
An idealized representation of the relationship between comprehension and production. The two variables shown interacting are the complexity of syntactic
structures and the amount of support (in terms of preserving the coalition of cues)
provided by the assessment method.

experience with English input, they notice a strong tendency for the first-mentioned noun to play the role of the agent (Bever 1970). In tests of comprehension of the passive, the child hears sentences whose cues are *not* in alignment. For phase II children, the consequences of this lack of alignment are evident when they misinterpret passive sentences; these children assume an alignment where there is none and treat the passive sentence as though it were a sentence in the active voice (e.g., the 24-month-old boys' misinterpreting intransitive "with" sentences as though they were transitive sentences; recall experiment 7 in chapter 6).

To fully investigate the role that language structure per se plays in the relationship between comprehension and production, researchers will need to compare language structures that have little extrasyntactic support in the form of semantic or prosodic cues with structures—such as canonical word order—that offer a great deal of potential support. If the prediction holds, then those structures that afford relatively more extra-syntactic support (the left half of figure 7.3) should appear to be comprehended earlier than those that do not (the right half of figure 7.3). Further, if these structures are examined in contexts in which children can capitalize on the coalition of sources in the input, then comprehension should appear well in advance of production for these forms (the bottom left-hand quadrant of figure 7.3). On the other hand, comprehension can appear to come *after* production, when a syntactic structure that requires sensitivity to complex structure is assessed with a method that makes many performance demands (such as truth-value judgments in binding tasks; see Grimshaw and Rosen 1990). By systematically varying the supports available to the child, researchers can begin to empirically examine the effect of each input source on comprehension and the potentially shifting weights that each input source is afforded over time.

In sum, the comprehension framework provided in section 7.1 sheds light on the comprehension/production debate. The comprehension of any particular structure develops from a more fragile state to a more resilient state (phase II to phase III). Those structures that are supported by redundant cues from the extrasyntactic context will be comprehended earlier than they will be produced. Further, those methods that test the child for knowledge of a structure without disrupting the natural ecology of the coalition of input sources are more likely to unveil precocious comprehension than those methods that do not preserve the coalition. In section 7.3 we suggest some ways in which the framework could be empirically validated.

7.3   Empirical Validation of the Comprehension Framework

Our incipient model of comprehension answers the question of what inputs drive the system forward by asserting that sentence comprehension is the *product* of the child's attempt to weave together information from a coalition of sources. That is, to construct a mental representation of the world, children must use information from perception, social interaction, semantic cues, the prosodic envelope in which sentences are spoken, and syntax. Different sources of information are prominent in different phases of the comprehension model. This approach leads to a number of obvious questions regarding the process of language comprehension and its development. What information in the sentence and the world do young children integrate to construct their mental models? For example, what are young children sensitive to in the various cooccurring inputs? How does the child weigh the various sources of information that are concurrent (and apparently often redundant) with language to form a mental representation? That is, what processes mediate guided distributional learning? How does the child then abstract the units and rules of language and learn how to map them onto representations of objects, actions, and events; and how do these mappings change with development?

These are empirical questions. One of the first challenges, for example, is to determine which sources of input are being used by children in different developmental periods. Rephrasing this question, we may ask, "What aspects of language and extralinguistic input are young children sensitive to at any given time?" The comprehension framework presented above makes clear predictions. Children will be sensitive first to properties of acoustic input (phase I and beginning phase II), then to a coalition of input sources (phase II) that includes social support and semantic, prosodic, and syntactic input (with a bias toward semantic input), and only later to features of the input that are predominantly syntactic (phase III).

Three types of experiments can be used to assess these claims, that is, to investigate the types of input that children use and their relative weighting. In the first type of experiment, *subtractive* studies, sources of input information are systematically subtracted from the natural coalition of cues to see which manipulations disrupt natural word or sentence comprehension. For example, if acoustic packaging of sentential units is paramount in phases I and II, then presenting words or sentences in adult-directed rather than infant-directed speech should hinder comprehension (see

Fernald, McRoberts, and Herrera, in press; Golinkoff et al. 1992). The partial elimination of prosody through the use of monotone might even disrupt the phase II child, depending on the complexity of the linguistic structure being investigated.

With respect to phase III, we argued that children in this phase can rely on syntactic cues to derive meaning even without the exaggerated prosody of infant-directed speech and without a high degree of semantic probability. Thus, the phase III child should function fairly well in a subtractive experiment where aspects of the coalition are systematically removed.

In *additive* studies, the inverse of subtractive studies, minimal cues are presented first, and new cues are added to the coalition until comprehension is achieved. For example, children might hear a sample of adult-directed speech that has been filtered so that only acoustic information is present. After examining what children understand in this condition, the filter might be removed and comprehension further assessed. Other sources of input (e.g., infant-directed prosody, situational cues) would then be systematically added, to assess their impact on comprehension.

In *conflict* studies, two sources of input are put into conflict to see which is considered more dominant for comprehension. The studies that tested comprehension of passive sentences by phase II children provide an excellent example. At a certain point in development, when semantic probability is put into conflict with syntactic cues, semantic probability rules the day. Eventually, however, as Strohner and Nelson (1974) found, children come to be able to rely on the syntax of the sentence. Similarly, in assessing phase II, we claimed that all the sources of input would have to be "in alignment" for comprehension of a fragile structure to be revealed. If comprehension of a structure is "lost" as input sources are systematically put into conflict, then there is some support for the claim that the sources of the coalition have to be in alignment for comprehension to occur.

Each of these methodological approaches—subtractive, additive, and conflict—allows researchers to examine the sources of information that children are marshaling to comprehend language input in a particular context and at a particular time in development. Studies of this sort can also help researchers to chart the shift from fragile to resilient knowledge of language structures and to examine which structures will be inherently more difficult to master within a particular language. To be most informative, however, these methods should be used in the context of longitudinal studies. Only by examining how the coalition of sources contributes to the interpretation of language across time can researchers examine the impact of one source of input over the others throughout the course of language acquisition.

Studies of this nature can also help in developing a more complete answer to the question of mechanism. If infants rely on different cues in the coalition in different ways at different times, researchers can begin to chart the *process* of acquisition. One would also expect memory for different aspects of the coalition to be reflected in tests of the mental models that children use. For the phase I child, for example, memory for a non-linguistic event should be influenced by the acoustic information that accompanies it.

Thus, each phase of the proposed model raises a number of questions that are empirically testable. Much of the empirical work remains to be done. The ideas presented above only provide a way of organizing some of the data and of asking questions that can lead to a new way of thinking about children's language comprehension.

7.4 Conclusions

In this chapter we took seriously two questions that are too rarely considered in the literature on developmental psycholinguistics, namely, "What is language comprehension, and why should comprehension precede production?" We proposed that language comprehension is best thought of in the context of mental model building. The mental model construct itself was expanded to include internalization and interpretation. Work on early event perception, acoustic processing, and so on, all becomes relevant to an understanding of how the child begins to process language input and to internalize information as a foundation for mental model building. The framework that we have proposed highlights the fact that children do not rely on a single type of input as they negotiate sentence meaning; rather, they live in a world of multiple inputs that they piece together to build interpretation through guided distributional learning. Under this view, comprehension—one route to mental model building— proceeds as children move from using language as a tool for internalization to using language as a tool for interpretation. Comprehension begins with a strong reliance on acoustics, moves to a reliance on coordinated input cues from syntax, prosody, extralinguistic context, and semantics (with a bias toward semantics), and culminates in a reliance mainly on syntax. In this context, we suggested that the comprehension of any linguistic structure is best thought of as falling on a continuum of development from fragile to resilient. Only in the latter case can the child use syntactic cues to derive meaning.

To the question of why comprehension might precede production, we answered that only fragile comprehension precedes production. Resilient comprehension and production develop in tandem. That is, production, by its very nature, demands more resilient knowledge of a structure. Without extralinguistic supports or a method of testing the child that keeps these supports intact, fragile comprehension will not be revealed and the two processes—resilient comprehension and production—will show the same course of development.

The ideas presented here are only speculative. In section 7.3, we raised some of the questions and predictions that emerge in the context of this framework and suggested ways in which these questions can be empirically investigated. Indeed, many of the ideas explored in this chapter are consistent with those emerging from "dynamic systems theory" treatments of language acquisition (Thelen and Smith 1994; Tucker and Hirsh-Pasek 1994; Hirsh-Pasek, Tucker and Golinkoff 1995). Dynamic systems theory is an old theory newly imported into psychology, which can accommodate the complexity of the different systems that contribute to the development of language comprehension. The theory proposes that cognitive and behavioral systems are organized, highly interdependent, and mutually informing. To this end, the theory "expressly seeks to integrate information from multiple interacting subsystems with asynchronous developmental pathways [such as the prosodic, semantic, and syntactic systems] which cooperate to engender qualitative developmental shifts (Thelen and Smith 1994, 24). Although the use of a dynamic systems model for language acquisition is just now being explored (see Hirsh-Pasek, Tucker, and Golinkoff 1995; Tucker and Hirsh-Pasek 1994), it offers the promise of explaining how the integrated language inputs work concurrently to result in language comprehension. It may also offer ways to think about and explain children's differential reliance on acoustics, then semantics, and then syntax in their early comprehension of language. As Hirsh-Pasek, Tucker, and Golinkoff (1995) write:

The crux of the story is this: Rather than characterizing the different language inputs as always being in some hierarchic relation to each other, it is much more useful to think of these inputs as systems of developing knowledge that are mutually informing and always available, but with differing weights at different developmental points. Such a vision provides us with a non-linear framework for development. (p. 485)

This view impels us to continue to study language comprehension in some of the ways suggested above. It impels us to uncover how this coalition of redundant sources of information feeds into the child's burgeoning ability to process language and how language processing works with other cues to enrich developing mental models.

7.5 Final Thoughts

In this book we have attempted to make the case that comprehension can serve as a window onto the developing language system in the same way that language has been viewed as a window onto the mind. The position we developed for how comprehension, and thus language, is acquired adopts neither a nativistic nor an environmental stance. Rather, it embraces newer developmental theories that call for early selectivity and constraints on the way in which the organism processes the input, along with the construction of cognitive representations through the interaction of these selected inputs with context (see Thelen and Smith 1994; Gelman and Greeno 1989; Karmiloff-Smith 1992). Children discover language because they are predisposed to notice cues to language units and relations. As was highlighted in some of the experiments reviewed earlier, these sensitivities to language cues are not all present at birth. Nor do they merely unfold in the course of maturation. Children, equipped with some predispositions to attend to language cues from various input domains, must discover the cooccurring patterns in the input that provide the skeleton for language learning. They must then construct their grammar and even their mental models through guided distributional learning. Indeed, what is new information at one stage becomes the backdrop for more detailed analysis and for the richer representation that emerges at the next stage (Peters 1985). Under this view, language learning is a dynamic process in which children continually redescribe their current language model, matching it against the input while relying less and less on external support for their conclusions about grammar (see Karmiloff-Smith 1992; Hirsh-Pasek, Tucker, and Golinkoff 1995).

The study of comprehension in its fragile state allows researchers to peer in on children's early sensitivities to language input; to observe the processes that children use as they move from an understanding of grammar realized in a coalition of input sources to a grammar that is internally consistent and self-sufficient; and to examine the kinds of predispositions that children bring to the language-learning task and the weights that they place on the various input sources over time.

The studies reported here represent only a beginning effort to chart the course of comprehension by examining infants' and toddlers' knowledge of syntactic structures. We believe, however, that with the advent of more sensitive methods for the exploration of fragile comprehension, like the intermodal preferential looking paradigm, researchers will be able to investigate both infant sensitivities to language cues and the ways in which infants exploit the coalition of language-relevant cues as they attempt to decipher the meaning of the language they hear. By focusing on infant sensitivity to language-relevant cues, the study of early language comprehension should help researchers to better understand language development and the way in which infants' and toddlers' interpretation of language interacts with the developing mind.

Notes

Chapter 3

1. In our studies we calculate visual fixation across the entire 6-second trial. Fernald, McRoberts, and Herrera (in press) have divided this period up into three, 2-second segments and find that the first 4 seconds are the most informative. By the last 2 seconds of a trial, children's visual fixation to the match or the nonmatch did not differ. Preliminary analyses indicate that this method of coding does not affect our results. This may be due to the fact that Fernald, McRoberts, and Herrera used single, static objects in their videos whereas we used dynamic events.

2. Some of our studies (e.g., Golinkoff et al. 1987) have employed a second dependent variable: *latency to look* at the matching versus the nonmatching screen. This is the time it takes the child to look to the match or the nonmatch from the central fixation point during the intertrial interval that precedes a test trial. Since the latency measure usually yields information that is redundant with the information obtained from the visual fixation analysis, we no longer use this measure.

3. The computer program is available from either author on request.

Chapter 5

1. The use of the terms "noun" and "verb" does not necessarily imply that these word classes have this formal status for the young child. Indeed, the source of these classes is an ongoing issue in language acquisition research (see, e.g., Braine 1987; Pinker 1984; and chapter 2).

2. For ease of identification, experiments are numbered consecutively throughout the book.

Chapter 6

1. This chapter discusses studies carried out in collaboration with Henry and Lila Gleitman (University of Pennsylvania).

2. The study reported in Naigles 1990, based on a dissertation under the supervision of L. Gleitman, was carried out at the Temple and Delaware laboratories after experiment 5.

3. The same argument has been made by Eilers and Oller (1988) with respect to the demonstrations of phoneme discrimination that scientists elicit under ideal conditions in the laboratory.

Chapter 7

1. Portions of this chapter appeared in Golinkoff and Hirsh-Pasek 1995.

2. The metaphor of language functioning as a "zoom lens," which gives a particular perspective on an event, was suggested by Gleitman (1990). Whether she would have carried the analogy to the lengths we have is another matter!

3. These ages are listed as prototypical ages at which these developments take place and should not be taken rigidly. The stages through which language comprehension passes are more important than the ages themselves.

4. Experiment 1 in chapter 4 did not, however, preserve the semantic part of the coalition since it used pairs of events designed to be equally improbable.

5. Our intent here is not to reproduce the errors made in the literature on "derivational complexity" in the late 1960s! That is, we are not claiming that we can sequence structures in order of complexity by the number of syntactic operations (however conceived) that are required to generate them. What we are claiming is that, roughly speaking, syntactic structures (in a particular language) that require fewer syntactic computations and correspond more readily to events in the world are simpler than structures requiring computation of sentence dependencies.

References

Acredolo, L. P. 1978. Development of spatial orientation in infancy. *Developmental Psychology* 14, 224–234.

Acredolo, L. P. 1980. Laboratory versus home: The effect of environment on the nine-month-old infant's choice of spatial reference system. *Developmental Psychology* 15, 666–667.

Acredolo, L. P., and D. Evans. 1980. Developmental changes in the effects of landmarks on infant spatial behavior. *Developmental Psychology* 16, 312–318.

Adamson, L. B. 1995. *Communication development during infancy.* Madison, Wisc.: Brown and Benchmark Publishers.

Aslin, R. N. 1981. Experiential influences and sensitive periods in perceptual development: A unified model. In R. N. Aslin, J. R. Alberts, and M. R. Petersen, eds., *Development of perception.* Vol. 2. New York: Academic Press.

Aslin, R. N. 1992. Segmentation of fluent speech into words: Learning models and the role of maternal input. In B. de Boysson-Bardies, S. Schonen, P. Jusczyk, P. MacNeilage, and J. Morton, eds., *Developmental neurocognition: Speech and face processing in the first year of life.* Dordrecht: Kluwer Academic Publishers.

Atkinson, M. 1985. How linguistic is the one-word stage? In M. Barrett, ed., *Children's single-word speech.* New York: John Wiley and Sons.

Atkinson, M. 1987. Mechanisms for language acquisition: Parameter-setting, triggering and learning. *First Language* 7, 3–30.

Atkinson, M. 1992. *Children's syntax: An introduction to principles and parameters theory.* Oxford: Blackwell.

Au, T. K., M. Dapretto, and Y.-K. Song. 1994. Input vs. constraints: Early word acquisition in Korean and English. *Journal of Memory and Language* 33, 567–582.

Austin, J. L. 1962. *How to do things with words.* New York: Oxford University Press.

Baillargeon, R. 1995. Physical reasoning in infancy. In M. S. Gazzaniga, ed., *The cognitive neurosciences.* Cambridge, Mass.: MIT Press.

Baker, C. L. 1979. Syntactic theory and the projection problem. *Linguistic Inquiry* 10, 535–581.

Baldwin, D. A., and E. M. Markman. 1989. Mapping out word-object relations: A first step. *Child Development* 60, 381–398.

Barrett, M. 1995. Early lexical development. In Fletcher and MacWhinney 1995.

Bates, E., I. Bretherton, and L. Snyder. 1988. *From firstwords to grammar: Individual differences and dissociable mechanisms.* Cambridge: Cambridge University Press.

Bates, E., and B. MacWhinney. 1987. Competition, variation, and language learning. In B. MacWhinney, ed., *Mechanisms of language acquisition.* Hillsdale, N.J.: Lawrence Erlbaum Associates.

Bates, E., and B. MacWhinney. 1989. Functionalism and the competition model. In B. MacWhinney and E. Bates, eds., *The crosslinguistic study of sentence processing.* Cambridge: Cambridge University Press.

Beilin, H. 1975. *Studies in the cognitive basis of language development.* New York: Academic Press.

Benedict, H. 1979. Early lexical development: Comprehension and production. *Journal of Child Language* 6, 183–200.

Berko Gleason, J. 1993. *The development of language.* New York: Macmillan.

Bernstein Ratner, N. 1995. Acoustic/phonetic characteristics of child-directed speech: Possible phonological and grammatical consequences. In J. L. Morgan and K. Demuth, eds., *Signal to syntax: Bootstrapping from speech to grammar in early acquisition.* Hillsdale, N.J.: Lawrence Erlbaum Associates.

Berwick, R. C. 1986. *The acquisition of syntactic knowledge.* Cambridge, Mass.: MIT Press.

Bever, T. G. 1970. The cognitive basis for linguistic structures. In Hayes 1970.

Bever, T., and B. McElree. 1988. Empty categories access their antecedents during comprehension. *Linguistic Inquiry* 19, 34–43.

Bickerton, D. 1984. The language bioprogram hypothesis. *Behavioral and Brain Sciences* 7, 173–221.

Bloom, L. 1970. *Language development: Form and function in emerging grammars.* Cambridge, Mass.: MIT Press.

Bloom, L. 1973. *One word at a time.* The Hague: Mouton.

Bloom, L. 1974. Talking, understanding and thinking. In R. L. Schiefelbusch and L. L. Lloyd, eds., *Language perspectives: Acquisition, retardation and intervention.* Baltimore, Md.: University Park Press.

Bloom, L. 1978. The semantics of verbs in child language. Paper presented at the Eastern Psychological Association Meeting, New York, N.Y., April 1978.

Bloom, L. 1991a. *Language development from two to three.* Cambridge: Cambridge University Press.

Bloom, L. 1991b. Representation and expression. In N. A. Krasnegor, D. M. Rumbaugh, R. L. Schiefelbusch, and M. Studdert-Kennedy, eds., *Biological and behavioral determinants of language development.* Hillsdale, N.J.: Lawrence Erlbaum Associates.

Bloom, L. 1993. *The transition from infancy to language: Acquiring the power of expression.* New York: Cambridge University Press.

Bloom, L. 1994. Meaning and expression. In W. F. Overton and D. S. Palermo, eds., *The nature and ontogenesis of meaning.* Hillsdale, N.J.: Lawrence Erlbaum Associates.

Bloom, L., J. B. Capatides, and J. Tackeff. 1981. Further remarks on interpretive analysis: In response to Christine Howe. *Journal of Child Language* 8, 403–411.

Bloom, L., and M. Lahey. 1978. *Language development and language disorders.* New York: John Wiley & Sons.

Bloom, L., P. Lightbown, and L. Hood. 1975. Structure and variation in child language. *Monographs of the Society for Research in Child Development* 40(Serial No. 160).

Bloom, L., P. Miller, and L. Hood. 1975. Variation and reduction as aspects of competence in language development. In A. Pick, ed., *Minnesota Symposia on Child Psychology.* Vol. 9. Minneapolis: University of Minnesota Press.

Bloom, L., E. Tinker, and C. Margulis. In press. The words children learn. *Cognitive Development.*

Bloom, P. 1990. Syntactic distinctions in child language. *Journal of Child Language* 17, 343–356.

Bloomfield, L. 1933. *Language.* New York: Henry Holt.

Bohannon, J. N., and L. Stanowitz. 1988. The issue of negative evidence: Adult responses to children's language errors. *Developmental Psychology* 24, 684–689.

Borer, H., and K. Wexler. 1987. The maturation of syntax. In T. Roeper and E. Williams, eds., *Parameter setting.* Dordrecht: Reidel.

Bowerman, M. 1973. Structural relationships in children's early utterances: Syntactic or semantic? In T. E. Moore, ed., *Cognitive development and the acquisition of language.* New York: Academic Press.

Bowerman, M. 1979. The acquisition of complex sentences. In P. Fletcher and M. Garman, eds., *Language acquisition.* Cambridge: Cambridge University Press.

Bowerman, M. 1985. What shapes children's grammars? In D. I. Slobin, ed., *The crosslinguistic study of language acquisition.* Vol. 2, *Theoretical issues.* Hillsdale, N.J.: Lawrence Erlbaum Associates.

Bowerman, M. 1988. The role of meaning in grammatical development: A continuing challenge to theories of language acquisition. Paper presented at the Boston Child Language Conference, Boston, Mass., October 1988.

Braine, M. D. S. 1974. Length constraints, reduction rules and holophrastic processes in children's word combinations. *Journal of Verbal Learning and Verbal Behavior* 13, 448–456.

Braine, M. D. S. 1976. Children's first word combinations. *Monographs of the Society for Research in Child Development* 41(Serial No. 164).

Braine, M. D. S. 1987. What is learned in acquiring word classes: A step toward an acquisition theory. In B. MacWhinney, ed., *Mechanisms of language acquisition*. Hillsdale, N.J.: Lawrence Erlbaum Associates.

Braine, M. D. S. 1988. Modeling the acquisition of linguistic structure. In Y. Levy, I. M. Schlesinger, and M. D. S. Braine, eds., *Categories and processes in language acquisition*. Hillsdale, N.J.: Lawrence Erlbaum Associates.

Bresnan, J. 1978. A realistic transformational grammar. In M. Halle, J. Bresnan, and G. A. Miller, eds., *Linguistic theory and psychological reality*. Cambridge, Mass.: MIT Press.

Brown, R. 1973. *A first language*. Cambridge, Mass.: Harvard University Press.

Bruner, J. 1975. The ontogenesis of speech acts. *Journal of Child Language* 2, 1–19.

Bruner, J. 1983a. The acquisition of pragmatic commitments. In R. M. Golinkoff, ed., *The transition from prelinguistic to linguistic communication*. Hillsdale, N.J.: Lawrence Erlbaum Associates.

Bruner, J. 1983b. *Child's talk: Learning to use language*. New York: W. W. Norton.

Chafe, W. 1971. *Meaning and structure of language*. Chicago: University of Chicago Press.

Chapman, R. S., and L. L. Kohn. 1978. Comprehension strategies in two- and three-year-olds: Animate agents or probable events. *Journal of Speech and Hearing Research* 21, 746–761.

Chapman, R. S., and J. F. Miller. 1975. Word order in early two- and three-word utterances: Does production precede comprehension? *Journal of Speech and Hearing Research* 18, 355–371.

Chien, Y.-C., and K. Wexler. 1987. Children's acquisition of reflexives and pronouns. *Papers and Reports on Child Language Development* 26, 30–39.

Choi, S., and M. Bowerman. 1991. Learning to express motion events in English and Korean: The influences of language specific lexicalization patterns. In B. Levin and S. Pinker, eds., *Lexical and conceptual semantics*. Cambridge, Mass.: Blackwell.

Chomsky, N. 1957. *Syntactic structures*. The Hague: Mouton.

Chomsky, N. 1964. Formal discussion. In U. Bellugi and R. Brown, eds., The acquisition of language. *Monographs of the Society for Research in Child Development* 29(1, Serial No. 92).

Chomsky, N. 1965. *Aspects of the theory of syntax*. Cambridge, Mass.: MIT Press.

Chomsky, N. 1972. *Studies on semantics in generative grammar*. The Hague: Mouton.

Chomsky, N. 1975. *Reflections on language*. New York: Random House.

Chomsky, N. 1981. *Lectures on government and binding*. Dordrecht: Foris.

Chomsky, N. 1988. *Language and problems of knowledge: The Managua lectures*. Cambridge, Mass.: MIT Press.

Clark, E. V. 1994. *The lexicon in acquisition*. Cambridge: Cambridge University Press.

Clark, R., S. Hutcheson, and P. Van Buren. 1974. Comprehension and production in language acquisition. *Journal of Language* 10, 39–54.

Cocking, R. R., and S. McHale. 1981. A comparative study of the use of pictures and objects in assessing children's receptive and productive language. *Journal of Child Language* 8, 1–13.

Cohen, J. 1960. Coefficient of agreement for nominal scales. *Educational Psychological Measurement* 20, 37.

Cohen, L. B., J. DeLoache, and M. S. Strauss. 1979. Infant visual perception. In J. Osofsky, ed., *Handbook of infant development*. New York: John Wiley & Sons.

Cohen, L. B., and L. M. Oakes. 1993. How infants perceive a simple causal event. *Developmental Psychology* 29, 421–433.

Comrie, B. 1981. *Language universals and linguistic typology*. Chicago: University of Chicago Press.

Cook, V. J. 1989. *Chomsky's universal grammar: An introduction*. New York: Blackwell.

Cooper, R. P., and R. N. Aslin. 1990. Preference for infant-directed speech in the first month after birth. *Child Development* 61, 1584–1595.

Crain, S., and M. Nakayama. 1987. Structure dependence in grammar formation. *Language* 63, 522–543.

Crain, S., and R. Thornton. 1991. Recharting the course of language acquisition: Studies in elicited production. In N. A. Krasnegor, D. M. Rumbaugh, R. L. Schiefelbusch, and M. Studdert-Kennedy, eds., *Biological and behavioral determinants of language development*. Hillsdale, N.J.: Lawrence Erlbaum Associates.

Cutler, A. 1993. Phonological cues to open- and closed-class words in the processing of spoken sentences. *Journal of Psycholinguistic Research* 22, 109–131.

Dale, P. S., E. Bates, S. J. Reznick, and C. Morisset. 1989. The validity of a parent report instrument of child language at 20 months. *Journal of Child Language* 16, 239–250.

Deutsch, W., C. Koster, and J. Koster. 1986. What can we learn from children's errors in understanding anaphora? *Linguistics* 24, 203–225.

de Villiers, J. G., and P. A. de Villiers. 1973. Development of the use of word order in comprehension. *Journal of Psycholinguistic Research* 2, 331–342.

Eilers, R. E., and K. Oller. 1988. Precursors to speech: What is innate and what is acquired? *Annals of Child Development* 5, 1–32.

Fauconnier, G. 1985. *Mental spaces: Aspects of meaning construction in natural language*. Cambridge, Mass.: MIT Press.

Fenson, L., P. S. Dale, J. S. Reznick, E. Bates, D. Thal, and S. J. Pethick. 1994. Variability in early communicative development. *Monographs of the Society for Research in Child Development* (Serial No. 242).

Fernald, A. 1985. Four-month-old infants prefer to listen to motherese. *Infant Behavior and Development* 8, 181–195.

Fernald, A. 1991. Prosody in speech to children: Prelinguistic and linguistic functions. In R. Vasta, ed., *Annals of child development*. Vol. 8. London: Jessica Kingsley Publishers.

Fernald, A., G. McRoberts, and C. Herrera. In press. Effects of prosody and word position on lexical comprehension in infants. *Journal of Experimental Psychology*.

Fillmore, C. 1969. The case for case. In E. Bach and R. T. Harms, eds., *Universals in linguistic theory*. New York: Holt, Rinehart & Winston.

Fisher, C. 1994. Structure and meaning in the verb lexicon: Input for a syntax-aided verb learning procedure. *Language and Cognitive Processes* 9, 473–518.

Fisher, C., H. Gleitman, and L. R. Gleitman. 1991. On the semantic content of subcategorization frames. *Cognitive Psychology* 23, 331–392.

Fisher, C., D. G. Hall, S. Rakowitz, and L. R. Gleitman. 1994. When it is better to receive than to give: Syntactic and conceptual constraints on vocabulary growth. *Lingua* 92, 333–375.

Fletcher, P., and B. MacWhinney, eds. 1995. *The handbook of child language*. Cambridge, Mass.: Blackwell.

Fodor, J. A. 1975. *The language of thought*. New York: T. Y. Crowell.

Fodor, J. D. 1989. Empty categories in sentence processing. *Language and cognitive processes* 4, 155–209.

Fodor, J. D., and S. Crain. 1987. Simplicity and generality of rules in language acquisition. In B. MacWhinney, ed., *Mechanisms of language acquisition*. Hillsdale, N.J.: Lawrence Erlbaum Associates.

Fraser, C., U. Bellugi, and R. Brown. 1963. Control of grammar in imitation, comprehension, and production. *Journal of Verbal Learning and Verbal Behavior* 2, 121–135.

Friedman, S., and M. Stevenson. 1975. Developmental changes in the understanding of implied motion in two-dimensional pictures. *Child Development* 46, 773–778.

Furrow, D., K. Nelson, and H. Benedict. 1979. Mothers' speech to children and syntactic development: Some simple relationships. *Journal of Child Language* 6, 423–442.

Gallistel, C. R., A. L. Brown, S. Carey, R. Gelman, and F. C. Keil. 1991. Lessons from animal learning for the study of cognitive development. In S. Carey and R. Gelman, eds., *The epigenesis of mind: Essays on biology and cognition*. Hillsdale, N.J.: Lawrence Erlbaum Associates.

Gauker, C. 1990. How to learn a language like a chimpanzee. *Philosophical Psychology* 3, 31–53.

Gelman, R. 1991. Epigenetic foundations of knowledge structures: Initial and transcendent constructions. In S. Carey and R. Gelman, eds., *The epigenesis of mind: Essays on biology and cognition*. Hillsdale, N.J.: Lawrence Erlbaum Associates.

Gelman, R., and C. R. Gallistel. 1979. *The young child's understanding of numbers: A window on early cognitive development*. Cambridge, Mass.: Harvard University Press.

Gelman, R., and J. G. Greeno. 1989. On the nature of competence: Principles for understanding in a domain. In L. B. Resnick, ed., *Knowing and learning: Essays in honor of Robert Glaser*. Hillsdale, N.J.: Lawrence Erlbaum Associates.

Gentner, D. 1983. Why nouns are learned before verbs: Linguistic relativity versus natural partitioning. In S. A. Kuczaj, ed., *Language development*. Vol. 2, *Language, cognition, and culture*. Hillsdale, N.J.: Lawrence Erlbaum Associates.

Gentner, D. 1988. Cognitive and linguistic determinism: Object reference and relational inference. Paper presented at the Boston Child Language Conference, Boston, Mass., October 1988.

Gerken, L. 1994. Child phonology: Past research, present questions, future directions. In M. A. Gernsbacher, ed., *Handbook of psycholinguistics*. San Diego, Calif.: Academic Press.

Gerken, L., B. Landau, and R. E. Remez. 1990. Function morphemes in young children's speech perception and production. *Developmental Psychology* 27, 204–216.

Gerken, L., and B. J. McIntosh. 1993. Interplay of function morphemes and prosody in early language. *Developmental Psychology* 29, 448–457.

Gernsbacher, M. A. 1988. Cognitive processes and mechanisms in language comprehension: The structure building framework. Paper presented at the meeting of the Western Psychological Association, San Francisco, April 1988.

Gernsbacher, M. A. 1990. *Language comprehension as structure building*. Hillsdale, N.J.: Lawrence Erlbaum Associates.

Geyer, H., L. R. Gleitman, and H. Gleitman. 1995. Subcategorization as a predictor of verb meaning: Evidence from modern Hebrew. Manuscript, University of Pennsylvania.

Gibson, E. 1992. On the adequacy of the competition model. *Language* 68, 812–830.

Gleitman, L. R. 1981. Maturational determinants of language growth. *Cognition* 10, 103–114.

Gleitman, L. R. 1990. The structural sources of verb meanings. *Language Acquisition* 1, 3–55.

Gleitman, L. R., and J. Gillette. 1995. The role of syntax in verb learning. In Fletcher and MacWhinney 1995.

Gleitman, L. R., and E. Wanner. 1982. Language acquisition: The state of the state of the art. In E. Wanner and L. R. Gleitman, eds., *Language acquisition: The state of the art*. Cambridge: Cambridge University Press.

Gleitman, L. R., and E. Wanner. 1988. Current issues in language learning. In M. H. Bornstein and M. E. Lamb, eds., *Developmental psychology: An advanced textbook*. Hillsdale, N.J.: Lawrence Erlbaum Associates.

Gold, E. M. 1967. Language identification in the limit. *Information and Control* 16, 447–474.

Goldfield, B. A. 1993. Noun bias in maternal speech to one-year-olds. *Journal of Child Language* 20, 85–99.

Golinkoff, R. M. 1981. The case for semantic relations: Evidence from the verbal and nonverbal domains. *Journal of Child Language* 78, 413–438.

Golinkoff, R. M. 1983. The preverbal negotiation of failed messages: Insights into the transition period. In R. M. Golinkoff, ed., *The transition from prelinguistic to linguistic communication*. Hillsdale, N.J.: Lawrence Erlbaum Associates.

Golinkoff, R. M. 1986. "I beg your pardon?": The preverbal negotiation of failed messages. *Journal of Child Language* 13, 455–476.

Golinkoff, R. M. 1993. When is communication a "meeting of minds"? *Journal of Child Language* 20, 199–207.

Golinkoff, R. M., and A. Alioto. In press. Infant-directed speech facilitates lexical learning in adults hearing Chinese: Implications for language acquisition. *Journal of Child Language*.

Golinkoff, R. M., A. Alioto, K. Hirsh-Pasek, and D. Kaufman. 1992. Infants learn lexical items better in infant-directed than in adult-directed speech. Boston Child Language Conference, Boston, Mass., October 1992.

Golinkoff, R. M., and L. Gordon. 1983. In the beginning was the word: A history of the study of language acquisition. In R. M. Golinkoff, ed., *The transition from prelinguistic to linguistic communication*. Hillsdale, N.J.: Lawrence Erlbaum Associates.

Golinkoff, R. M., C. G. Harding, V. Carlson-Luden, and M. E. Sexton. 1984. The infant's perception of causal events: The distinction between animate and inanimate objects. In L. P. Lipsitt, ed., *Advances in infancy research*. Vol. 3. Norwood, N.J.: Ablex.

Golinkoff, R. M., and K. Hirsh-Pasek. 1995. Reinterpreting children's sentence comprehension: Toward a new framework. In Fletcher and MacWhinney 1995.

Golinkoff, R. M., K. Hirsh-Pasek, K. M. Cauley, and L. Gordon. 1987. The eyes have it: Lexical and syntactic comprehension in a new paradigm. *Journal of Child Language* 14, 23–46.

Golinkoff, R. M., K. Hirsh-Pasek, C. B. Mervis, W. Frawley, and M. Parrillo. 1995. Lexical principles can be extended to the acquisition of verbs. In Tomasello and Merriman 1995.

Golinkoff, R. M., R. Jacquet, and K. Hirsh-Pasek. 1994. Lexical principles underlie verb learning. Manuscript, University of Delaware.

Golinkoff, R. M., and J. Markessini. 1980. "Mommy sock": The child's understanding of possession as expressed in two-noun phrases. *Journal of Child Language* 7, 119–136.

Golinkoff, R. M., C. B. Mervis, and K. Hirsh-Pasek. 1994. Early object labels: The case for a developmental lexical principles framework. *Journal of Child Language* 21, 125–155.

Goodluck, H. 1991. *Language acquisition: A linguistic introduction*. Cambridge, Mass.: Blackwell.

Greenberg, J. 1963. Some universals of grammar with particular reference to the order of meaningful elements. In J. Greenberg, ed., *Universals of language*. Cambridge, Mass.: MIT Press.

Grimshaw, J. 1981. Form, function, and the language-acquisition device. In C. L. Baker and J. J. McCarthy, eds., *The logical problem of language acquisition*. Cambridge, Mass.: MIT Press.

Grimshaw, J., and S. T. Rosen. 1990. Knowledge and obedience: The developmental status of the binding theory. *Linguistic Inquiry* 21, 187–222.

Gropen, J., S. Pinker, M. Hollander, and R. Goldberg. 1991. Affectedness and direct objects: The role of lexical semantics in the acquisition of verb argument structure. *Cognition* 41, 153–196.

Haith, M., C. Hazen, and G. Goodman. 1988. Expectation and anticipation of dynamic visual events by 3.5-month-old babies. *Child Development* 59, 467–480.

Harris, M. 1992. *Language experience and early language development*. Hillsdale, N.J.: Lawrence Erlbaum Associates.

Harris, M., M. Barrett, D. Jones, and S. Brookes. 1988. Linguistic input and early word meaning. *Journal of Child Language* 15, 77–94.

Harris, M., D. Jones, S. Brookes, and J. Grant. 1986. Relations between the non-verbal context of maternal speech and rate of language development. *British Journal of Developmental Psychology* 4, 261–268.

Harris, M., D. Jones, and J. Grant. 1983. The nonverbal context of mothers' speech to infants. *First Language* 4, 21–30.

Harris, M., D. Jones, and J. Grant. 1984. The social-interactional context of maternal speech to infants: An explanation for the event-bound nature of early word use? *First Language* 5, 89–100.

Hayes, J. R., ed. 1970. *Cognition and the development of language*. New York: John Wiley & Sons.

Haywood, K. M. 1986. *Lifespan motor development*. Champaign, Ill.: Human Kinetics Publishers.

Held, R. 1989. Development of cortically mediated visual processes in human infants. In C. von Euler, H. Forssberg, and H. Lagercrantz, eds., *Neurobiology of early infant behavior*. London: Macmillan.

Hirsh-Pasek, K., and R. M. Golinkoff. 1993. Skeletal supports for grammatical learning: What the infant brings to the language learning task. In C. K. Rovee-Collier and L. P. Lipsitt, eds., *Advances in infancy research*. Vol. 8. Norwood, N.J.: Ablex.

Hirsh-Pasek, K., R. M. Golinkoff, S. Braidi, and L. McNally. 1986. "Daddy throw": On the existence of implicit negative evidence for subcategorization errors. Boston Child Language Conference, Boston, Mass., October 1986.

Hirsh-Pasek, K., R. M. Golinkoff, G. Hermon, and D. Kaufman. 1995. Evidence from comprehension for the early knowledge of pronouns. In E. Clark, ed., *The Proceedings of the Twenty-sixth Annual Child Language Research Forum.* Stanford, Calif.: Center for the Study of Language and Information.

Hirsh-Pasek, K., D. G. Kemler Nelson, P. W. Jusczyk, K. W. Cassidy, B. Druss, and L. Kennedy. 1987. Clauses are perceptual units for young infants. *Cognition* 26, 269–286.

Hirsh-Pasek, K., R. Treiman, and M. Schneiderman. 1984. Brown and Hanlon revisited: Mother's sensitivity to ungrammatical forms. *Journal of Child Language* 11, 81–88.

Hirsh-Pasek, K., M. Tucker, and R. M. Golinkoff. 1995. Dynamical systems: Reinterpreting prosodic bootstrapping. In J. L. Morgan and K. Demuth, eds., *Signal to syntax: Bootstrapping from speech to grammar in early acquisition.* Hillsdale, N.J.: Lawrence Erlbaum Associates.

Holcomb, P. J., S. A. Cofey, and H. Neville. 1992. Visual and auditory sentence processing: A developmental analysis using event-related brain potentials. *Developmental Neuropsychology* 8, 203–241.

Horowitz, F. D., ed. 1974. Visual attention, auditory stimulation, and language discrimination in young infants. *Monographs of the Society for Research in Child Development* (Serial No. 158).

Howe, C. J. 1976. The meanings of two-word utterances in the speech of young children. *Journal of Child Language* 3, 29–48.

Huttenlocher, J. 1974. The origins of language comprehension. In R. L. Solso, ed., *Theories in cognitive psychology.* New York: John Wiley & Sons.

Hyams, N. 1986. *Language acquisition and the theory of parameters.* Dordrecht: Reidel.

Ihns, M., and L. B. Leonard. 1988. Syntactic categories in early child language: Some additional data. *Journal of Child Language* 15, 673–678.

Ingram, D. 1989. *First language acquisition.* Cambridge: Cambridge University Press.

Jackendoff, R. S. 1972. *Semantic interpretation in generative grammar.* Cambridge, Mass.: MIT Press.

Jackendoff, R. S. 1983. *Semantics and cognition.* Cambridge, Mass.: MIT Press.

Jaeggli, O. A. 1986. Passive. *Linguistic Inquiry* 17, 587–622.

Jakubowicz, C. 1984. On markedness and binding principles. In C. Jones and P. Sells, eds., *Proceedings of NELS 14.* GLSA, University of Massachusetts, Amherst.

Johnson-Laird, P. 1983. *Mental models: Towards a cognitive science of language, inference, and consciousness.* Cambridge, Mass.: Harvard University Press.

Jusczyk, P. W., and R. N. Aslin. In press. Infants' detection of the sound patterns of words in fluent speech. *Cognitive Psychology.*

Jusczyk, P. W., K. Hirsh-Pasek, D. G. Kemler Nelson, K. Kennedy, A. Woodward, and J. Piwoz. 1992. Perception of acoustic correlates of major phrasal boundaries by young infants. *Cognitive Psychology* 24, 252–293.

Karmiloff-Smith, A. 1989. Commentary. *Human Development* 32, 272–275.

Karmiloff-Smith, A. 1992. *Beyond modularity*. Cambridge, Mass.: MIT Press.

Kaufman, D. 1987. "Who's him?": Evidence for Principle B in children's grammar. Paper presented at the Boston Child Language Conference, Boston, Mass., October 1987.

Kaufman, D. 1994. Grammatical or pragmatic: Will the real Principle B please stand? In Lust, Hermon, and Kornfilt 1994.

Keil, F. C. 1981. Constraints on knowledge and cognitive development. *Psychological Review* 88, 197–227.

Kelly, M. H. 1992. Using sound to solve syntactic problems: The role of phonology in grammatical category assignments. *Psychological Review* 99, 349–364.

Kelly, M. H., and S. Martin. 1994. Domain-general abilities applied to domain-specific tasks: Sensitivity to probabilities in perception, cognition, and language. *Lingua* 92, 105–140.

Kemler Nelson, D. G., K. Hirsh-Pasek, P. W. Jusczyk, and K. Wright Cassidy. 1989. How the prosodic cues in motherese might assist language learning. *Journal of Child Language* 16, 53–68.

Kuczaj, S. A. 1977. On the acquisition of regular and irregular past tense forms. *Journal of Verbal Learning and Verbal Behavior* 16, 589–600.

Kuhl, P. K., and A. N. Meltzoff. 1982. The bimodal perception of speech in infancy. *Science* 218, 1138–1141.

Landau, B., and L. R. Gleitman. 1985. *Language and experience: Evidence from the blind child*. Cambridge, Mass.: Harvard University Press.

Landau, B., and E. Spelke. 1988. Geometrical complexity and object search in infancy. *Developmental Psychology* 24, 512–521.

Lederer, A., and M. Kelly. 1991. Prosodic correlates to the adjunct/complement distinction in motherese. *Papers and Reports in Child Language*, 30.

Lenneberg, E. H. 1967. *Biological foundations of language*. New York: John Wiley & Sons.

Levin, B. 1985. Lexical semantics in review: An introduction. In B. Levin, ed., *Lexical semantics in review*. Lexicon Project Working Papers 1. MITWPL, Department of Linguistics and Philosophy, MIT.

Levy, Y. 1988. On the early learning of formal grammatical systems: Evidence from studies of the acquisition of gender and countability. *Journal of Child Language* 15, 179–188.

Li, P., L. R. Gleitman, and H. Gleitman. 1994. Subcategorization as a predictor of verb meaning: Cross-language study in Mandarin. Manuscript, University of Pennsylvania.

Lightfoot, D. 1989. The child's trigger experience: 'Degree-0' learnability. *Behavioral and Brain Sciences* 12, 321–334.

Lightfoot, D. 1991. *How to set parameters: Arguments from language change.* Cambridge, Mass.: MIT Press.

Lovell, K., and E. M. Dixon. 1967. The growth of the control of grammar in imitation, comprehension, and production. *Journal of Child Psychology and Psychiatry* 8, 31–39.

Lust, B., G. Hermon, and J. Kornfilt, eds. 1994. *Syntactic theory and first language acquisition: Cross-linguistic perspectives.* Vol . 2, *Binding dependencies, and learnability.* Hillsdale, N.J.: Lawrence Erlbaum Associates.

Lust, B., and R. Mazuka. 1989. Cross-linguistic studies of directionality in first language acquisition: The Japanese data—a response to O'Grady, Suzuki-Wei, and Cho (1989). *Journal of Child Language* 16, 665–682.

Lust, B., M. Suñer, and J. Whitman, eds. 1994. *Heads, projections, and learnability.* Hillsdale, N.J.: Lawrence Erlbaum Associates.

Lyons, J. 1977. *Semantics.* Vol. 1. Cambridge: Cambridge University Press.

Macnamara, J. 1972. Cognitive basis of language learning in infants. *Psychological Review* 79, 1–13.

MacWhinney, B. 1978. The acquisition of morphophonology. *Monographs of the Society for Research in Child Development* (Serial No. 175).

MacWhinney, B. 1987. The competition model. In B. MacWhinney, ed., *Mechanisms of language acquisition.* Hillsdale, N.J.: Lawrence Erlbaum Associates.

MacWhinney, B., and E. Bates. 1989. Functionalism and the competition model. In B. MacWhinney and E. Bates, eds., *The crosslinguistic study of sentence processing.* Cambridge: Cambridge University Press.

Mandler, J. M. 1988. How to build a baby: On the development of an accessible representational system. *Cognitive Development* 3, 113–136.

Mandler, J. M. 1992. How to build a baby: II. Conceptual primitives. *Psychological Review* 99, 587–604.

Maratsos, M. 1988. The acquisition of formal word classes. In Y. Levy, I. M. Schlesinger, and M. D. S. Braine, eds., *Categories and processes in language acquisition.* Hillsdale, N.J.: Lawrence Erlbaum Associates.

Maratsos, M., and M. A. Chalkley. 1980. The internal language of children's syntax: The ontogenesis and representation of syntactic categories. In K. Nelson, ed., *Children's language.* Vol. 2. New York: Gardner Press.

Marcus, M. 1980. *A theory of syntactic recognition for natural languages.* Cambridge, Mass.: MIT Press.

Markman, E. M. 1989. *Categorization and naming in children.* Cambridge, Mass.: MIT Press.

Mazuka, R. 1995. Can a grammatical parameter be set before the first word? Prosodic contributions to early setting of a grammatical parameter. In J. L. Morgan and K. Demuth, eds., *Signal to syntax: Bootstrapping from speech to grammar in early acquisition*. Hillsdale, N.J.: Lawrence Erlbaum Associates.

McDaniel, D., H. Cairns, and J. Hsu. 1990. Binding principles in the grammars of young children. *Language Acquisition* 1, 121–138.

McNeill, D. 1970. *The acquisition of language: The study of developmental psycholinguistics*. New York: Harper & Row.

Meltzoff, A. N. 1990. Towards a developmental cognitive science: The implications of cross-modal matching and imitation for the development of representation and memory in infancy. In A. Diamond, ed., *The development and neural bases of higher cognitive functions*. Annals of the New York Academy of Sciences 608. New York: New York Academy of Sciences.

Meltzoff, A. N., and R. W. Borton. 1979. Intermodal matching by human neonates. *Nature* 282, 403–404.

Menyuk, P., J. Liebergott, and M. Schultz. 1995. *Patterns of early development in full term and premature infants*. Hillsdale, N.J.: Lawrence Erlbaum Associates.

Merriman, W. E., and L. Bowman. 1989. The mutual exclusivity bias in children's word learning. *Monographs of the Society for Research in Child Development* 54 (Serial No. 220).

Messer, D. J. 1983. The redundancy between adult speech and nonverbal interaction: A contribution to acquisition? In R. M. Golinkoff, ed., *The transition from prelinguistic to linguistic communication*. Hillsdale, N.J.: Lawrence Erlbaum Associates.

Messer, D. J. 1994. *The development of communication*. Chichester, U.K.: John Wiley & Sons.

Miller, G. A. 1981. Comments on the symposium papers. Presented at the symposium The Development of Language and of Language Researchers: Whatever Happened to Linguistic Theory? Society for Research in Child Development, Boston, Mass., April 1981.

Miller, G. A. 1990. The place of language in a scientific psychology. *American Psychological Society* 1, 7–14.

Mills, J., S. A. Cofey, and H. Neville. In press. Language acquisition and cerebral specialization in 20-month-old children. *Journal of Cognitive Neuroscience*.

Moerk, E. L. 1983. *The mother of Eve—as a first language teacher*. Norwood, N.J.: Ablex.

Molfese, D. L. 1983. Event related potentials and language processes. In A. W. K. Gaillard and W. Ritter, eds., *Tutorials in ERP research: Endogenous components*. Amsterdam: North Holland Publishing.

Molfese, D. L., L. Burger-Judisch, L. Gill, R. M. Golinkoff, and K. Hirsh-Pasek. In press. Evoked responses discriminate nouns from verbs during a visual-auditory matching task. *Brain and Language*.

Molfese, D. L., P. Morse, and C. Peters. 1990. Auditory evoked responses to names for different objects: Cross-modal processing as a basis for infant language acquisition. *Developmental Psychology* 26, 780–795.

Morgan, J. L., and J. R. Saffran. In press. Emerging integration of sequential and suprasegmental information in preverbal speech segmentation. *Child Development.*

Morgan, J. L., R. Shi, and P. Allopenna. 1995. In J. L. Morgan and K. Demuth, eds., *Signal to syntax: Bootstrapping from speech to grammar in early acquisition.* Hillsdale, N.J.: Lawrence Erlbaum Associates.

Naigles, L. 1990. Children use syntax to learn verb meanings. *Journal of Child Language* 17, 357–374.

Naigles, L., L. R. Gleitman, and H. Gleitman. 1993. Children acquire word meaning components from syntactic evidence. In E. Dromi, ed., *Language and cognition: A developmental perspective.* Norwood, N.J.: Ablex.

Naigles, L., and E. Hoff-Ginsberg. 1992. Input to verb learning: Verb frequency and frame diversity in mother's speech predicts children's verb use. Manuscript, Yale University.

Naigles, L., and E. T. Kako. 1993. First contact in verb acquisition: Defining a role for syntax. *Child Development* 64, 1665–1687.

Neisser, U., and R. Becklen. 1975. Selective looking: Attending to visually specified events. *Cognitive Psychology* 7, 480–494.

Nelson, K. 1973. Structure and strategy in learning to talk. *Monographs of the Society for Research in Child Development* 38(1–2 Serial No. 149).

Nelson, K. 1985. *Making sense: The acquisition of shared meaning.* Orlando, Fla.: Academic Press.

Nelson, K., J. Hampson, and L. Shaw. 1993. Nouns in early lexicons: Evidence, explanations and implications. *Journal of Child Language* 20, 61–84.

Nelson, K. E. 1977. Facilitating children's syntax acquisition. *Developmental Psychology* 13, 101–107.

Oviatt, S. L. 1980. The emerging ability to comprehend language: An experimental approach. *Child Development* 51, 97–106.

Perlmutter, D. M. 1978. Impersonal passives and the unaccusative hypothesis. In *Proceedings of the Fourth Annual Meeting of the Berkeley Linguistics Society.* Berkeley Linguistics Society, University of California, Berkeley.

Peters, A. M. 1985. Language segmentation: Operating principles for the perception and analysis of language. In D. I. Slobin, ed., *The crosslinguistic study of language acquisition.* Vol. 2, *Theoretical Issues.* Hillsdale, N.J.: Lawrence Erlbaum Associates.

Piaget, J., and B. Inhelder. 1971. *Mental imagery in the child.* London: Routledge & Kegan Paul.

Piatelli-Palmarini, M. 1980. *Language and learning: The debate between Chomsky and Piaget.* Cambridge, Mass.: Harvard University Press.

Pinker, S. 1984. *Language learnability and language development.* Cambridge, Mass.: Harvard University Press.

Pinker, S. 1987. The bootstrapping problem in language acquisition. In B. MacWhinney, ed., *Mechanisms of language acquisition*. Hillsdale, N.J.: Lawrence Erlbaum Associates.

Pinker, S. 1989. *Learnability and cognition: The acquisition of argument structure*. Cambridge, Mass.: MIT Press.

Pinker, S. 1990. Language acquisition. In D. Osherson and H. Lasnik, eds., *Language: An invitation to cognitive science, volume 1*. Cambridge, Mass.: MIT Press.

Pinker, S. 1994. How could a child use verb syntax to learn verb semantics? *Lingua* 92, 377–410.

Plunkett, K. 1995. Connectionist approaches to language acquisition. In Fletcher and MacWhinney 1995.

Quine, W. V. O. 1960. *Word and object*. Cambridge: Cambridge University Press.

Radford, A. 1990. *Syntactic theory and the acquisition of English syntax*. Oxford: Blackwell.

Reed, C., and P. Schreiber. 1982. Why short subjects are harder to find than long ones. In E. Wanner and L. R. Gleitman, eds., *Language acquisition: The state of the art*. Cambridge: Cambridge University Press.

Rescorla, L. 1991. Identifying expressive delay at age 2. *Topics in Language Disorders* 11, 14–20.

Roberts, S. 1983. Comprehension and production of word order in stage I. *Child Development* 54, 443–449.

Roeper, T. 1987. The acquisition of implicit arguments and the distinction between theory, process and mechanism. In B. MacWhinney, ed., *Mechanisms of language acquisition*. Hillsdale, N.J.: Lawrence Erlbaum Associates.

Rovee-Collier, C. K., and H. Hayne. 1987. Reactivation of infant memory: Implications for cognitive development. In H. W. Reese, eds., *Advances in child development and behavior*. Vol. 20. New York: Academic Press.

Sachs, J., and L. Truswell. 1978. Comprehension of two-word instructions by children in the one-word stage. *Journal of Child Language* 5, 17–24.

Savage-Rumbaugh, E. S., J. Murphy, R. Sevcik, K. E. Brakke, S. L. Williams, and D. M. Rumbaugh. 1993. Language comprehension in ape and child. *Monographs of the Society for Research in Child Development* (Serial No. 233).

Schieffelin, B. B. 1990. *The give and take of everyday life: Language socialization of Kaluli children*. Cambridge: Cambridge University Press.

Schlesinger, I. M. 1971. Production of utterances and language acquisition. In D. I. Slobin, eds., *The ontogenesis of grammar*. New York: Academic Press.

Schlesinger, I. M. 1977. *Production and comprehension of utterances*. Hillsdale, N.J.: Lawrence Erlbaum Associates.

Schlesinger, I. M. 1979. Cognitive and linguistic structures: The case of the instrumental. *Journal of Linguistics* 15, 307–324.

Schlesinger, I. M. 1988. The origins of relational categories. In Y. Levy, I. M. Schlesinger, and M. D. S. Braine, eds., *Categories and processes in language acquisition*. Hillsdale, N.J.: Lawrence Erlbaum Associates.

Schmidt, C. 1991. The scrutability of reference: Ostensive naming events in caregiver-child interaction. Manuscript, Albert Einstein College of Medicine.

Searle, J. R. 1969. *Speech acts*. Cambridge: Cambridge University Press.

Shatz, M. 1978. On the development of communicative understanding: An early strategy for interpreting and responding to messages. *Cognitive Psychology* 3, 271–301.

Shipley, E. F., C. S. Smith, and L. R. Gleitman. 1969. A study in the acquisition of language: Free responses to commands. *Language* 45, 322–342.

Shrout, P. E., and J. L. Fleiss. 1979. Intraclass correlation: Uses in assessing rate reliability. *Psychological Bulletin* 86, 420.

Skinner, B. F. 1957. *Verbal behavior*. New York: Appleton-Century-Crofts.

Slobin, D. I. 1966. Developmental psycholinguistics. In F. Smith and G. A. Miller, eds., *The genesis of language*. Cambridge, Mass.: MIT Press.

Slobin, D. I. 1973. Cognitive prerequisites for the development of grammar. In C. Ferguson and D. I. Slobin, eds., *Studies of child language development*. New York: Holt, Rinehart & Winston.

Slobin, D. I. 1985a. Cross linguistic evidence for the language-making capacity. In D. I. Slobin, ed., *The crosslinguistic study of language acquisition*. Vol. 2, *Theoretical issues*. Hillsdale, N.J.: Lawrence Erlbaum Associates.

Slobin, D. I. 1985b. *The crosslinguistic study of language acquisition*. Vol. 1, *The data*. Hillsdale, N.J.: Lawrence Erlbaum Associates.

Slobin, D. I. 1992. Introduction. In D. I. Slobin, ed., *The crosslinguistic study of language acquisition*. Vol. 3. Hillsdale, N.J.: Lawrence Erlbaum Associates.

Slobin, D. I., and T. Bever. 1982. Children use canonical sentence schemas: A crosslinguistic study of word order and inflections. *Cognition* 12, 229–265.

Snow, C. E. 1986. Conversations with children. In P. Fletcher and M. Garman, eds., *Language acquisition*. Cambridge: Cambridge University Press.

Snow, C. E. 1989. Understanding social interaction and language acquisition: Sentences are not enough. In M. H. Bornstein and J. S. Bruner, eds., *Interaction in human development*. Hillsdale, N.J.: Lawrence Erlbaum Associates.

Snow, C. E., and C. A. Ferguson. 1977. *Talking to children: Language input and acquisition*. Cambridge: Cambridge University Press.

Snow, C. E., and B. J. Gilbreath. 1983. Explaining transitions. In R. M. Golinkoff, ed., *The transition from prelinguistic to linguistic communication*. Hillsdale, N.J.: Lawrence Erlbaum Associates.

Snow, C. E., and M. Tomasello. 1989. Data on language input: Incomprehensible omission indeed! *Behavioral and Brain Sciences* 12, 357–358.

Sokolov, J. L., and C. E. Snow. 1994. The changing role of negative evidence in theories of language development. In C. Gallaway and B. J. Richards, eds., *Input and interaction in language acquisition*. Cambridge: Cambridge University Press.

Spelke, E. 1979. Perceiving bimodally specified events in infancy. *Developmental Psychology* 15, 626–636.

Spelke, E. 1990. Principles of object perception. *Cognitive Science* 14, 29–56.

Spelke, E., K. Breinlinger, J. Macomber, and K. Jacobson. 1992. Origins of knowledge. *Psychological Review* 99, 605–632.

Starkey, P., E. S. Spelke, and R. Gelman. 1983. Detection of intermodal correspondences by human infants. *Science* 222, 179–181.

Sternberg, R. J. 1988. Intellectual development: Psychometric and information-processing approaches. In M. H. Bornstein and M. E. Lamb, eds., *Developmental psychology: An advanced textbook*. Hillsdale, N.J.: Lawrence Erlbaum Associates.

Strohner, H., and K. E. Nelson. 1974. The young child's development of sentence comprehension: Influence of event probability, nonverbal context, syntactic form and strategies. *Child Development* 45, 564–576.

Tardif, T. 1994. Nouns are not always learned before verbs, but why? Evidence from Mandarin Chinese. Paper presented at Stanford Child Language Research Forum, Stanford, Calif., April 1994.

Thelen, E., and L. Smith, eds. 1994. *A dynamic systems approach to the development of cognition and action*. Cambridge, Mass.: MIT Press.

Thomas, D. C., J. J. Campos, W. Shucard, D. S. Ransay, and J. Shucard. 1981. Semantic comprehension in infancy: A signal detection analysis. *Child Development* 52, 798–803.

Tomasello, M. 1992. *First verbs: A case study of early grammatical development*. Cambridge: Cambridge University Press.

Tomasello, M., and J. Farrar. 1986. Joint attention and early language. *Child Development* 57, 1454–1463.

Tomasello, M., and W. Merriman, eds. 1995. *Beyond names for things: Young children's acquisition of verbs*. Hillsdale, N.J.: Lawrence Erlbaum Associates.

Tucker, M. L., and K. Hirsh-Pasek. 1994. Systems and language: Implications for acquisition. In Smith and Thelen 1994.

Valian, V. 1986. Syntactic categories in the speech of young children. *Developmental Psychology* 22, 562–579.

Wanner, E., and M. Maratsos. 1978. An ATN approach to comprehension. In M. Halle, J. Bresnan, and G. A. Miller, eds., *Linguistic theory and psychological reality*. Cambridge, Mass.: MIT Press.

Waxman, S. R., and M. T. Balaban. 1992. The influence of words vs. tones on 9-month-old infants' object categorization. Paper presented at International Conference on Infant Studies, Miami, Fla. May 1992.

Weinberg, A. 1987. Comments on Borer and Wexler. In T. Roeper and E. Williams, eds., *Parameter setting*. Dordrecht: Reidel.

Werker, J. F., J. E. Pegg, and P. J. McLeod. 1994. A cross-language investigation of infant preference for infant-directed communication. *Infant Behavior and Development* 17, 323–333.

Wetstone, H., and B. Friedlander. 1973. The effect of word order on young children's responses to simple questions and commands. *Child Development* 44, 734–740.

Wexler, K. 1982. A principle theory for language acquisition. In E. Wanner and L. R. Gleitman, eds., *Language acquisition: The state of the art*. Cambridge, Mass.: MIT Press.

Wexler, K., and Y.-C. Chien. 1985. The development of lexical anaphors and pronouns. *Papers and Reports on Child Language Development*, 24, 138–149.

Wexler, K., and P. Culicover. 1980. *Formal principles of language acquisition*. Cambridge, Mass.: MIT Press.

Woodward, A., E. M. Markman, and C. Fitzsimmons. 1994. Rapid word learning in 13- and 18-month olds. *Developmental Psychology* 30, 553–556.

Younger, B. A., and L. B. Cohen. 1983. Infant perception of correlations among attributes. *Child Development* 54, 858–867.

Younger, B. A., and L. B. Cohen. 1986. Developmental changes in infants' perception of correlations among attributes. *Child Development* 57, 803–815.

Index

Acoustic cues, 75–76, 166–167
  sensitivity to, 97, 169–170, 196
Acoustic packaging, 161, 263, 165–171,
  178, 185
  ability to use, 165–166
  formation of, 168
  internalization and, 168, 170, 171
  and mapping, 166, 168, 173–174, 189
  roles for, 168–169, 196
Action, 109
Agent, 104, 109, 114–115, 117, 180
Allopenna, P., 188
Ambiguity, 73–74
Analogy, 131, 141
Anaphors, 181, 183
Atkinson, M., 103

Baker's paradox, 1–2
Balaban, M. T., 77
Bates, E., 22–23, 25
  children's infrastructure in, 24–25
  Competition Model of, 22–23, 120
  and domain-general language learning, 22
  and functional cues, 8, 22–23
Bellugi, U., 56
Biased learners, 2–5, 9, 11, 51, 73
Binding principles, 181–184, 193
Binding theory, 34, 179, 181–183
Bloom, L., 7, 26, 38, 121
  contextual cues of, 6
  language acquisition theory of, 29–30, 39,
    78, 171, 189
  and mental models, 160, 162–163,
    177–178, 189
  and redundancy, 177
Bloom, P., 76
Borton, R. W., 62
Bowerman, M., 25, 172
Boys
  language development of, 88–89

use of syntactic frames by, 138–139, 146,
  181
vocabulary of, 88, 105
and word order, 112, 113
Braine, M. D. S., 25
Brown, R., 56
Bruner, J., 20–21

Chalkley, M. A., 120
Chapman, R. S., 102, 103
Child-directed speech, 65–66, 192
Chinese, 13
Choi, S., 172
Chomsky, N.
  and binding, 181
  and cognitive processes, 42
  parameters of, 5, 34
  and poverty of the stimulus, 27
  and social understanding, 42
  theories of, 5, 31–32, 33, 40
Clause boundaries, 167
Coalition-of-cues model, 185–190, 196, 197
Cocking, R. R., 57
Cofey, S. A., 58
Cognitive categories, 22, 25–26
Cognitive language-acquisition theories,
  22–23, 33
Cognitive processes
  development of, 160–161
  in language acquisition, 42, 120–121
Communication, 163
Competition Model, 22–23, 45
  children's infrastructure in, 24–25
  critique of, 28
  word order in, 120
Constituents, 15
  ability to find, 79
  comprehension of, 159
  mapping of, 76
  operation of, 74